Challenging Family Therapy Situations

Joan D. Atwood, PhD, is the Director of the Graduate Programs in Marriage and Family Therapy at Hofstra University. Dr. Atwood is also the Director of the Marriage and Family Clinic located in the Saltzman Community Center at Hofstra. She is the past-President of the New York State Association for Marriage and Family Therapists and was awarded the Long Island Family Therapist of the Year award for outstanding contributions to the field. She teaches courses in Couples Therapy, Family Therapy, Gender Issues in Marriage and Family Therapy, Sexual

Photo by Jay Gassman

Issues in Marriage and Family Therapy, Families in Transition, Social Construction Theory and Therapy, and Supervision and Advanced Supervision. Dr. Atwood has published six books: *Making Contact With Human Sexuality; Treatment Techniques for Common Mental Disorders; Family Therapy: A Cognitive-Behavioral Perspective; Counseling Single Parents; Family Scripts;* and *Challenging Family Therapy Situations.* In addition, she has published numerous journal articles on social construction theory and therapy, families in transition, human sexuality issues, and family health issues. She is a clinical member and approved supervisor of the American Association of Marriage and Family Therapy; she holds Diplomate Status and is a Clinical Supervisor on the American Board of Sexology; she is a certified Imago therapist; and she has served on the President's Commission for Domestic Policy. Among her many projects, Dr. Atwood is the codeveloper of the P.E.A.C.E. (Parent Education and Custody Effectiveness) Program, a court-based educational program for parents obtaining a divorce, and the L.I.F.E. (Looking Into Feelings and Emotions) Program, a school-based K–12 curriculum that helps children learn to express feelings and emotions. She has made numerous TV appearances and radio newspaper interviews. She is in private practice in individual, marriage, and family therapy in Rockville Centre, New York.

Challenging Family Therapy Situations

Perspectives in Social Construction

Joan D. Atwood, PhD
Editor

Springer Publishing Company

Springer Publishing Company, Inc.
536 Broadway
New York, NY 10012-3955

Cover design by Margaret Dunin
Acquisitions Editor: Bill Tucker
Production Editor: Jeanne Libby

97 98 99 00 01 / 5 4 3 2 1

Library of Congress Cataloging-in-Publication Data

Challenging family therapy situations : perspectives in social
    construction / Joan D. Atwood, editor.
        p.   cm.
    Includes bibliographical references and index.
    ISBN 0-8261-9820-1
    1. Family psychotherapy.   2. Constructivism (Psychology)
    3. Schemas (Psychology)   I. Atwood, Joan D.
    RC488.5.C455   1997
    616.89'156—dc21   97-23148
                                                              CIP

Printed in the United States of America

Contents

v

Preface

RATIONALE

In American society, romantic love is not only an expectation for a potential marriage partner but a demand. This, combined with socially transmitted, often impractically based, sets of expectations around the institution of marriage and unrealistic definitions of family life, results in the notion that those who do not achieve the ideal are failures. It is not surprising, therefore, that situations less than the ideal are often shrouded in myth, misconception, and misunderstanding and have remained hidden from view for centuries in the closely guarded sanctuary of the home. Profound disappointment results when individuals fall in love with the man or woman of their dreams only to find they are not living happily ever after. Even worse, they may silently suffer, living secret lives, hiding their true family situation. This book seeks to dissect painful family situations into their chameleon-like elements to give beginning therapists as well as seasoned therapists an in-depth look at some of the most complex and frustrating, yet challenging, dilemmas they will ever face. Examples and explanations from current literary works and personal communications are used to give full accounts of hurtful situations in as many realms as possible. Existing theoretical orientations and treatments are discussed as well as the problems associated with them. Implications for treatment are presented in each chapter.

Social Construction

What we consider knowledge is rooted in our way of seeing the world. When we accept a given item as known, we are also accepting the validity of many rules for establishing the reality of truth of something that exists outside of ourselves. Generally, we are unaware of these rules, or the particular "world" in which they belong. And generally we do not think about the means by which these worlds become established and can be challenged and overturned.

The examination of such social constructions—definitions of reality under which humans and their families operate—is one purpose of this analysis. A second purpose is to analyze the various current socially constructed family scripts and relate them to the social worlds in which they are anchored. Berger and Luckmann (1966), in their classic work, *The Social Construction of Reality,* described the human origin of social realities very simply as a process by which individuals who repeatedly confront a task or situation relevant to their lives develop habitual ways of dealing with it. A situation once typified this way often leads to the development of roles or functions which cooperating partners perform in connection with the task involved. Often individuals bring their personal realities into line with the social constructions. Sometimes the personal reality becomes a basis for attacking or rejecting the social construction. The dialectical relationship between personal realities and social constructions is a recurring focus of this book.

Social Scripts

Another major concept used as a theoretical backdrop for the book is social scripts. The notion of scripts was first introduced by Gagnon and Simon (1973) in reference to sexuality theory. In a series of articles, they challenged Freudian theory that posed the reduction of sexuality to biological explanations. They believed instead that individuals are like actors with parts in a play and used the term *scripts* to mean a repertoire of acts and statuses that are recognized by a social group, together with the rules, expectations, and sanctions governing these acts and statuses. Scripts, they believed, exist for the sexual life as they do for other areas of life.

It is this notion of social scripts that forms one of the basic tenets of the theoretical formulations proposed in this book. Human beings expect their lives to follow certain scripts and they make efforts to follow them. They try to make their experiences congruent with these scripts, sometimes even reinterpreting reality so as to make it "fit" them better. These scripts are usually recognizable to us: "the good mother," "the good husband," "the happy marriage." While there are perhaps gaps, such as when we are between scripts (i.e., identity transition during divorce), scripts provide us with a general idea of what is supposed to happen.

The Social Construction of Family Scripts

A social construction includes not only the routines and the scripts for educating or socializing the youngsters in the system, but also the means for maintaining the definition of reality on which the system is based and the subjective loyalty of the family members. Thus, in applying the idea of social constructions to the system of the family, a major assumption is that family behavior is scripted. Competing constructions and their resultant scripts are on the periphery of each person's life, barely visible. The denigration and denial of alternative scripts maintains the dominant constructions and scripts and prevents others from appearing as options. General family scripts as well as painful scripts are taken for granted. Family members construct a rationale for why undesirable behavior continues and how they can live their lives in spite of it. This is evident in a family with an alcohol abuser as well as the family of a sexual abuser. Using this model, therapy, then, assists families in developing their barely visible alternative constructions and scripts.

This book is more than an introduction to issues in family therapy. It focuses on the most current theoretical issues in the field, applies recent theory to challenging family situations, and presents practical techniques and information on special issues in family therapy. Each chapter follows basic social constructionist assumptions, putting solution-focused techniques into practical, understandable language. The topics that are included were selected because of their challenging and frequent appearance in therapists' offices. Although the book is comprehensive in its treatment of the subject areas identified in the table of contents, not all violent or painful situations in the field of family therapy are included. The topics selected were those that the authors believed clinicians most often experience in their professional lives. The goal was to give both students and seasoned family therapists a new view of what knowledge and skills they might need when confronted with clients presenting any one of the problems identified in the book.

Chapter 1 discusses the transition of the mental health field from premodern to modern to postmodern assumptions. It presents ideas about therapy from first and second order cybernetics, along with a discussion of the narrative therapies and social construction theory and therapy. Notions of meaning systems and scripts are presented and the idea of shadow scripts is discussed in relation to couple therapy. The chapter concludes with a section on social constructionist assumptions, setting in place the theoretical formulation of the book.

Chapters 2 through 8 present specific family therapy issues, illustrated with case studies. Each chapter's reference section offers plentiful suggestions for further reading. Chapter 2, "Extramarital Affairs and Constructed Meanings," examines research and explores the literature on extramarital sex (EMS). Chapter 3, "AIDS and the Family Narrative," explores how this devastating illness affects families. Chapter 4, "Depression," discusses the problem of depression, its incidences and symptoms, and then explores its shadow script, hope. Chapter 5, "Suicide," presents the predispositions to suicide, including its warning signs. Chapter 6, "Dueling Couples," explores the issue of chronic conflict in couples. Chapter 7, "Physical Violence in the Family," presents an overview of wife battering and explores the problem from a theoretical and practical point of view. Chapter 8, on intimacy dissolution, discusses divorce and its aftermath, and presents the stages of emotional responses. Chapter 9 discusses the effect chronic illness has on the family. It looks at these effects from multiple levels and derives suggestions for therapy.

A NOTE ON RESEARCH

In general, although family therapy has espoused the process of rigorous scientific research, this theoretical commitment is often honored in the breach. There is a need for models in family therapy to be empirically tested and examined. In addition, there is a tendency by family therapy theorists (along with other mental health professionals who see themselves as doing "soft science") to attribute more authenticity to biologically based events and more artificiality to psychologically or socially based events.

This false dichotomy in thinking can be particularly misleading in the analysis of the family. Even if we examine what we define as biological "facts," we learn that they do not have a direct effect on experience in humans. With nonhuman species, researchers have been able to demonstrate direct connections between hormones and behavior, but for humans, behavior is mediated by meaning systems. The decision to have a child for women is generally a direct function of the state of the relationship between the individual and her partner. Even the effect of childbirth, a seemingly nonsocial event, depends on social meanings that are attached to it. And we know from Durkheim (1951) that even suicide, a very individual act, is influenced by macrosociological factors. Looking to the "hard sciences" for "social realities" has led family therapists to neglect the study of the meaning systems of the persons. So that while we have accumulated data about who does what, with whom, and where, we still know very little about the ways people learn to consider themselves part of a family, a society or even married or a parent.

To the extent that we relate to social or physical events in terms of their meanings for us—for example, what to do about them—we are acting on the basis of social constructions, that is, knowledge received through socialization. The exploration of persons' social constructions—definitions of reality under which individuals operate—is one purpose of this analysis. A second purpose is to analyze various current constructions of family scripts and relate them to the social worlds in which they are anchored. A third purpose is to examine family scripts under deconstruction.

SUMMARY

The field of family therapy has grown into a new stage of life (perhaps adolescence) in which it is questioning existing assumptions and realities of its traditional theoretical models. In so doing, current thought has embraced social construction theory, emphasizing the importance of language and the social environment. The new work has only recently been applied to therapeutic situations. We have applied it to challenging family therapy situations. If we are to go forward as a field, we must develop our theories practically to assist people with problems in living. The present volume addresses this significant problem.

REFERENCES

Durkheim, E. (1951). *Suicide.* New York: Free Press.
Gagnon, J. H., & Simon, W. (1973). *Sexual conduct.* Chicago: Aldine de Gruyters.

Contributors

Nancy Cohan, MA, is the supervising social worker of the Family Mediation Project at Children's House in Mineola, Long Island, New York.

George J. Meyer, EdD, is a New York State licensed psychologist and approved supervisor of the American Association for Marriage and Family Therapists and is the President-elect of the New York Chapter. He is a professor of psychology at Suffolk Community College, Selden, New York.

Teri Pakula, PhD, is a Gestalt therapist, a marriage and family therapist, and a hypnotherapist. She is in private practice in Hewlett, New York. She is the President of the Alumni Association of the Gestalt Center of Long Island, has presented at the annual Gestalt Conference, and has taught in the center's elective program. She is also a provisional instructor for the National Board of Certified Hypnotherapists.

Madeline Seifer, MA, is clinical member of the American Association for Marriage and Family Therapists and is a clinical member of the American Association for Clinical Hypnosis. She is currently working in the area of chronic pain management and is in private practice in Jericho, New York.

Estelle Weinstein, PhD, is the Chair and Coordinator of the Graduate Programs in Health, Hofstra University, Hempstead, New York. She has published extensively on health counseling and adolescent sexuality. She is a clinical member of the American Association for Marriage and Family Therapists, and is certified by the American Association of Sex Educators, Counselors, and Therapists as a sex educator and counselor.

CHAPTER 1

Social Construction Theory and Therapy

Joan D. Atwood

> *You live in a universe; and within you, you form pictures of the universe*
> *as it appears to you. And you know nothing of that universe and*
> *can know nothing except for the pictures. But the pictures*
> *within you of the universe are not the universe . . .*
> A. E. van Vogt (quoted in *Omni,* February, 1986, p. 31).

In all societies, there is a world view (a story) according to which all is understood and evaluated. This world view shapes our attitudes, incorporates new knowledge, dictates the form of our methodologies, and acts as the context through which we process all knowledge. It determines which measuring techniques we will invent to better understand the concepts we have invented about our behavior. When we consider knowledge as being embedded in our way of seeing the world, when we accept any given item or event as known, we are also accepting the notion that there is a reality of truth—something that exists outside of ourselves. In general, we are unaware of the rules we follow, or the particular "world" in which they belong. We do not think about the means by which these worlds become established nor do we think about the ways they can be challenged and overturned. World views are questioned when faced with alternative views. Recently, an alternative view has emerged in the field of marriage and family therapy. This chapter explores the historical development of the new world view, describes social construction theory and presents a model for psychotherapy.

FIRST-ORDER CYBERNETICS, MODERNISM, AND PSYCHOTHERAPY

Up until around the 1800s, most theoreticians believed, based on Newtonian physics, that there was an objective reality—a world "out there" waiting to be discovered. In the early pathology models, behavior was seen as the external manifestation of internal characteristics, traits, and conflicts. For example, the delusions of a paranoid schizophrenic were deemed to result from the projection of unacceptable sexual and aggressive drives (e.g., see Masterson, 1976).

Traditional analytic psychotherapies would fall into this category. By diagnosing and assessing the original cathexis, the therapist then provides a reparative parenting experience for the client who then works through the pain and hurt. The client is, thus, freed to psychologically grow and the personality structure changes.

Traditional psychoanalytic therapies adhere to the following assumptions:

- There is an objective reality and it is knowable.
- There can be models of normalcy.
- The therapist is an expert.
- The therapist is a diagnostician who does assessment.
- The therapist is transparent, in that the therapist is a toneless sounding board.
- The client has one self, not very malleable.
- The symptom is caused by the pathology which is located in the self.
- Change is an either/or process.
- A client is dependent on the therapist to fix future problems.

Later, the field of psychotherapy evolved to a problem-focused (behavioral, systemic) or a problem-solving stance. Behavior was explained within a causal or functional system. "I did x because he did y" or "He does x in order to protect his parents from arguing." These ideas are also referred to as first-order cybernetics, utilizing the metaphor from engineering because similar to family therapy the field of cybernetics concerns itself with form, pattern, organization, and openness.

In this view, the therapist is outside the client system, acting upon it as an expert who diagnoses and intervenes to cure the client or the problem. If the therapy does not work, it means the client was resistant or in denial or not ready. The therapist adheres to a model of normalcy and compares the client to this model in order to assess how far or deviant the client is from the norm. The therapeutic task then becomes bringing the client closer to the normative model.

Traditional psychological approaches adhere to first-order cybernetics. Objectivity is assumed to be a singular truth that can be found if we dig deeply enough. In this model, there is a search for scientifically predictable essences and structures and the therapist is a rational, objective expert who discovers facts and prescribes corrective measures. If the client does not agree, the therapist is then justified in confronting the client or in imposing ideas or assignments on the client. In this view, in order that the therapist can best know how to deal with the problem or the problematic person, he or she gathers assessment information, assuming that detailed information about the problem, its cause, its history, its frequency, will lead to ideas about solutions. The tradition further assumes that psychological qualities or emotional qualities exist as measurable entities and that there are standard or normative criteria for determining mental health. Therapists operating from these assumptions pose as experts, gathering information as a basis for planning interventions, for identifying deficits, weaknesses or wounds. Therapy in this world view then attempts to change, remediate, or heal. For the traditional therapist, truth is knowable, normality is identifiable, and both can be discovered (Gergen, 1985; 1988; 1992).

Behavioral psychotherapies also fall into this category. The following situations illustrate practice based on the assumptions listed above:

1. Clients come in for couple counseling because they continually argue about whether the air conditioner should be on or off in the bedroom. After giving the couple a marital satisfaction profile and assessing it, the therapist decides that the couple are within the "normal" range of marital satisfaction and suggests to the couple that they take turns with the air conditioner, one day on and one day off.

2. A mother brings in her child for therapy because he is getting poor spelling grades. The therapist sets up a behavior modification

chart and instructs mother and child how to use the chart. For every good spelling grade (defined as over 90), the child will receive a gold star, and after collecting four gold stars for the month the child will receive a prize, something that is reasonable, that the child defines.

- there is an objective reality.
- adhere to models of normalcy.
- the therapist is an expert.
- the therapist is a diagnostician who does assessment.
- the therapist is visible and leading at times.
- the client has a malleable self.
- the symptom is caused by problems in living.
- change is either/or.
- client is dependent on the therapist to fix future problems.

Again, the therapist is the expert, the diagnostician, who holds ideas about normalcy, who acts upon the client system in order to effect a change in the problem behavior.

Traditional models of family therapy are also based on modernist assumptions: They embrace a position of certainty that there is a model of normalcy to which the therapist compares the person/family in therapy. In so doing, the focus is on how different the family is from the norm (deficit focus), and decision are made as to which interventions are needed to bring the family closer to the norm. A brief overview of two major models of family therapy will illustrate these points.

While strategic family therapy and structural family therapy were born on different coasts of the United States, they share many similar assumptions and are representative of the traditional view. *Strategic* family therapy generally is characterized by its use of specific strategies for addressing family problems (Madanes & Haley, 1977). Therapy is directly geared toward changing the presenting complaint and is typically accomplished by the therapist's first assessing the cycle of family interaction, then breaking that cycle through straightforward or paradoxical directives. Therapy is oriented to change, not growth; and the therapist is responsible for successful therapeutic outcomes. The therapist focuses on present interaction, not interpretation of family members' behavior or exploration of the past. Therapy is terminated when the presenting problems have ceased.

Haley's (1976) approach to therapy is method oriented and problem focused, with little or no attempt to instill insight. Concepts of power and control are important in his description of family patterns, for he sees communication sequences and symptoms as attempts to control or influence. In this model, symptoms are behaviors that are beyond one's control. They are, however, very controlling in terms of the alternatives available to other persons in relationships with the symptom bearer. Haley believes that problems are maintained by a faulty hierarchy within the family. One of the goals of therapy, therefore, is to alter the family's interactions, thereby changing the family's hierarchical structure. Also, he contends that the presenting problem is often a metaphor for the actual problem (Haley, 1976; Madanes, 1981). So, through the use of directives, the strategic therapist seeks to change symptomatic metaphors in order to allow more adaptive ones to emerge.

In contrast with the strategic approach, Minuchin (1974) emphasizes the dynamic orderings of the system itself, the actual structure within which elements of communication take place. *Structural* family therapy is an active, problem-solving approach to a dysfunctional family context. Minuchin believes that the structure of the family is "an open sociocultural system in transformation" (p. 14). The family structure is sociocultural in that it integrates the demands of society, as well as those of the internal family system, in shaping the individual. Minuchin sees the transformation of structure through boundary negotiation as the key to successful adaptation. Structural family therapy focuses on the patterns of interaction within the family that give clues to the basic structure and organization of the system. For Minuchin, structure refers to the invisible set of functional demands that organizes the way the family interacts. Thus, observations of patterns of interactions in the family provide information about how the family is organized or structured to maintain itself.

For structural theorists, diagnosis is directed toward and treatment is predicated upon a system's organizational dynamics. They also believe that boundaries are critically important. *Boundaries* are the rules and regulations that separate the system from its environment, the manifestation of the system's rules and regulations. A boundary can be highly permeable so that thoughts and feelings are easily exchanged, or it can be impermeable, so that thoughts and feelings are either not exchanged at all or are exchanged with much difficulty. The *clarity* of the boundaries refers to how well the lines of responsibility have been thought out and how clearly the designation of authority has been defined.

Minuchin charges the therapist with three major tasks: to join with the family as a leader, to unearth and evaluate the underlying family structure, and to create circumstances that will allow for the transformation of this structure. The therapist's tasks then are to form the therapeutic system and to restructure the family system. Structural family therapy focuses on two kinds of live, here-and-now activities: enactments and spontaneous behavioral sequences. If the therapist successfully joins the family, the family will begin to reveal pieces of its structure through enactments and spontaneous behavioral sequences. The structural therapist is an expert, either neutral and detached or self-employed as a lever to offset the balance in the family. In addition, the therapist is generally a diagnostician and assessor who acts upon the family to "fix" their fusion, disengagement, rigidity, overprotection, conflict avoidance, symetricality, complementarity, hurts, wounds, dysfunctional patterns, or communications.

To summarize, in traditional family therapies the following assumptions are found:

- There are multiple interpretations of one objective reality.
- Models of normalcy should be adhered to.
- The role of the therapist is to be an expert.
- The therapist is a therapeutic tool, a lever intending to create change in the system.
- The therapist is very visible.
- There are multiple aspects of self.
- Pathology is located in the family system.
- The symptom functions to maintain the system.
- Change is an either/or process.
- A client is dependent upon the therapist to fix future problems.

Traditional family therapies adhere to modernist assumptions and work from a first-order cybernetics stance. It is clear that both models, strategic and structural, tend to fit families into or compare them to a normative template. Inherent in this type of approach is the assumption that there is such a thing as the "normal family" and that anything outside this range is less than normal, or negative. This creates a construction that inclines clinicians to perceive families' problems or deficits, by focusing on and documenting how far the family is from the norm. Therapy then involves bringing the family closer to normative. The therapist, entrenched in theoretical groundings, defines the situation, discovers the truth.

In response to the traditional psychological and family therapy deficit approach and in an attempt to respond to the developing postmodernist milieu, the solution-focused therapies appeared (deShazer, 1991; Dolan, 1991; Lipchik & deShazer, 1986; O'Hanlon & Weiner-Davis, 1989; Walter & Peller, 1992). Solution-focused therapists address and focus on the competencies and strengths of the clients, thereby replacing the deficit story with one of success. In this model, active participation in the solution by the client is required as the more positive aspects of the client's life become foreground—via finding exceptions—and the trauma or the problem fades into the background. Table 1.1 compares traditional/modernist and solution-focused/postmodernist therapy assumptions.

DeShazer (1985) was one of the first theorists responsible for solution-focused therapy. His work led him away from a focus on the problem in therapy to a focus on finding a solution the client deemed helpful. He stated that often the solution a client constructed had very little to do with the problems he saw, but that it "fit" with the client's definition of the problem. Consequently, the therapy moved in a direction away from the therapist trying to understand the client's problem and design a solution to it to a focus on questioning the client about personal goals and encouraging self-exploration as a potential resource for problem solving. Molnar and deShazer (1987) noticed that there were "exceptions" to the client's story—times when the problem was not happening. These therapists then focused on what that exceptional experience was like, and developed the solution-focused therapy model. Instead of focusing on the trauma or problem and its effects, as do the traditional psychotherapies, or the function of the problem, as do the early systemic therapies, solution-focused therapy instead highlights the competencies and strengths of the clients.

Briefly, in solution-focused approaches, the client comes in with a problem, tells the problem to the expert, who then focuses on aspects of the client's story that did not contain the problem, and who will ultimately project the client into the future without the problem.

Solution-focused therapies diverge from traditional ones along some, but not all, parameters:

- There may be a reality but it is unknowable.
- There is no adherence to models of normalcy.

TABLE 1.1   Comparison of Problem/Deficit Models of Therapy with Solution-Focused Models

Traditional Approaches	Solution Focused Therapy
• Therapist is an expert—has special knowledge regarding the problem to which the client needs to submit (colonialization/ missionary model)	• Client and therapist both have particular areas of expertise (collaborative model)
• Client is viewed as damaged by the abuse (deficit model)	• Client is viewed as influenced but not determined by abuse history, having strengths and abilities (resource model)
• Remembering abuse and the expression of repressed affect (catharsis) are treatment	• Goals are individualized for each client, but do not necessarily involve goals of catharsis or remembering
• Interpretation	• Acknowledgment, valuing, and opening possibilities
• Past oriented	• Present/future oriented
• Problem/pathology oriented	• Solution focused
• Must be long-term treatment	• Variable/individualized length of treatment
• Invites conversations for insight and working through	• Invites conversations for accountability and action and declines invitations to blame and invalidation

From O'Hanlon, W. In J. Atwood & F. Genovese (Eds.) (1993). *Counseling the single parent family*. Alexandria, VA: American Counseling Association

- The role of the therapist is as expert.
- The client is a diagnostician who does assessment.
- The therapist is visible and leading at times.
- The client has many selves.
- The symptom is caused by problems in living.
- Change is either/or, a replacement process.
- The client is dependent on the therapist to fix future problems.

In general, questions that flow from modernist assumptions have right or wrong answers related to socially accepted norms and are designed more to validate the therapist's thoughts and premises than to uncover the family's definition of the situation. Traditional therapies have a tendency to escalate into cycles which serve to reinforce a problem-focused view of the couple/family and/or therapist. Solution-based therapies have a tendency to escalate into cycles of "positiveness" which serve to reinforce the positive view of the couple and the therapist.

These methods, though, tend to overshadow information about other aspects of behavior which could expand existing descriptions. In this sense, modernist therapies leave out important aspects of the picture. They have in common an adherence to an either/or perspective, tending to leave out half of the picture. In an attempt to correct this omission, the narrative therapies developed, with the goal of assisting clients to *expand* their reality rather than assisting them to *replace* it. These newer models emphasize "in addition to" rather than "instead of."

SECOND-ORDER CYBERNETICS, POSTMODERNISM, AND THE NEW EPISTEMOLOGY

With Einstein's theory of relativity (in Capra, 1983; Zukav, 1989) and Heisenberg's (1958) uncertainty principle, the certain, predictable, reductionistic universe was pulled out from under us. The finding that human observations at the quantum level could actually change what was being observed moved us into a new way of understanding *seeing*. The resulting paradigmatic shift (Kuhn, 1970) infiltrated the social sciences in the 1960s and now, supported by Maturana's (1980) research and Gergen's (1985) theory, has made its way into the family therapy literature as constructivism and social constructionism, the new epistemology or second-order cybernetics, holding profound implications not only for family therapy theory but also for family therapy practice.

For example, Hoffman (1987) describes a therapy that respects a second-order cybernetic epistemology and Epston and White (1990) elaborate on its therapeutic application. In Hoffman's view, the therapist initially assists the couple in learning processes that help them to amplify (be aware of) their couple process, provides techniques that the couple can use to generate new possibilities, and is someone who creates a safe environment where the couple can explore their process, generate new possibilities, consider the implications of the possibilities, and negotiate a shared frame around the chosen change. These ways of learning can be used by the couple outside therapy. In the sense that the therapist provides opportunities for the couple, there is initially some "therapist residue"; however, over time as the couple learn to rely on their own self-healing processes, they become more confident in the processes and in their own abilities to generate growth and change.

The therapist assists clients to become aware of their present frame through an exploration of the issue. In so doing, clients decide what, where, and how to change. In a second-order cybernetic stance, the therapist does not prescribe specifically, but instead works with clients to establish mechanisms for generating and for seeing alternative points of view. The therapist helps clients to develop abilities to determine for themselves when change is necessary and then, through questioning and exploring, assists them in implementing the change. With second-order cybernetics, clients become their own diagnosticians, their own generators of possibilities, and experts on their process.

Second-order cybernetics tends to incorporate constructivism or constructionist perspectives. Constructivism is not new and may be traced back to philosophers Kant (in Atwood, 1992), Hume (1934), Wittgenstein (in Atwood, 1992), and Husserl (in Nathanson, 1963). Piaget (1951) and Kelly (1969) represent proponents from psychology. Biologists Maturana (1980, 1987, 1988) and Varela (1979, 1981), cybernetician and biophysicist, von Foerster (1981a, 1981b, 1984b), physicists Heisenberg (1958) and Prigogine and Stengers (1984); constructivist von Glaserfeld (1984); and anthropologist, Bateson (1972, 1978, 1980, 1991) also share this perspective. The social psychologists, Cooley (1902), Mead (1934), Berger and Luckman (1966), Reiss (1981), Gergen and Gergen (1983), and Gergen (1985) taking into account the larger sociocultural environment, contributed to the notion that our knowledge about the world is constructed by the observer and laid the groundwork for social construction theory. In family therapy, the proponents of the new epistemology included Dell (1982), Keeney (1983, 1985), Tomm (1987), Anderson and Goolishian (1988) and Hoffman (1987, 1990). Constructivism and social constructionism offer new epistemological explanations of how we know what we know and are representative of second-order cybernetics.

Both constructivists and social constructionists believe that how we know what we know is *not* through an exact pictorial duplication of the world; the map is not the territory. Rather, reality is seen experientially, in terms of how we subjectively interpret the constructions (von Glasserfeld, 1984). In a sense, we are responsible for what we believe, feel, and see. What this means is that our story of the world and how it works is not the world, although we behave as though it is. Our experiencing of the world is limited to our description of it. Von Foerster (1981a, 1981b, 1984a, 1984b) states, "If you desire to see, learn how to act [take action]." Using language ("languaging") is action and it is through language that persons define and experience reality. It is therefore through languaging in therapy that an environment conducive to change is created.

Postmodernism is philosophically rooted in Nietzsche's views that there are no facts, only "interpretations," that each perspective originates from a "lust to rule," and that claims to "truth" mask the workings of the "will to power." The postmodernists of the quantum world assume that our relations with the world do not always correspond with the world; the way we explain the world arises from active cooperation of persons in relationship; whether or not knowledge is maintained depends on social exchanges; and constructed meanings are social activities and are not separate from the rest of our social life (Gergen, 1988).

The Narrative Therapies

There are two strands of narrative therapies: one represented by a problem-determined or collaborative language systems approach (Anderson & Goolishian, 1988; Andersen, 1987; Hoffman, 1990) and the other by the externalization approach (Epston, 1989; Tomm, 1987 & White, 1989). White (1986, 1989), building on Bateson's (1972) notion of restraints, proposed a similar model of "alternate descriptions." As defined by Bateson (1972), restraints are the limitations placed on people by their beliefs and values that make them less likely to notice other aspects of their problem-saturated life. White termed these other aspects "subjugated knowledge" and developed a narrative therapy through which people explore their ongoing story. Therapy in this case involves assisting individuals to reauthor their lives. Following White's tradition, one of the purposes of this book is to explore the processes by which individuals tell themselves stories, give themselves meanings, and interpret their behaviors.

Andersen's *reflective team* illustrates this new epistemology in that it attempts to expand the client's reality by providing therapeutic observations, hoping that some of these observations will be taken in by the family. The therapy team describes their observations to the family with the hope that the client family will take in ideas for new possibilities. The role of the therapist here is that of an idea generator. Although the couple (family) can assimilate from the team's ideas what they want and discard what they do not want, they are still therapist dependent in that they have not been given procedures for promoting their own new possibilities the next time they have a problem.

Epston and White (1990) believe that, "When persons are established as consultants to themselves, to others, and to the therapist, they experience themselves as more of an authority on their own lives, their problems, and the solution to these problems" (p. 28). White's work in terms of subjugated knowledge clearly puts him into a second-order cybernetic stance and a therapy of expanding realities.

Tomm (1991), in his notions of reflective questions and therapeutic unfolding or expansion, is closest to what is meant by a second-order cybernetics stance. His method is to ask questions with the intent to facilitate self-healing in an individual or family by activating the reflexivity among meanings within pre-existing belief systems that enable family members to generate or generalize constructive patterns of cognition and behavior on their own (p. 172), and represents a therapy of third-order change. The goal is self-healing. Tomm (1991), through his concept of *therapeutic loving,* touches on aspects of the therapist's self essential to helping clients expand their capacity to experience the world on a new level. He defines therapeutic loving as increasing options and opening space. He compares it to therapeutic violence, whereby the therapist imposes his or her will on the client. By a play on words, Tomm's characterization gives us "the rapist."

Therapists who adhere to a second-order cybernetic stance believe:

- Reality is socially created through social interaction.
- The client defines what is normal.
- The role of the therapist is to collaborate with client to co-construct new stories that hold new possibilities.
- The client is a diagnostician who does assessment.
- The therapist is transparent (attempts to keep all biases and assumptions out of the therapy arena).

- The client has many selves.
- The client is having a problem in living. The problem persists because the client does not know how to fix it.

Compare the narrative language (co-create, co-construct, social constructs, narrative, themes, stories, scripts, audience, meaning systems, etc.) with the language of the earlier models.

SOCIAL CONSTRUCTION THEORY

Social construction theory and therapy are also based on a second-order therapeutic stance. Although narrative therapy is used throughout this book, our approach to therapy is more socially based, taking the socially defined meanings and scripts as the target for restorying. However, it is necessary to first explore the theoretical underpinnings of social construction theory, socially constructed meaning systems, and socially constructed scripts. Berger and Luckmann; (1966) describe social constructions as the consensual recognition of the realness and rightness of a constructed reality, plus the socialization process by which people acquire this reality. A social construction includes not only the routines and the mechanisms for socializing the children of the system, but also the means for maintaining the definition of reality on which the system is based.

The Development of a World View

Social Routines

As stated earlier, many of the insights into the nature of social constructions are derived from the work of Berger and Luckmann (1966). They describe the origin of social realities very simply as a process by which individuals who repeatedly confront a task or situation relevant to their lives develop habitual ways of dealing with it. People first recognize the recurrent nature of a situation; then, they develop roles or functions for cooperating individuals to perform in connection with the task involved.

If social arrangements are examined in detail, it is easy to see that each individual interaction involves processes of reciprocal accommodation and negotiations, with individuals making frequent attempts to disclose their own subjective reality and grasp each other's realities. At this small-scale level, before the routines are institutionalized, the interactions between individuals appear to be fluid and flexible. They are adopted because they seem to work, and changing them is as easy as setting them up; it merely requires further communication.

Though one could define these fluid arrangements as forms of social structure, it is not implied that they will last, nor do we have any indication how long they will survive. At this rudimentary stage of social organization, social routines are heuristic devices; however, routinization is a small step away from the establishment of a problem-solving process in which all possibilities are considered. A routine is a solution to a problem that is available and on call. With continued usage of routines, over time, other elements of institutionalization develop. When speaking of full-fledged social constructions, the implication is that they contain all the stages of institutionalization: the consensual recognition of the realness and rightness of the constructed reality and the specification of the socialization processes by which people acquire the definition of the reality.

Just as routines are one step from spontaneous problem solving, the establishment of roles is one step away from ways of relating to total persons. For example, roles focus attention on some highlighted function or attribute of persons. To a degree, once roles are established, persons become interchangeable once they can fulfill the role expectations. Their identity is based on their functions in the division of labor, rather than on themselves as total persons. If they perform their functions effectively, the need for communication, accommodation, and negotiation is reduced.

Social Constructions

Social constructions that have survived over time and have become standard are called institutions. Institutions have a history. They arise under specific material and historical conditions (for example, a war) to which they are exactly the kind of heuristic solutions we have been discussing. They are products of individual agencies, not impersonal forces. Once they are reified, members of society lose sight of their origins and the related possibility that they may change. They also forget that responses to problems can vary and carelessly slip into thinking that the form that they observe as a social institution is its only normal and/ or natural form. This is fallacy similar to the often-made assumption that the nuclear family, with father as breadwinner and wife and children as economic dependents, is the normal and best way of life and all other family forms are suspect. If problems appear to be associated with aspects of family life, the solution proposed is often to reinforce the dominant nuclear family form, rather than explore new forms, which might be more effective, in light of the recent social and economic changes.

Socialization: Getting Others to Share the World View

As previously stated, at a small-scale level of analysis, individuals' inter-actions appear to be fluid and flexible. However, if the individuals attempt to extend social constructions, whether by including more individuals or by bringing in a new generation, much of the flexibility is lost. A new person who is to take part in the system must be taught the routines the others have worked out. The rules must be made explicit. Often in these situations, the system becomes frozen in its assumptions, and the new members perceive its features as absolutes, "the way things are." It is this understanding that is brought in by families entering therapy: they are "stuck" in their story and see no alternative ways of behaving. As Berger and Luckmann (1966) point out, the social structure they have inherited is "opaque" (p. 55). The ways in which it is constructed are invisible to individuals as are the elements that compose it, and so they do not see the possibilities for combining these elements in new and different ways. Individuals seem to be unaware of the existence and characteristics of the social environment. Although social arrangements are developed with conscious intent, that intent is neither perceived nor questioned by those in future generations. They are accepted as ends in themselves rather than as means to ends.

The Socialization of Subjective Reality

Socialization is the group of processes by which subjective realities and social constructions are brought into congruence. The social world we are born into is experienced by the child as the sole reality. The rules of the world we are born into are not problematic, they require no explanation, and they are neither challenged nor doubted. However, as

Foucault (1978) points out, the most powerful knowledge is often the most taken for granted. Through socialization, the socially constructed meanings are internalized; they are filtered and understood through meaningful symbols. Though socialization continues throughout the life cycle, it is primary (early) socialization to which we must ascribe the greatest impact (Berger & Luckmann, 1966).

The Socialization of Identity

Through socialization, social constructions are internalized, and as experience is filtered and understood through meaningful symbols, the essence of individual identity is formed. Identity is built upon the foundation of family identity. The construction is the same as the construction of all identity: young children learn to use verbal labels for themselves and their behavior, as well as for others and their behavior. These labels then come to have the same meaning for the learners as they do for the "old hands." Social constructions thus embodied in the language shared within a group come to be embedded in the foundation of individual identities by means of language. Individuals observe and judge their own behavior and the behavior of others. In making these judgments, they use the scripts (the social plans of action) provided by society. The meanings of behaviors and the judgments that individuals attach to them are part of these scripts.

The evolution of identity thus involves individuals' attempts to match their experience with the available scripts. They learn not only the language that is applied to feelings and events, but also society's expectations for persons of their ages and genders. They learn reciprocal behaviors, attitudes, and postures expected of the opposite sex as well. In this way they learn and prepare to enact the scripts which are deemed appropriate by their culture.

A child is born into a social world which has the experienced characteristic of being the sole reality. To the young child, the family is the world. His or her mother is not one mother among many or one of a class; she is "Mother" (Berger & Luckmann 1966, p. 124). The routines and the social arrangements are not problematic for the young child; they require no explanation, and they are neither challenged nor doubted. The child's suspension of questioning and doubt is not only functional for the society, but it simplifies daily life for the individuals involved. Any challenge to the dominant social constructions of the individual's reality serves to complicate the individual's life and ultimately society. Thus there are various social mechanisms in place to maintain the subjective credibility of the dominant realities.

The perceived absoluteness of subjective reality resulting from primary socialization appears to be a function of two factors: the cognitive immaturity of the young child and the effective quality of the teaching and learning that take place at this developmental stage. The early socializing agents (most often the parents) have control over important outcomes for the child and the child's reliance on these early caretakers is total. They determine what and when the child's physical needs will be taken care of, which realities the child will be exposed to, and what conceptual tools the child will be given for solving problems. From the viewpoint of the child, he or she is physically, psychologically, and informationally dependent. The early caretakers affect the child's feelings of dependence and contribute to the perceived power of the socializing agents and the probability of internalization (Jones & Gerard, 1967). Those individuals and events involved in subsequent socialization (teachers, peers, and/or media) have less power relative to the agents of primary socialization, and less monopolistic power simply because the child is not so completely dependent on them.

The other factor in the intensity of primary socialization is the emotional investment of the caretakers in the child and in what they are teaching the child. This affective quality of primary socialization is generally not found to the same degree in subsequent socialization, including formal academic education. The latter tends to be (at least in Western cultures) deliberately affect-free, objective, and impersonal. The reality claimed by such learning is "fugitive" and more easily bracketed (Berger & Luckmann, 1966, p. 131). An individual's reality is maintained by developing a personal sense of self that is congruent with the social constructions. Thus, based on early interactions and ongoing socialization, individuals construct realities around meanings which include a preferred way of relating to others. These constructed realities become the basis for how we view others and how we expect others to view us. In many ways, these perceptual sets determine predictable ways of interacting with others. The self is experienced as the most vividly real aspect of reality (Berger & Luckmann, 1966) and the "reality" for the individual is usually perceived as unitary (p. 124). It is maintained by the kinds of social arrangements described above and by a developing personal identity congruent with learned social constructions.

Meaning Systems

Not only do social constructions contain routines and structures, they contain meaning systems as well. Meaning systems refer to the complex and unique definitions in each individual that can influence behavior. Meanings are components of interpersonal interaction. They originate in childhood and are maintained by ongoing interpersonal interactions. The meanings that events and behaviors have for individuals are determined by their social position and cultural indoctrination. Meanings can be individual (subjective), interpersonal (shared), and cultural (social). They are frames of reference for understanding—for making sense. The culture (or subculture) thus equips individuals with ways of understanding and judging many aspects of behavior, ranging from the biological functions of their bodies to moral systems. These ways of making sense of experiences are embedded in a world view which is accepted as reality by all those around each of us and in the scripts that are part of the world view.

Take for example the following vignettes:

Account Number 1.

She awakened from a deep sleep, only to realize she was fifteen minutes behind schedule. Skipping breakfast, she rushed to her car and drove to school. If she didn't hit any traffic, she would be on time for her class. Luckily the roads seemed empty and she didn't hit any traffic lights. She pulled into the university parking lot, noticing how empty it was. She then commented to herself on how many students had come down with the flu this year.

It was only when she walked into her empty classroom that she realized it was Saturday and she didn't have to go to class.

Account Number 2.

She drove off the parkway because her car was making an awful sound and shaking all over. It appeared to be bumping down the street. She commented to herself how she must stop procrastinating and take the car for its needed tune up. She was convinced that the dirty oil was clogging up the engine causing it to bump.

It was only when the person in the next car gestured to the rear of her car that she realized she had a flat tire.

The kinds of interpretations presented in accounts 1 and 2 occur every day, all day. Individuals attempt to make sense out of everyday life. The persons in the above accounts were fitting their experiences into their meaning systems attempting to make sense out of experiences that appeared to be nonsensical. Making sense is an ever changing and ever emerging process. The processes we utilize in making sense out of our everyday life are socially constructed, learned from and embedded in the larger sociocultural environment and operate at the social, interpersonal, and intrapersonal levels.

Maintaining Meaning Systems

A well-developed social construction includes not only the routines and the mechanisms for educating and socializing the youngsters in the system, but also the means for maintaining the definitions of reality on which it is based and the subjective loyalty of individuals. A community and a language that the community reaffirms as its dominant reality and the discrediting of competing social constructions are the two basic mechanisms that function to maintain the subjective reality of social constructions. Therefore, contact with both the community and its language must be consistent (Berger & Luckmann, 1966). There must be face-to-face contact that repeatedly reinforces the desired definitions of individuals within the context of the social constructions for the subjective reality to be maintained. Moreover, competing constructions, even the awareness of them, must be kept at the periphery of each individual's life and identity. Thus, alternative or "shadow" constructions tend to be denigrated or denied. Dominant or institutionalized constructions cannot permit alternatives from appearing as viable options. This limiting function has profound implications for application to the way the family defines reality. It is important to keep in mind that social constructionists believe that our explanations are not only created by individuals in society but modifiable in the same way.

Scripts

From socially constructed meaning systems flow socially constructed scripts. Individuals' meaning systems determine the content of their scripts. A person attempts to match experience with the available meanings and scripts. In this way, the person learns the language, the appropriate behavior according to gender, age, and culture. Reiss (1981) points out that scripts exist for intrapsychic, interpersonal, and cultural levels.

The concept of scripts was first discussed by Gagnon and Simon in 1973 when they introduced the idea of sexual scripts. In a series of articles, they challenged Freudian theory and the reduction of sexuality to biological explanations. Instead, they believe that we are like actors with parts in scripts. These scripts exist for all areas of life, including sexual life. Scripts are involved in learning the meaning of internal states, organizing the sequences of specific acts, decoding novel situations, setting the limits on responses, and linking meanings from other aspects of life to specific experience (Gagnon, 1990, p. 6). A script is a "device for guiding action and for understanding it" (p. 6). Scripts are plans that people have about what they are doing and what they are going to do. They justify actions which are in agreement with them and challenge those which are not. Scripts are the "blueprints for behavior," specifying the whos, whats, whens, and whys of behavior. ". . . Scripts constitute the available repertoire of socially recognized acts and statuses, and roles and the rules governing them" (Laws & Schwartz, 1977, p. 217).

Scripts operate at a social, personal, and intrapsychic level. They are embedded in social institutions and are thence internalized by individuals. The overriding, dominant scripts receive most attention because of their primacy and potency among people's options. It is against the dominant social scripts that people attempt to match or reject their own personal social scripts. But the match is never perfect and what occurs in actuality is often far from the ideal. The ideal scripts are usually recognizable to us: "the good mother," "the good husband," "the happy marriage." By attempting to make our experiences accord with our scripts, we sometimes internalize only part of the ideal script. At other times we reinterpret reality so as to make it fit them better.

In addition, there are unscripted areas of experience. Where there is neither widespread comprehension nor common gauges to facilitate comprehension. An example of an unscripted area is the period between scripts, such as the identity transition that occurs during divorce. Backwards sequences, such as when a child dies before the parents, are also unscripted. In these situations, individuals tend to feel at a loss or report they feel out of control. Scripts also prepare us for events of the future. Rehearsal precedes performance, and while others may coach us or guide us in our parts, it is the social scripts that get us ready for situations we are about to encounter. Through socialization, we learn the dominant scripts and the expectations that our lives will follow certain scripts. Figure 1.1 presents a model of the social constructionist world view.

Non-Dominant Scripts

The dialectical relationship between personal realities and social constructions is a recurring focus in this book. While the pluralistic nature of the contemporary American climate is emphasized, it is important to note that not every individual is equally aware of the existence of a variety of life scripts. Individuals choose a particular dominant script generally because of their location in the social structure. While some may know that certain other dominant scripts; exist, others may not. By the nature of the social construction of reality, the received reality is the only reality; hence, what is different is not merely lacking in validity, but is either hard to imagine—unthinkable—or unacceptable.

Thus, while the sequences of life stages are scripted and the transitions tend to be scripted within the dominant scripts, it is not apparent to most individuals that there could be other scripts at each stage. Our socialization makes areas outside the chosen dominant script appear vague—irrelevant or inappropriate. The unfamiliar script, however, is an area that holds promise for the therapeutic setting. Possibilities for new ways lie in the other, opaque dominant scripts just beyond our view.

Alternative Scripts

Following the dominant scripts is not an automatic process, like growing taller. It is not a maturational process; it is a social one. Even the most well-socialized, for whom inner reality and social reality are in agreement, sooner or later encounter claims for the invalidity of dominant scripts. Any challenge to the accepted social constructions of reality presents a problem for individuals, but unless alternative scripts have personal relevance for them, they will not be adopted. Even when the individual conforms to the dominant script, awareness of the other scripts has therapeutic relevance because awareness brings awareness of choice. And whenever choice is present, the automatic unquestioned acceptance of social constructions is disrupted. In most cases, the subjective reality of the dominant scripts remains unshaken with the force of primary socialization behind it.

While many individuals find the accepted scripts adequate guidelines for making sense of their own experience and thus form coherent

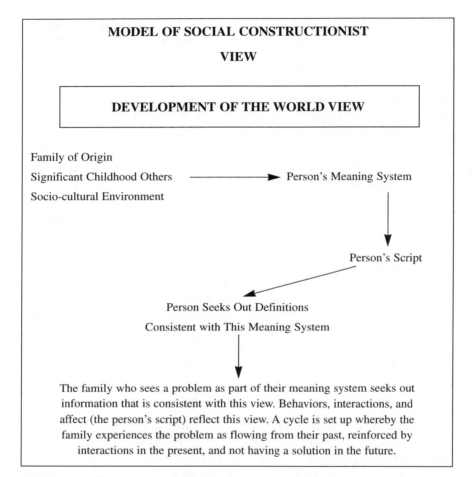

FIGURE 1.1   Development of a worldview.

identities basically in line with these scripts, others find that the available scripts do not fit their experience. Sometimes the personal reality becomes a basis for attacking or rejecting the social construction. Sometimes the source of discomfort is not under our control, as when there is chronic illness in a family member or when a child dies before the parent. It is a fact of the multiply-scripted world that many individuals make unscripted transitions in the course of their life histories. It is even possible to conceptualize a script for being scriptless.

Finding and articulating options outside the dominant script is more risky—both socially and psychologically—than following the dominant script. The development of identity for the people who do so is more problematic. They usually suffer from an absence of validation as well as invalidation or negative sanctions imposed by those who assume roles in the dominant scripts. There is no standard language to describe or express experiences and identities that are not socially recognized. Consequently it is difficult for individuals to communicate about such phenomena. But, as Berger and Luckmann (1966, p. 141) point out, without such communication, the validation of these experiences by others is practically impossible, and their reality, for lack of verbal recognition, becomes shaky.

Because of the social nature of constructed realities, it is difficult for individuals to achieve and maintain their identities in social isolation. In this case, such persons will generally submit to or create alternative lifestyles. Communities where alternative lifestyles are sustained are often sought out or created by such individuals. These communities facilitate resocialization, which can be as intense a process as primary socialization and include mechanisms for displacing or discrediting the reality of the dominant script. This process is evident, for example, in the lives of many homosexuals. Accounts of publicly "coming out" indicate the powerful process of personal change under social influence when individuals assume a gay identity and join a gay community.

The Shadow Scripts

As stated earlier, the strength of social scripts often disallows perception of other scripts. Persons use "selective noticing" of experiences, scanning the environment and taking in only those aspects that are in agreement with their socially constructed realities. But in the background, always present, primed to move forward if triggered, are the *shadow scripts* (Atwood, in press), the scripts just beyond our view, those scripts within which the seeds of change lie. Shadow scripts follow Derrida's (1976) notion of *difference*. Difference is the tension between what is said and what is not said. Shadow scripts are connected to the individuals' dominant scripts because they are composed of the opposite, the trace, of what individuals present to others as their dominant script. They are composed of what is not said, behaviors that are not acted out, gestures that are not made. Therapy in this model then becomes an act of deconstruction, exploring the trace of the script, the part called into existence at the mere mention of a certain aspect of the person's dominant script.

Similar to the "subjugated knowledges" of White and Epston (1990) or deShazer's "exceptions" (1991), shadow scripts are the opaque elements or fragments from past, present, and future that are just beyond our awareness. Shadow scripts are socially constructed and operate at all levels: the social, the cognitive, the behavioral, and the emotional. Shadow scripts are not analogous to the unconscious because the individual is not unaware of the shadow script; rather, shadow scripts are just outside, peripheral to the person's awareness and, if triggered, are accessible. Figure 1.2 presents a comparison view of exceptions and shadow scripts.

Past Shadow Scripts

Scripts of the past contain the fragments of our childhoods—those memories we hold that define for us our view of how we were raised, whether we had a happy or sad childhood, whether we did well in school or not. These scripts are the explicit scripts of our childhood; they are central to our perception, containing relatively clear definitions of what our experience of our childhood was like. Past shadow scripts are the implicit scripts of the past that are peripheral to our perception but that also affect our current meaning system or behavior. An example would be an implicit, nonverbal negative definition of sexual expression modeled to us by our parents, which affects our sexual expression as an adult. While dominant scripts tend to be explicit and direct, shadow scripts tend to be implicit and covert. Shadow scripts contain the information that was left out.

Current Shadow Scripts

Current scripts give us information about how to behave, what meanings events have for us, whom to date, and other relevant data. They are the dominant explicit scripts of society, transmitted to us by our families—the scripts that teach us appropriate meanings and behaviors. Current shadow scripts contain the traces of these scripts. If, for example, we have a current family script in which the men in the family are strong, then each family member who has internalized this definition has also internalized the shadow script which contains a model for weak men, along with all the meanings that entails.

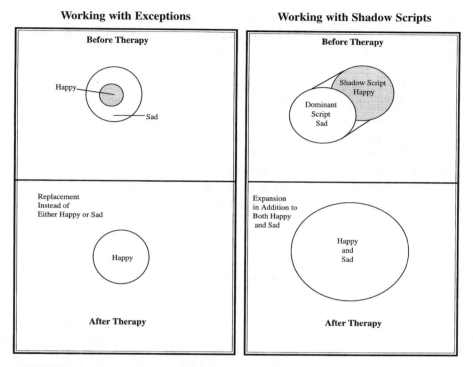

FIGURE 1.2   Comparison view of exceptions and shadow scripts.

Future Shadow Scripts

Future scripts hold our vision of how things will be for us in the future. These are the fragments of possibility, yet to be developed. The future shadow scripts are the traces of the opposite view. For example, a person could have a future script where he sees himself as depressed and alone. This person's view of his future then also contains, by definition, the shadow script where he is happy and interacting with friends or family.

Irrelevant Scripts

Irrelevant scripts contain fragments of discarded scripts that are no longer relevant. For example, they may simply be age inappropriate, (e.g., an adult jumping up and down on the bed). Or they could be role inappropriate. Discarded pieces of a couple's premarital scripts (e.g., going out with the boys on Friday nights) contain behaviors, attitudes, or meanings that do not fit well with their newly developed couple script. Not as frequent but still possible, irrelevant scripts might be socially inappropriate or unavailable (e.g., the aspiring cowboy or behaving like a hippie in the nineties). These are the scripts that individuals are aware of, may have experienced, and have discarded because they are unavailable or no longer relevant. In times of stress, these scripts may become relevant again as the person struggles to solve problems. For example, a newly divorced person may revert to adolescent behavior. Figure 1.3 summarizes the different types of scripts available to individuals and Figure 1.4 depicts how individuals are only "aware" of their dominant scripts. Other scripts available to them are either invisible, defined as irrelevant, or seen as inappropriate.

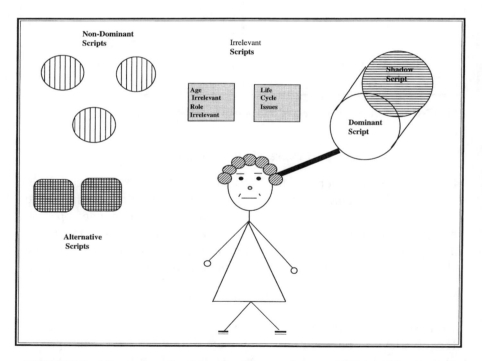

FIGURE 1.3   Many types of scripts exist. They are in constant flux and impact each other and individuals. However, people only "see" scripts that confirm their chosen social script. Shadow scripts contain the opposite, what is not in the dominant script.

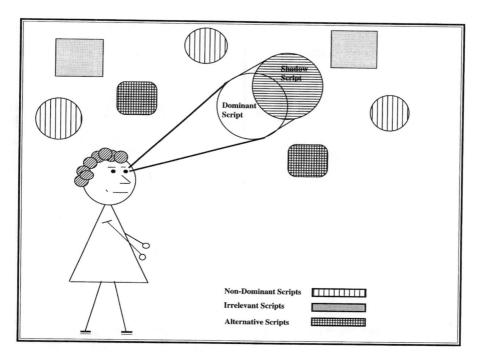

FIGURE 1.4   Depiction of how individuals are only "aware" of their dominant scripts. Other scripts available to them are either invisible, defined as irrelevant, or seen as inappropriate.

Shadow Scripts Applied to Couples

During dating and marriage two separate individuals with two separate meaning systems and two separate sets of scripts develop, recognize, and negotiate a coupled or shared meaning system and script. This coupled meaning system now includes not only both of their individual scripts, but also contains, like overlapping Venn diagrams (see Figure 1.5), the social scripts that define for them what it means to be a couple. Their view of what it means to become a couple may arise from a similarity in social background characteristics but as Berger and Luckmann (1966) point out, it is more likely that it involves a negotiation of a shared process. Within the newly formed marital relationship, the languaging of the couple leads to new definitions of self, other, relatives, and so forth. Thus, the two individuals bring two separate scripts into their

FIGURE 1.5   Depiction of how two individuals' scripts merge to form a third script, the couple script, when individuals marry.

relationship, then negotiate a newly formed script as a couple. It is this team script that they now present to the social world, including their parents, in-laws, bosses, and religious figures. As the Venn diagram indicates, however, parts of the individual scripts have no overlap. These remaining individual scripts are reserved for when the individuals within the couple pursue their own interests or develop their own individual opinions about topics.

Shadow scripts have enormous implications for therapy, for they indicate from the beginning where the possibilities for change are. Shadow scripts are relevant for couple counseling. For example, a particular couple may have negotiated a couple script that contains what a good marriage entails. For them a good marriage might mean that each person is open to new ideas presented by the other. However, for the couple to have ideas about a good marriage, they also must have ideas about a bad marriage. That definition might include one or the other's being opinionated. The definitions that are the opposite of what the couple presents are part of the couples' shadow script, existing peripherally, just below their awareness.

Shadow scripts are also relevant for premarital counseling. Because of the high divorce rate in U.S. society, more and more couples seek premarital counseling. When the therapist asks each partner what he or she likes best about the other, within the response lies the shadow script— the potential trouble spots of the marriage. A partner who describes the other as having a quiet strength, signals that there are traces of "not quiet" and "not strong." A partner who defines her fiancée as protective also announces to the therapist that there might be a time when she defines him as non-protective. The meaning system associated with this also has a shadow script. For example, if she feels safe and cared for when she defines him as protective in premarital counseling, she may later feel unsafe and unloved when she sees him as not protective of her.

The shadow scripts are also those pieces of information that simply do not fit with the individual's definition of the situation. They draw on times when one partner felt the argument was unresolved, times when the nonjudgmental husband expressed a critical statement, when the passionate, loving wife did not want to have sex, when the "laid back" wife had a temper tantrum, when one criticized the other in front of friends—all the times when the behavior was discrepant from the ongoing definition of a good marriage. A couple in therapy because of a boring marriage indicates immediately to the therapist that they have notions of what an exciting marriage is. A couple who reports that there's no passion in their lovemaking verifies to the therapist that they have ideas about passion.

While these notions sound like de Shazer's ideas about exceptions, they are fundamentally different. As stated earlier, exceptions refer to those times when the problem behavior is not happening. The goal of therapy is to replace the problem behavior with the exception. Assisting the client to explore his or her shadow scripts is an invitation to expansion, to include the information that is contained in the shadow script in the current definition of the situation. See Figure 1.2 for a comparison of working with exceptions and working with shadow scripts.

Shadow scripts may contain intense emotional material, and similar to White's notions of restraints, require energy to keep them below the surface. Take for example, the wife who defines her marriage as good and who finds some evidence that her husband is having an affair. When he tells her he's going on a business trip, it might take energy for her to retain her definition of her marriage as good. The more evidence of infidelity she accumulates, the more difficult it becomes to follow the original marriage is "good" script. Eventually the shadow script may become the foreground in the relationship. In so doing, the meaning system has been altered as the definition of the "good marriage" changes. This process also works in reverse.

The Importance of Scripts

In sum, the view in this book is that of the social construction of scripts. It is assumed that there is a developmental aspect which is dynamic rather than static. It is assumed that change is normal and that choice has a part in change. Our knowledge about how to behave is patterned by the family scripts embedded in the larger sociocultural environment. It is assumed that there are multiple family scripts in society. However, while there are a number of family scripts available to us, some of us are only exposed to some of the family scripts and only some are acceptable to us. It is here that such factors as socioeconomic status, level of education, multicultural factors, gender, and unique individual choice come into play. In this book, it is my aim to examine the prevailing constructions in some of the scripts that families bring to the therapeutic situation.

The focus of our model of intervention is on meaning systems and scripts. It is similar to Epston and White's (1990) recent work whereby the therapist initially assists persons in learning how to amplify (be aware of) their psychological processes, provides techniques for generating new possibilities, and creates a safe environment for the client to explore his or her process, generate new possibilities, consider the implications of the possibilities, and negotiate a frame around the chosen change. Tomm's (1987) notions of therapeutic loving are seen as a basis for all therapist/client interactions. We are also influenced by O'Hanlon's notions of possibility therapy which appears to represent ". . . a balance between acknowledgment of existing realities and the creation of new possibilities" (O'Hanlon & Weiner-Davis, 1989, p. 7).

These ways of learning can then be used by the person outside therapy. Over time, as the person learns to rely on self-healing processes, confidence grows and with it, the ability to generate growth and change. The result is new structures that are of a higher order—more connected and integrated, more complex, more flexible, and more susceptible to further change and development than the ones they replaced.

Thus, the approach to family therapy presented in this book is based on the belief that we create our own reality. Individuals make sense of their ongoing experience and it is this process of making sense that is the object of therapy. Social construction therapy takes as its focus the client's meaning system, viewed from the past, present, and future— both negative and positive. The initial focus of the past is affective— understand how clients' meanings developed and how they believe these meanings effected them in the past. Once the past is put in perspective, the second focus of the approach is cognitive—on present scripts for behavior as well as the shadow scripts and on the maintenance of the meaning system. The therapist helps the person, couple, or family to be aware of what and how they think, and facilitates learning about and amplifying exceptions to the process in order to provide possibilities for new solutions. Future focus enables clients to form images of how different meanings and the resultant scripts could effect their lives. "Re-visioning" their lives, or their relationship, or their family is the last stage of this style of therapy and emphasizes future visions of their life. Figure 1.6 presents a therapeutic model flowing from a social constructionist perspective.

SOCIAL CONSTRUCTION THERAPY

Basic Premises of a Social Constructionist Approach

- There are no absolute truths and there are no absolute realities.
- We co-construct reality through language with another or others and in a continual interaction with the sociocultural environment. Thus, what is real is the product of those interactions.
- The social cultural environment contains socially created scripts for behavior, blueprints or plans of action that tell us about behaviors that are appropriate or inappropriate to the given culture.
- Through the process of socialization which occurs through family interaction, children learn the dominant scripts in society.
- People do not incorporate these scripts in the same way. They tend to select out that information corresponding to their individual, couple, or family scripts by noticing behavior in others that confirms

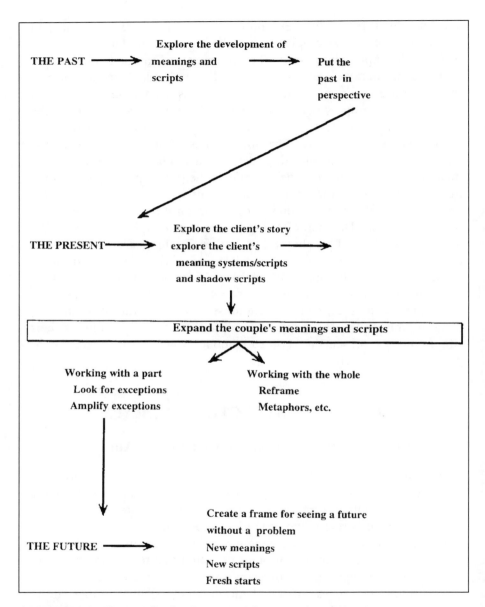

FIGURE 1.6   Therapy flowing from a social construction approach.

their self-definitions and definitions of situations and by selectively ignoring disconfirmatory behavior.

• Always present in the background are shadow scripts, scripts which are just beyond one's awareness. Shadow scripts contain traces, fragments of what is not included in a person's awareness. They could also contain repetitive knowledge of behavior that is discrepant or contradictory to the individual's chosen dominant script.

• Shadow scripts hold possibilities for therapeutic change because their exploration is likely to uncover new knowledge or unique outcomes. Other possibilities for change are the irrelevant scripts, those that contain the fragments of early, no longer useful scripts; the nondominant scripts; the opaque, tenuous, other dominant scripts present in the culture yet outside the person's dominant script and the alternative scripts; and those scripts in society which are not deemed appropriate or normative.

• Individuals, couples or, families who come for therapy are experiencing problems. They have tried many solutions—most of which have been unsuccessful. The problems they report are not seen as being functional in maintaining the system or as a manifestation of underlying pathology. They are seen as problems—problems which have negative effects for them. The language they use to talk about problems reveals how they can use language to co-construct new possibilities.

• Social constructionist therapy focuses on exploring the family's view of themselves to bring their shadow scripts to the foreground, so that possibilities for new ways might emerge.

Figure 1.7 presents a summary of the therapy flowing from this view.

The Concept of Time

The concept of time is an important part of social constructionism (Atwood, 1991; Penn, 1985; White, 1989). For example, by asking How long has this problem been around? or When did you first start becoming depressed about the sexual part of your relationship?, the therapist introduces the historical context of a beginning, a middle, and hopefully, an end. These types of questions give couples and families information about the origins and persistence of problems over time. They also help to dispel beliefs that people were "born this way," are just like one of their parents, or suffer genetic causality.

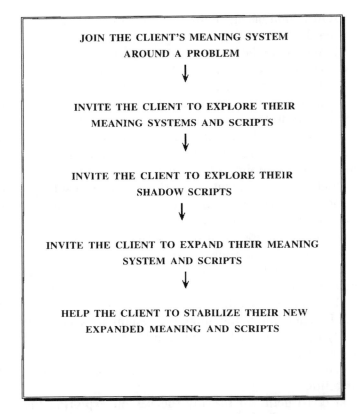

FIGURE 1.7   The therapist's role in social constructionist therapy.

The Concept of Change:
First, Second, and Third Order

Often confused with first- and second-order cybernetics, change refers to the way the client is viewed, while cybernetics refers to the positioning of the therapist. Watzlawick, Weakland, and Fisch (1974) describe two types of therapeutic change: first- and second-order change.

First order changes are consistent with the already existent frame, the changes are reinforcing of the present levels of understanding, and are incremental modifications that make sense within an established frame. First-order change is exemplified by traditional psychotherapy and by the more behaviorally oriented therapies: Change occurs in the elements within the system.

Second-order changes are changes in the frames themselves. First-order change maintains homeostasis, whereas second-order changes are changes in the premises governing the system as a whole. Second-order change is represented by the approaches of Minuchin (1979) and Haley (1976) and involves changes in the system itself.

Third-order change is expansion. Synonyms for *change* generally bring to mind notions of moving something out and bringing something in (e.g., *alter, convert, correct, modify,* and even *mutate*). Within the therapeutic context, it generally has implied that the thing brought in is better than the thing taken out, thereby implying judgment. Synonyms found for *expand,* however, are *extend, open up, spread out, enlarge, develop,* and *unfold.* I feel these words are more descriptive of third-order change.

The Therapist's Stance in Second-Order Cybernetics

Earlier it was stated that second-order cybernetics refers to the positioning of the therapist. But it is more than the therapist's position. It is the therapist's tone, demeanor, and ability to connect. While we say that therapist transparency is a requirement for the second-order stance, it is really therapist connection that is characteristic of this view. For example, a therapist working at the level of second-order, must be able to interchange with the client. As particles and waves become each other, the transparency occurs when the bounds that typically separate people are relaxed and the therapist and client truly understand each other's humanness.

In a second-order cybernetic model, the therapist is a curious observer who takes great care to understand the client. So in this view it is not the client who must "get it," it is the therapist. The therapist asks and reasks "Am I understanding you correctly?" and then asks more questions in order to deepen both their views around the issue. Through language, the issue begins to take on expanded clarity. Simultaneously, the relationship between the client and the therapist develops and deepens, creating increasing levels of safety and respect so that the client feels free to explore new ways of being.

This process is not rational, and since language is logical, it is difficult to describe. It seems that a true therapy of second order is one where the role of the therapist is to create a connection, establish a relationship with the client on a human and spiritual level, where both collaborate in safety to explore and expand their realities so that new possibilities arise around the client's issue. This can result in what Bateson (1972) described as the ability to know that one's perspective exists within many possible frameworks. This kind of knowledge seems to provide both the therapist and the client an opportunity to move among different frameworks or paradigms as is appropriate or useful.

A second-order cybernetic therapy also must enable the client to become therapist independent. In first-order cybernetics, clients are dependent on their therapist for solving their problems. Witness the many jokes about the patients who are dependent on their analysts for minute decisions or who fall to pieces when their therapist goes on vacation in August. This is also true of the traditional family therapists: Called in as consultants, they go in and, with one clean sweep, knock the system on its side. The family is not only dependent on their therapist, but the therapist is often dependent on the master therapist or supervisor for direction. Thus, as one navigates the client-therapist-supervisor-master therapist systems, a hierarchy of dependency exists.

From a second-order therapeutic stance, the therapist becomes part of the system and, as such, acts in collaboration with the client to co-create new stories, new possibilities, new ways of seeing and being. Together they work, fostering awareness and growth that will affect both. Their agreement is nothing more than to come together for a time, one human being to another, to work together by talking to each other about their realities. Ultimately, through trust and mutual respect, they will "see" with expanded vision. The process that is generated is one where both are motivated to mobilize processes in each other that will ultimately promote psychological growth and expand realities. There is no therapist/client dependency; both therapist and client are equal and they are both equally dependent, for all things are dependent on all other things in perfect balance; they have connected with each other on a different plane. There is only process dependency, and this is for both. The process works; they feel its power. Both know when it is operating because they become one, and like the particles and waves, they become each other. They connect with a reality that holds no bounds, yet they feel their boundaries. At that moment they experience the human condition, and its force is healing, nurturing, and loving.

REFERENCES

Andersen, H., & Goolishian, H. (1987). Human systems as linguistic systems: Preliminary and evolving ideas about the implication for clinical therapy. *Family Process, 27,* 371–393.

Andersen, T. (1987). The reflecting team: Dialogue and meta-dialogue in clinical work. *Family Process, 26,* 415–428.

Atwood, J. (1991). Killing two slumpos with one stone. *Family Therapy Case Studies, 5,* 43–50.

Atwood, J. (1992). *Family therapy: A systemic behavioral approach.* Chicago: Nelson Hall.

Atwood, J. (1997, in press). Using shadow scripts in couple therapy. *Journal of Couples Therapy.*

Atwood, J., & Genovese, F. (Eds.) (1993). *Counseling the single parent family.* Alexandria, VA: American Counseling Association.

Bateson, G. (1972). *Steps to an ecology of mind.* New York: Ballantine Books.

Bateson, G. (1978). The birth of a matrix or double-bind epistemology. In M. Berger (Ed.), *Beyond the double bind.* New York: Brunner Mazel.

Bateson, G. (1980). *Mind and nature: A necessary unity.* New York: Bantam.

Bateson, G. (1991). *A sacred unity.* New York: HarperCollins.

Berger, P., & Luckman, T. (1966). *The social construction of reality.* New York: Irvington.

Capra, F. (1983). *The tao of physics.* New York: Bantam.

Cooley, C. (1902). *Human nature and the social order.* New York: Free Press.

Dell, P. F. (1982). Beyond homeostasis: Toward a concept of coherence. *Family Process, 21,* 21–24.

Derrida, J. (1976). *Of grammatology.* Baltimore: Johns Hopkins University Press.

deShazer, S. (1985). *Keys to solutions in brief therapy.* New York: Guilford.

deShazer, S. (1991). *Putting differences to work.* New York: Norton.

Dolan, Y. (1991). *Resolving sexual abuse: Solution-focused therapy and Ericksonian hypnosis for adult survivors.* New York: Norton.

Epston, D. (1989). *Collected papers.* Adelaid South Australia: Dulwich Center Newsletter.

Epston, D., & White, M. (1990). *Consulting your consultants: The documentation of alternative knowledges.* Dulwich Center Newsletter, p. 4.

Foucault, M. (1978). *The history of sexuality.* Vol. 1: *An introduction.* New York: Vintage.

Gagnon, J. (1990). Scripting in sex research. *Annual Review of Sex Research, 1,* 1–39.

Gagnon, J. H., & Simon, W. (1973). *Sexual conduct.* Chicago: Aldine.

Gergen, K. (1985). The social constructionist movement in modern psychology. *American Psychologist, 40,* 266–275.

Gergen, K. (1988). Knowledge and social process. In D. Bar-Tal & A. W. Kruglanski (Eds.), *The social psychology of knowledge* (pp. 30–47). Cambridge, England: Cambridge University Press.

Gergen, K. (1992). Toward a postmodern psychology. In S. Kvale (Ed.), *Psychology and postmodernism: Inquiries in social construction* (pp. 17–30). London: Sage.

Gergen, K., & Gergen, J. (1983). *Historical social psychology.* Hillsdale, NJ: Erlbaum Associates.

Gergen, K. J., & Gergen, M. M. (1988). Narrative and self as relationship. In L. Berkowitz (Ed.), *Social psychological studies of self: Perspectives and programs* (pp. 17–56). San Diego, CA: Academic.

Goldner, V. (1985). Feminism and family therapy. *Family Process, 24,* 31–47.

Haley, J. (1976). *Problem-solving therapy.* San Francisco: Jossey-Bass.

Heisenberg, W. (1958). *Physics and philosophy.* New York: Harper Torchbooks.

Hoffman, L. (1987). Toward a second order family systems therapy. *Family Systems Medicine, 3,* 381–386.

Hoffman, L. (1990). Constructing realities: An art of lenses. *Family Process, 29,* 1–12.

Hume, R. E. (1934). *The thirteen principal upanishads.* New York: Oxford University Press.

Jones, T., & Gerard, J. (1967). Families in developed countries: Determinants and policies. *Family Planning Perspective, 17,* 53–63.

Keeney, B. (1983). *Aesthetics of change.* New York: Guilford.

Keeney, B. (1985). *Mind in therapy: Constructing systemic family therapies.* New York: Basic Books.

Kelly, G. (1969). Man's construction of his alternatives. In R. Maher (Ed.), *Clinical psychology and personality; the second papers of George Kelly.* New York: Wiley.

Kuhn, T. (1970). *The structure of scientific revolutions* (2nd ed.). Chicago: University of Chicago Press.

Laws, J., & Schwartz, P. (1977). *Sexual scripts.* Hinsdale, IL: Dryden.

Lipchik, E., & DeShazer, S. (1986). The purposeful interview. *Journal of Strategic and Systemic Therapies, 5*(1), 27–41.

Madanes, C. (1981). *Strategic family therapy.* San Francisco: Jossey-Bass.

Madanes, C., & Haley, J. (1977). Dimensions of family therapy. *Journal of Nervous and Mental Disorders, 165,* 88–98.

Masterson, J. (1976). *Borderline narcissistic personality and borderlines: An integrated and developmental approach.* New York: Brunner/Mazel.

Maturana, H. (1980). Biology of cognition. In H. R. Maturana & F. Varela (Eds.), *Autopsies and cognition* (pp. 60–83). Boston: Reidel.

Maturana, H. (1987). The biological foundation of self-consciousness and the physical domain of existence. In E. Caianiello (Ed.), *Physics of cognitive processes.* Singapore, Hong Kong: World Scientific.

Maturana, H. (1988). Reality: The search for objectivity or the quest for a compelling argument. In V. Kenny (Ed.), *Irish Journal of Psychology,* [special issue on 'Radical Constructivism,' Autopsies and Psychotherapy] *9*(1), 25–55.

Mead, G. H. (1934). *Mind, self and society.* Chicago: University of Chicago Press.

Minuchin, S. (1974). *Families and family therapy.* Cambridge: Harvard University Press.

Molnar, V., & deShazer, S. (1987). Solution-focused therapy: Toward the identification of therapeutic tasks. *Journal of Marriage and Family Therapy, 13,* 349–358.

Nathanson, M. (1963). *The philosophy of the social sciences.* New York: Random House.

O'Hanlon, W., & Weiner-Davis, M. (1989). *In search of solutions: A new direction in psychotherapy.* New York: W. W. Norton & Co.

Penn, P. (1985). Feed forward: Future questions, future maps. *Family Process, 24,* 299–311.

Piaget, J. (1951). *Play, dreams and imitation in childhood.* London: Routledge and Kegan Paul.

Prigogine, I., & Stengers, I. (1984). *Order out of chaos: Man's new dialogue with nature.* New York: Bantam.

Reiss, D. (1981). *The family's construction of reality.* Cambridge, MA: Harvard University Press.

Tomm, K. (1987). Interventive interviewing: Part I. Strategizing as a fourth guideline for the therapist. *Family Process, 26,* 3–13.

Varela, F. (1979). *Principles of biological autonomy.* New York: Elsevier.

Varela, F. (1981). Describing the logic of the living. In M. Zeleny (Ed.), *Autopsies: A theory of living organization* (pp. 45–70). Oxford: North Holland.

von Foerster, H. (1981a). On cybernetics of cybernetics and social theory. In G. Roth & H. Schwegler (Eds.), *Self-organizing systems: An interdisciplinary approach* (pp. 55–67). New York: Campus.

von Foerster, H. (1981b). *Observing systems.* Seaside, CA: Intersystems.

von Foerster, H. (1984a). On constructing a reality. In P. Watzlawick (Ed.), *The invented reality.* New York: Norton.

von Foerster, H. (1984b). Apropos epistemologies. *Family Process, 24,* 517–521.

von Glaserfeld, E. (1984). An introduction to radical constructivism. In P. Watzlawick (Ed.), *The invented reality* (pp. 91–104). New York: Norton.

Walter, J., & Peller, J. (1992). *Becoming solution-focused in brief therapy.* New York: Brunner/Mazel.

Watzlawick, P., Weakland, J. H., & Fisch, R. (1974). *Change: Principles of problem-formulation and problem resolution.*

White, M. (1986). Negative explanation, restraint, and double description: A template for family therapy. *Family Process, 25,* 169–184.

White, M. (1989, Summer). *The externalizing of the problem.* Dulwich Centre Newsletter.

Zukav, D. (1989). *The dancing Wuli masters: An overview of the new physics.* New York: William Morrow.

CHAPTER 2

Extramarital Affairs and Constructed Meanings: A Social Constructionist Therapeutic Approach

Joan D. Atwood and Madeline Seifer

> *The world of nature, as explored by the natural scientist, does not "mean" anything to molecules, atoms, and electrons. But the observational field of the social scientist—social reality—has a specific meaning and relevance structure for the human beings living, acting, and thinking within it.*
> A. Schutz, (1962, p. 58).

INTRODUCTION

It is estimated that up to 66% of males and 55% of married women engage in extramarital sex (EMS) at some time during their marriage (Gass & Nicols, 1988). Affairs are given as a reason for marital separation by 31% of men and 45% of women, with 17% of the men and 10% of the women who report affairs eventually filing for divorce (Humphrey, 1985a). While some couples appear to cope effectively with extramarital affairs, others turn to couple therapists for help. Humphrey and Strong (1976) polled clinical members of the American Association for Marriage and Family Therapy (AAMFT), who reported that almost half of their clients came to therapy because of involvement of one or both spouses in extramarital affairs. Marett (1990) also reports that extramarital affairs are given as a common reason for couples entering therapy.

This chapter presents information on extramarital affairs and discusses the sociocultural definitions of extramarital sex which influence the reasons couples construct for involving themselves in EMS. It presents information on typical psychological reactions, taking into account current research. A six-stage social construction therapeutic model addressing the meaning systems of couples who experience EMS is then presented.

Definitions

Definitions of marital behavior and extramarital behavior in the United States are socially constructed. These definitions are heavily influenced by religious teachings which almost universally condemn extramarital sex. They are reinforced by our legal system, which restricts sexual behavior to within marriage. As a result, in this society, socialization around dating patterns and marital scripts usually lead couples to antic- ipate sexual faithfulness from their marital partners. At the same time, however, extramarital sex is glorified by the media. The mass media blatantly uses sex—without regard to the marital status of the partici- pants—to sell movies, perfumes, liquor, cars, soap, and all sorts of non- erotic items. Thus, we get many contradictory messages about EMS. On the one hand, the religious and legal systems are restrictive toward EMS; on the other, the media often encourages it. Both the socially con- structed traditional and liberal prescriptions for EMS present explicit and implicit scripts for conduct. Examining the two positions as important elements of the social world in which extramarital relationships are avoided or approached should yield important information for the couple therapist. While for the most part there is a social proscription against EMS, there are times when there is a haltingly grudging tolerance of EMS in a limited way. This tolerance is extended primarily to men and is manifested in the belief that men have stronger sex drives than women so EMS is a natural fulfillment of the male's need for sexual variety, frequency, and eroticism. It is further accompanied by the social constructions that men have animal natures that prohibit sexual monogamy and that "men will be men."

The language used to describe EMS is fraught with negative meaning. The word *adultery* conjures up images of scarlet letters and infidelity is defined as falseness or disloyalty. Basically, intimate relations with another person by a married person is likely to be defined as infidelity and sexual intercourse with another person is legally considered adultery—a crime against the state as well as the partner. Negative definitions are not only restricted to religion and law; family therapists perpetuate negative images as well. For example, Pittman (1989) uses the term *infidel* for the EMS spouse and *cuckold* for the non-EMS spouse. Moultrup's (1990) language is more neutral. He defines EMS as a relationship between a person and someone other than the spouse that has an impact on the level of intimacy, emotional distance, and overall dynamic balance in the marriage.

Percentages

Percentages of those who engage in extramarital sex vary from survey to survey. (Kinsey, Pomeroy, & Martin, 1948; Kinsey, Pomeroy, Martin, & Gebhard, 1953) reported that about half of all married men and 26% of women have intercourse with persons other than their partners at some time during their marriage. Other studies (Athanasiou, Shaver, & Tavris, 1970; Bell, Turner, & Rosen , 1975; Blumstein & Schwartz, 1983; Hite, 1981; Hunt, 1974; Johnson, 1970; Levin, 1975; Maykovich, 1976; Nass, Libby, & Fisher, 1981; Pietropinto & Simenauer, 1978; Wolfe, 1980) have found similar or higher incidences. More recent surveys (Gass & Nicols, 1988) indicate that up to 66% of males and 55% of females engage in extramarital affairs at some point in their marriage.

There are some discrepancies among the studies. Given that surveys used different sampling techniques (i.e., face-to-face interview vs. mailed-in questionnaire), samples were often quite limited (e.g., restricted to readers of magazines, specific geographic location, etc.), and underreporting due to embarrassment and other causes is possible, it is not surprising that results differ. However, it is reasonable to conclude that more men than women engage in extramarital sex, and that EMS appears to have increased among both genders since the time of Kinsey.

EMS Typologies

EMS appears in several different forms: (a) incidents which are sexual in nature but involve no emotion—the "one-night stands" or encounters with a prostitute (Hurlbert, 1992); (b) relations that are both sexual and emotional, indicating a more intense emotional involvement (Thompson, 1984); and (c) relationships that are emotional but not sexual (Sarrel, 1984, Personal Communication). Pittman (1989) believes that any type of affair violates a couple's tacit agreements around issues of intimacy. Thompson (1984) found that 43% of his respondents were involved in at least one of the three types of extramarital affairs at some point during their marriage, with 21% involved in predominantly sexual affairs. Men were more likely to be involved in predominantly sexual affairs, while women were more likely to be involved in emotional affairs (Hurlbert, 1992). In addition, 19% were involved in affairs that were both sexual and emotional, while 18% reported involvement in emotional but nonsexual encounters (Thompson, 1984).

Lawson (1988) provides another typology: parallel, traditional, or recreational affairs. Parallel affairs are known by the spouse but tacitly condoned. Traditional affairs are not known to the spouse and would be a violation of the marital agreement. Recreational affairs are generally found in "open marriages." They usually involve inviting additional persons to the marital bed, are most often consensual, and are not usually in violation of any tacit agreements. Another discriminator with regard to extramarital activities assesses whether the affairs are single or bilateral. With singular involvement, only one spouse is engaging in extramarital activities; the bilateral designation is reserved for couples in which both partners are engaging in EMS. Finally, Humphrey (1987) distinguishes between heterosexual and homosexual affairs.

What We Know About EMS

The following research studies indicate that social background variables are minimally useful in accounting for EMS; however, some significant correlations were found. Bell, Turner, and Rosen (1975) found that political orientation and geographic location were significantly related to women's extramarital intercourse. Conservative women living in mountain and prairie regions of the United States were less likely to engage in EMS. Edwards and Booth (1976) found age negatively related to extramarital intercourse for husbands but not for wives. Kinsey et al. (1948, 1953), Wolfe (1982), and Tavris and Sadd (1977) found typical EMS to be infrequent, sporadic, and occurring with others who were married. Frequency was highest for younger men and older women. Those with higher education and lower levels of church attendance were more likely to be involved in EMS and erotic behavior. Edwards and Booth (1976), Humphrey (1985b), and Thompson (1983) found that the lower persons rated qualitative and sexual aspects of their marriage, the more likely they were to engage in EMS. On the other hand, Spanier and Margolis (1983) found that EMS may directly affect marital quality. Prior knowledge of an extramarital sexual partner may play a role as well. Humphrey (1985b) suggests that wives are more inclined than husbands (41% to 26%) to have their extramarital sex with a "friend." Humphrey (1985b) further suggests that the workplace may be a fertile breeding ground for affairs, noting that 39% of husbands and 36% of wives in his sample had indicated that their lover was a co-worker. The best predictor of EMS was liberal attitudes (Kinsey et al., 1948, 1953; Singh, Walton, & Williams, 1976). The more liberal individuals are, the more likely they are to hold permissive attitudes about extramarital sex, which influence whether or not they will engage in it.

From the above it can be concluded that EMS may be viewed as either a cause or consequence of marital problems or as unrelated to them. Also, we can conclude that old, friendless, uneducated, religious, conservative, unemployed, mountain women and young, friendless, uneducated, religious, conservative, unemployed, mountain men are least likely to engage in EMS.

Socially Constructed Beliefs and Rationales for EMS

Some of the more common beliefs about EMS are: Affairs are good for a marriage, can revive a dull marriage, or are a normal part of marriage. Affairs may mean that the love is gone from the marriage, that divorce is imminent, or that the lover is sexier or more handsome than the marital partner. In addition to socially constructed beliefs about EMS, couples construct rationales for EMS (Humphrey, 1986). One reason given for EMS is sexually based: Disagreements over the frequency of intercourse, over nudity, over techniques and coital positions, over sexual fatigue due to career, or household and childcare responsibilities. The "cup-of-coffee syndrome" is another reason given for extramarital sexual affairs (Humphrey, 1983). This rationale states that EMS affairs often result from attractions that are initially quite innocent and asexual in nature. They may begin when two persons, each married to someone else, begin to relax over a cup of coffee, whether at work or someplace else, and soon develop the "habit" of meeting regularly where they share more and more details of their lives and feelings. They develop a dependence on these coffee talks. Finally, sex enters as the next level of involvement. "It just happened," is a common statement of this situation.

Sometimes constructed EMS rationales have aspects of intentionality. The couple may want to adopt "alternative lifestyles" that are beyond jealousy and sexual possessiveness. Not infrequently such cases may involve married couples mate-swapping or "swinging," (less so today, in the AIDS era). Retaliation is also given as a rationale (Spanier & Margolis, 1983). Humphrey (1987) cites nearly 50 reasons constructed by clients for becoming involved in EMS: marital sexual frustration or boredom, unhappiness in the marriage, the need to be accepted, propinquity, variety, curiosity, rebellion, love, friendship, spouse encouragement or permission, reassurance of aging sexuality, pleasure and recreation, combating depression, infrequent or absent marital coitus, poor marital coitus, preserving the marriage, commitment failure, conquest, compensating for feeling inferior or inadequate, learning a new technique, being drunk or otherwise under the influence of drugs, gaining social status, getting promoted, frustration, escapism, curing sexual dysfunction, helping out a sexually deprived friend, asserting one's independence, hurting or challenging a spouse, unavailability of spouse, neurosis, mental illness, retardation, feeling vulnerable, being emancipated from conventional standards, clarifying sexual orientation, creating jealousy and gaining attention, becoming pregnant, earning money, rekindling a former romance with old beau or previous spouse, reducing marital intimacy, something lacking in the marriage, spouse just does not understand, spouse "made me to do it," and villainy. Other authors cite a sense of alienation (Maykovich, 1976); the need for intimacy, emotional independence, and sex role equalitarianism (Buunk, 1980); and for women, knowing someone who had engaged in an extramarital affair so they won't feel left out (Atwater, 1979). From the above we can conclude that individuals will give any and many reasons for engaging in EMS. Many people (including therapists) believe these constructions.

Reality Sets In: The Spouse Knows

Clients of individual therapists, social workers, and attorneys have acknowledged that affairs have led to the following consequences: breaking of religious teaching, the breaking of trust, guilt, dishonesty, lies, anger, humiliation, depression, suicide, homicide, marital conflict, separation, divorce, anxiety, regret, lost respect and love, disruption of careers, disruptions of marriages and families, loss of reputation, unwanted pregnancies, abortions, sexually transmitted diseases, loss of time and money, fears, jealousy, and sexual conflicts and dysfunctions (Humphrey, 1987).

In clinical samples of clients' reactions to learning of their spouses extramarital affair, the most common negative emotion experienced by husbands was anger (38%), followed by shock (19%). Wives ranked shock first (45%) and anger second (35%) (Humphrey, 1985, October). It was also noted that 8% of husbands and 7% of wives first reacted to their spouses' affairs with denial. None of the wives reacted first with calm acceptance, although 3% of husbands did so. In addition, 6% of husbands and 14% of wives never knew of their spouses' extramarital sexual involvement at the time therapy terminated (Humphrey, 1987). In some cases (26% of the EMS husbands; 21% of the EMS wives), marriages were improved as a result of the EMS. However it should be noted that it is not possible to conclude whether improvement was due to the affair, the therapy, both, or neither. Furthermore, these reactions may have been biased, in that they were representative of clinical populations and not necessarily representative of the EMS population in general. It is possible that the nonclinical EMS population had different reactions. Nevertheless, 46% of the husbands and 48% of the wives in Humphrey's clinical sample ended therapy either separated or divorced (Humphrey, 1985, October).

Most traditional methods of scientific inquiry (such as those described above) do not allow the individual's meanings to become known. The interviewer delineates response categories, determines which questions will be asked, and, in so doing, restricts answers. "All of these procedures," as Kohler-Reisman (1989) notes, "result in the dominance of the investigator's definition over that of the subject" (p. 743). In many ways the findings of the research tell us more about the interviewer than the interviewee! The point of this discussion is that based on different meaning systems, individuals give different meanings to, react differently to, and adjust differently to life events in general, and EMS in particular. A working hypothesis of this chapter is that changes in the meaning systems of EMS couples may influence the outcome for the couple.

SOCIALLY CONSTRUCTED MEANING SYSTEMS

Berger and Luckmann (1966) believe that the socially constructed meanings we hold are opaque (p. 55). By this they mean that the way our meanings are constructed is invisible to us, as are the elements that compose them. The social world we are born into is experienced by children as the sole reality. The rules of that world are not problematic; they require no explanation and they are neither challenged nor doubted. Through socialization the socially constructed meanings are internalized; they are filtered and understood through meaningful symbols. From these socially constructed meanings flow marital meanings and marital scripts. A person attempts to match his or her own experience with the available meanings and scripts and learns the language-appropriate behavior for his or her gender, age, and culture. In these ways a person develops an individual identity, an individual marital script and individual marital meanings using the dominant culture as a primary resource. For some, EMS becomes a part of their marital script.

An individual's reality is maintained by developing a personal sense of self that is congruent with the social constructions. As stated earlier, based on early interactions and ongoing socialization, individuals construct a reality around marital meanings that includes a preferred way of relating to others. This, then, becomes the basis for how they view others and how they expect others to view them. In many ways, this perceptual set determines predictable ways of interacting with others. We carry these socially defined ways of behaving into marital relationships.

Berger and Kellner (1979) define marriage as a definitional process. Two separate individuals come together with separate identities and begin to construct a life as a couple. What once were independent identities of the two individuals are now modified to incorporate the relationship identity. Now the two individuals construct a relationship reality where all conversations serve to validate this coupled identity. Gergen and Gergen (1983) used the term *self-narratives* to describe the social psychological processes whereby people tell stories about themselves to themselves and others. In this manner, individuals establish coherent connections in life events. They believe that individuals have a set of schema by which they attempt to understand life events as meaningful and systematically related. In this way, events are rendered understandable and intelligible because they are located in a sequence or as a part of an unfolding process. It is this process that enables individuals to make sense out of nonsense and to interpret events in a coherent, consistent manner. This chapter sees EMS as a sociocultural symbolic construct. Inquiry into the sources, processes, and consequences of the construction and organization of EMS is the therapy which flows from this view.

Applied to marriage, these narratives or marital meaning systems are originally created by and maintained by interactions with significant others. The process begins at birth and continues to death. A person holding a particular marital meaning system will seek out events and persons that are consistent with that meaning system. Marital meaning systems in turn lead to *states,* the emotional reaction to the meaning system, and *behaviors* actions consistent with the marital meaning system. Because these meanings are created, embedded in, and recognized by the larger social group, they operate at the social, interpersonal, and intrapersonal levels. "Because the meanings of the events and actions were different, the feelings and actions that followed varied as well," comments Kohler-Reisman (1989).

Individuals' marital meaning systems determine the content of their marital scripts (see Gagnon, 1973, for the notion of scripts as applied to sexuality). Marital "scripts are involved in learning the meaning of internal states, organizing the sequences of specific [marital] acts, decoding novel situations, setting the limits on [marital] responses, and linking meanings from [non-marital] aspects of life to specifically [marital] "experiences" (Gagnon, 1973, p. 6). People develop marital scripts out of their marital meaning systems. A script is a device for "guiding action and for understanding it" (p. 6). Scripts are plans that people have about what they are doing and what they are going to do. They justify actions that are in agreement with them and challenge those that are not.

Marital "scripts constitute the available repertoire of socially recognized acts and statuses, and roles and the rules governing them" (p. 217). They operate at a social, personal, and intrapsychic level. They are embedded in social institutions and as such are internalized by individuals. The overriding, dominant scripts receive the most attention because of their primacy and potency among people's behavioral options. It is against the dominant social script that people attempt to match or reject their own personalized version. "It is clear that the [marital] scripts that individuals bring to treatment exist at the intrapsychic and the interpersonal levels and most, though not all, interventions involve changes in both" (Gagnon, 1990, p. 33). Generally speaking, persons do not usually set out to have EMS. The EMS behavior is the result of an unfolding definitional process whereby a rationale for the activity is created over a period of time. For some individuals, EMS becomes part of their dominant personal marital script. Figure 2.1 describes these revising processes.

Couples make sense of their ongoing experience and it is this process of making sense that is the object of therapy. The therapy takes as its focus clients' marital meanings, viewed from the past, present, and future—both negative and positive (see Figure 2.1). The initial focus on the past is aimed at understanding how marital meanings developed and how the couple believe these meanings affected them in the past. Once the past is put in perspective, the second phase is cognitive, examining the couple's marital script and the maintenance of the couple's marital meanings, in the present, helping the couple to be aware of processes, and facilitating learning about and amplifying exceptions to their process in order to provide possibilities for new solutions. Future focus enables the couple to imagine how different marital meanings and the resultant marital scripts could affect their relationship in a positive way. Re-visioning the relationship is the last stage of this therapy and emphasizes future visions of the couple relationship without the EMS problem.

To Therapy We Go: Common EMS Therapeutic Issues

To Tell or Not to Tell

Some controversies still exist with regard to whether or not an affair should cease if therapy is to commence or continue (Green & Bobele, 1988; Hendrix, 1988; Marett, 1990; Moultrup, 1990). As far as telling the spouse about the affair, there are conflicting views. According to Guerin and Fay (1992), if and when the therapist finds out about the affair, a decision must be made whether to discuss the affair in a conjoint session. "While a theoretical argument can be made for doing so,"

MODEL OF THE DEVELOPMENT OF THE MEANING
SYSTEM

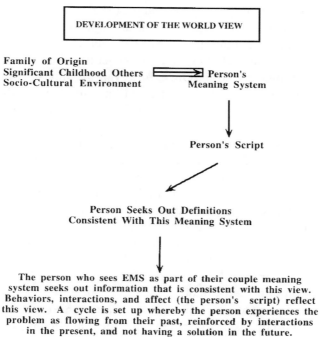

FIGURE 2.1   Model of the development of the meaning system.

they write, "it is our position that this should not generally be done" (p. 148). They point out that informing the unaware spouse of the affair will result in raising the couple's anxiety at the point in treatment where the main purpose is to reduce anxiety. The major exception to this rule is the case of "gaslighting," in which the unaware spouse, convinced of an affair, is severely depressed or even psychotic because she or he is constantly confronted with denial.

The term gaslighting was coined as a metaphor for the "head games" which occurred in the classic movie *Gaslight,* starring Charles Boyer and Ingrid Bergman. In the film, the husband systematically attempts to drive his wife mad by having the gaslights flicker and convincing his wife that she is imagining these events. It is only after the intervention of a Scotland Yard detective that her perceptions are validated and she realizes the full implications of her husband's plot to deceive her. What sometimes occurs when an affair is uncovered is that the accused attempts to convince his or her spouse that many of the incidents are imagined and/or the evidence misinterpreted. An attempt to falsify information often accompanies gaslighting (Gass & Nichols, 1988). Concealment is a simpler process than falsification, and generally occurs at the beginning of the extramarital affair. Once, however, the spouse begins to ask questions about specific actions, falsifications, and the creation of stories to account for one's time, the deception is likely to ensue (Gass & Nichols, 1988).

It is at this point that the gaslighting begins to become destructive, as more and more evidence of the affair is met with more assertions of the spouse's "wild imagination." The spouse "knows what was seen or heard, but is unable to have it validated," and typically begins to doubt his or her sanity. One might recall that Harry Stack Sullivan (1953) defined reality as that which can be consensually validated. In the case of a denied affair, the only person who could possibly validate one's perceptions will not confirm what the individual "knows." As a matter of fact, the accuser may be accused of "hearing things" or imagining them, reinforcing the self-doubt.

A therapist learns of an affair during or after an evaluation process faces three important tasks: (a) to make a clinical judgment as to whether a secret affair, past or present, ought to be made clinically definitive, (b) explain to the spouse having the affair that the affair must be terminated if progress is to be made in marital therapy, and (c) recognize and validate the pain and sense of loss which the person having an affair will experience. These tasks are accomplished in individual sessions (Guerin & Fay, 1992).

To Stop or Not to Stop

For persons who enter treatment over the issue of an ongoing affair, the first issue becomes, "to stop or not to stop" the affair. According to Moultrup (1990), any demand by the therapist that an affair discontinue presents multiple problems. First, he points out that the potential for deceit places the client in the position of having more power than the therapist. Second, if the involved spouse was the one to initiate individual treatment, requesting that the affair be kept confidential, and is then counseled to reveal it to the spouse and have the spouse enter therapy as well, it is unlikely that the client will agree to the stipulation. Third, a demand by a therapist to discontinue an affair, according to Moultrup (1990) may have more to do with the therapist's own issues than with the client's. He argues that the therapist's agenda may relate to issues of control or sexuality, or possibility to one's own history of involvement in extramarital affairs. In addition, he feels that if an affair has been of long duration, it has helped to maintain a comfortable emotional distance between spouses, which needs a slower reorganization than the cessation of an affair would allow.

Other theoreticians would certainly take issue with Moultrup's viewpoint. It has been a widely held belief of marriage and family therapists that triangular relationships of husbands, wives, and lovers must be ended before meaningful therapy can begin. Hendrix (1988) insists that couples who present for any type of marital therapy, including those with issues of EMS, must close off their exits. He insists upon a total commitment on their parts to the therapeutic process and works toward cutting them off from their typical ways of distancing from their partners. Recent trends would, however, support Moultrup's assertion that a negative therapist stance toward the affair often obligates the transgressing spouse to apologize, while the "wronged" spouse grants forgiveness. Further problems are felt to arise if the involved spouse perceives that the therapist is siding with the uninvolved spouse, acting as a confidante. On the other hand, failure to take sides can also be viewed as collusion with the involved spouse. (Smith, 1991). Another dilemma created by some sort of judgmental stance is the "loss of face" which can occur when spouses are asked to either confess or forgive. At times this creates a no-win situation for one or both partners, and might become an impediment to therapy (Smith, 1991).

SOCIAL CONSTRUCTION THERAPY WITH AN EXTRAMARITAL SEX ISSUE

In spite of the apparently high incidence of extramarital activity in today's society, very few specific models exist in the field of marriage and family therapy to assist a couple with an extramarital affair. Instead, extramarital affairs are perceived as not much different from any other presenting problem in therapy and are therefore treated via a variety of theoretical orientations (Marett, 1990). However since EMS can be framed as anything from moral transgression to romantic interlude, the beliefs that clinicians hold and the resulting method of therapy clinicians choose with regard to extramarital affairs affect their treatment options (Smith, 1991).

Couple therapists working with couples where one or both members have been involved in extramarital sex quickly recognize the multitude of issues and complexities of couple reactions to EMS. Extramarital involvement can be viewed by couples and their therapists as one of the most significant threats to marriage or it can be viewed as an unimportant transgression. This complexity of meaning is true not only for clients but for therapists as well and is further complicated in that the meaning therapists assign to extramarital sex affects the treatment options they choose. Couple therapists have generally been consistent with society's negative views, using a problem-oriented approach to studying EMS. Inherent in this type of approach is the assumption that the marital couple should be protected and any activity that threatens the marital unit is considered problematic. Thus, therapists' constructions of marriage and of EMS dictate a problem-oriented framework, or a deficit model. Focusing on the problems that EMS couples experience, while initially important, may create a negative therapeutic focus by amplifying the "EMS problem," and the couple may come to accept that their relationship will never be better.

Similarly, a therapist's orientation or serendipitously timely areas of investigation might also affect the assessment and treatment strategies utilized. As an example, suppose that the night before a couple presented in a therapist's office with an EMS issue the therapist had been reading a book on the family life cycle. With this model in mind, the therapist is likely to selectively amplify data in the course of the therapeutic conversation which is relevant to this model. As a consequence, the couple might generate a picture of their lives around the "empty nest syndrome," perhaps leading to a discussion of issues of intimacy.

On the other hand, if on the previous evening, the therapist had been reading an article on loss and mourning, the therapeutic conversation with the couple on the following day might take a different course, perhaps highlighting the fact that the EMS could have been a response which was intended to fill the void created by the loss of a parent. Again, suppose the therapist had been revisiting Minuchin and Fishman's (1974) structural approach to family therapy. The therapist might then be focusing on boundaries, alliances, and skewed structures within the family system. From this viewpoint, an assessment might be made that the father's extramarital affair was a response to feeling peripheral to the mother-daughter coalition in the family. In each case a plausible alternative story can be built conjointly by the couple and the therapist. Each story or narrative is structured around an available cultural theme, or theoretical orientation. Each story has a different cast of characters, logic, as well as moral and ethical assumptions.

In an effort to avoid a therapist-imposed narrative and therefore a therapist/theorist-imposed assessment and treatment strategy for the issue of EMS, a social constructionist therapeutic model emphasizes a collaborative approach, along with the avoidance of single explanations or viewpoints, in a search for multiple perspectives to describe clinical phenomena (Smith, 1991). The social constructionist model is principally concerned with describing and utilizing the *processes* by which people come to describe and explain the world, including themselves (Gergen, 1985). It attempts to articulate common forms of understanding as they have existed in both the past as well as in the present, and as they might exist in the future.

Basic Premises of a Social Construction Approach

All approaches to therapy hold certain assumptions. Social constructionism assumes the following:

- There are no absolute truths and there are no absolute realities. Rather, reality is experiential and therefore an outgrowth of how we subjectively interpret the world (vonGlaserfeld, 1984).
- People co-construct reality through language with another in a continual interaction with the sociocultural environment. What we call reality resides and is expressed in one's descriptions of events, people, feelings, and experiences. These descriptions evolve through social interactions that are themselves shaped by those descriptions. Discourse, or languaging, provides the frames within which social action takes place (Harre, 1984).
- An individual's inner world is a construct colored by the past, and the past is a construct.
- Couples tend to re-create an image of their world by noticing behavior in others that confirms their self-definitions and definitions

of situations and to selectively ignore disconfirming behavior (Atwood, 1993). ·

- Couples who come for therapy are experiencing problems in their relationship. They have attempted numerous solutions, many of which have been unsuccessful. The way that couples discourse about problems is the way they can use language to co-construct a new story. In the course of the therapeutic conversation about the problem, the therapist scans the couple's language system, attempting to transform the telling of the stories and the relationship between the stories (Atwood, 1993).

- Partner behavior that is discrepant with the perception of the other partner will result in a change in the observer's perceptual view. This change is accomplished by focus on and the amplification of exceptions in the observer's description of his or her world (Atwood, 1993).

- Social construction couple therapy with an EMS issue challenges the couple's view of the meaning the EMS holds by breaking up the meaning of the "problem" and questioning their marital script. This is achieved through the use of techniques (e.g., metaphors and reframes) that amplify the couple's process and by finding exceptions to the couple's process (deconstruction), thereby providing seeds (reconstruction) for transformation.

A THERAPEUTIC FLOW BASED ON SOCIAL CONSTRUCTION THEORY

I. Joining the Couple's Meaning System

In their discussion of the therapeutic process, Minuchin and Fishman (1974) highlight the need for creating an empathic rapport with the clients before any real work can begin. They describe this socialization process and encourage the therapist to utilize mimesis, whereby the clients' own language and affect are utilized by the therapist in an effort to create the safe therapeutic environment. Cimmarustu and Lappin (1985) refer to joining as creating a "workable reality." In workable realities, the view of the problem transforms from a paradigm of individual causality to one of interaction. The basic assumption is that the clients are the experts; the therapist assumes the role of the curious observer who is interested in learning the couple's story.

II. Proposing the Notion of the Couple's Meaning System

Using the above as a backdrop for constructing a therapeutic frame around an EMS issue, the couple therapy can be divided into three different stories: the couple's stories about their families of origin (how their meaning system concerning EMS developed in the first place), their story about their present relationship (how their belief system around the EMS is maintained), and their story about what they see for their future (how their meaning system and script about EMS can change). Knowledge of each of these three stories helps the therapist and the couple to understand the meaning system around the EMS.

Thus, clients are asked how they see the meaning of the EMS in the context of their society and culture. The couple interaction around the affair is viewed as a symbol to which society ascribes meaning, as it does to all other symbols as well. Therefore the approach to the problem is a matter of symbolic interpretation.

Constructing a Time Line

The concept of time is an important part of this model (White, 1989). By asking "How long has this problem been around? When did you first about the EMS?" the therapist introduces a historical context containing a beginning, a middle and hopefully an end (Atwood & Dershowitz, 1992). This contextual frame helps couples view their problem as being located in time rather than in themselves, thereby externalizing it so that its characteristics are examinable and observable (White, 1989; Atwood & Dershowitz, 1992).

The Past: The Development of the EMS Meaning System

When therapists feel an exploration into the past would be helpful (as indicated by their clients), therapists can use the rubber band to help the client move backwards in time. "If I were to take a rubber band and stretch it back to when you were a small child, can you remember any events that helped to define EMS for you?" Couples can explore how their meaning systems around EMS became established in the first place.

They can explore family of origin belief systems that contributed to their ability to construct a rationale for EMS in the present. The rubber band metaphor can be applied and stretch it to the time before when the EMS issue appeared "What was your relationship like then?" "Was there anything you wanted to change then?" The implied meaning around such an inquiry is that there was once a time when the problem was not there and that perhaps there were issues then that the couple could work on now, moving the emphasis away from the current EMS. The further implication is that perhaps at some point in the future the problem will also not be there (Atwood & Dershowitz, 1992).

Putting the Past to Rest

After both partners have told a story of how they first developed their marital meanings and their marital scripts, the past is put in perspective. Ritual can help clients lay the past to rest. For example, clients can write down all the important childhood events that relate to their developing marital meaning systems and marital scripts, both negative and positive, and place the paper in a shoe box and bury it (symbolically burying the past). Some clients may want to write a letter, which can be mailed or buried, to significant persons from their childhood. Or a ceremony, whereby clients symbolically let go of the past by setting a balloon or kite free at the beach, can be performed. Doing something special for caretakers can symbolically show appreciation for early gifts.

III. Inviting the Couple to Explore Their Present Meaning System

At this point in therapy, the couple is asked to tell the story of their current relationship. The focus is on how they combined their meaning systems and behavioral scripts to co-create a couple or marital script (Atwood, 1993). The therapist attempts to obtain a thorough understanding of the couple's story by investigating how the EMS was scripted into the couple relationship, at both the individual and couple levels. Clues are revealed in exploring the couple's linguistic symbolizations, metaphors, myths, and legends.

A further investigation of their meaning system is facilitated through questions associated with the beginnings of their relationship. Typical questions include: "How did you meet? What did you think about each other when you first met? How did you know this was it? How did the relationship evolve? How was your first encounter? How does each of you perceive your couple story—similarly or differently? Where is the story different?" (Atwood, 1993). When the investigation of the stories is complete, the therapist can focus on the themes and metaphors which run through the couple's construction of their meaning system (Atwood, 1993).

While discovering meaning within the couple's story about the EMS, the therapist and the couple learn what information the partners select out of their environment and how that information is selectively integrated into their meaning system, thereby reinforcing it. Patterned conversations and attempted solutions are noted as reflections of this meaning system. Relevant questions might be: "How do you think of the EMS issue? What meaning does it hold for you, for your relationship? What solutions have you attempted? Do you see any other options?"

Once the couple accepts that there are several different ways of looking at and observing reality, and that their meaning systems are socially constructed through interactions with others, it becomes possible to deconstruct it. The process of deconstruction involves the dismantling of the couple's meaning system. Only after this deconstruction has occurred can the couple begin to explore new, alternative meanings, and have them take hold. Change can occur only when partners begin to question their old definitions of their relationship. The role of the therapist now is to simultaneously attempt to break up the old meaning system, while planting seeds for a new one to develop.

When couples notice that their meaning systems are connected to the way they view their problems, they gather information about how they may have inadvertently contributed to the perpetuation of the problem, in this case the EMS. They might begin to notice the distance which the affair created between them and how that distance was maintained by both of them.

IV. Inviting the Couple to Expand Their Meaning Systems

Challenging the System

The following section elaborates the process by which a couple's marital meaning system can be challenged in order to create new experiences.

CLARIFYING THE COUPLE'S MODUS OPERANDI.   One method of assisting a couple to expand their meaning systems around EMS is to clarify the couple's process. Some useful ways of doing so are tracking (Minuchin & Fishman, 1974); circular (Boscolo, Cecchin, Hoffman & Penn, 1987) and reflexive questioning (Tomm, 1987); exaggeration (Haley, 1967); imagery (Papp, 1982); and sculpting (see Atwood, 1993). Tracking around the issue of EMS may help the couple to see the recursiveness of their language and the redundancy of their interactions concerning the issue. Circular questioning highlights the circular nature of the couple's interactions while reflexive questioning may lay the groundwork for change. As an example of reflexive questioning, the couple might be asked, "What would have to happen in order for you to realize that the problem was getting better? What would you notice if the EMS issue were becoming less of an impediment to your closeness and overall happiness?" Basically, the more the couple uses language to describe the effects of the EMS on their relationship, the more clarity they have about what it means for them, as individuals and as a couple.

EXPLORING THE EFFECTS OF EMS.   It is useful for the couple to focus on the effects of the EMS issue on the relationship rather than specifically on the details of the EMS (Durrant, 1991). In so doing, the problem begins to move to a location external to the couple. They begin to see themselves as not having an EMS issue, but rather as having a problem which has negative consequences for their marriage. "How has the affair influenced your relationship? How has it influenced your relationship with your friends? Your children? What was your relationship like before the affair happened? How was your relationship different? What was different about your relationship when the affair was not there? What has it taught you about your marriage? What positive direction could you go in as a result of the affair?" The therapist uses language that presupposes change.

Parts and Wholes

At this point the meaning the couple originally gave the EMS issue has loosened and the therapist has the option of intervening at the level of construction (the meaning system), either by focusing on a part of the meaning system or by concentrating on the whole. The therapist can move into finding and amplifying exceptions to the presenting problem by working on a portion of the couple frame or on the belief system as a whole. Both strategies will result in change. Working with a part is like chipping away at a brick wall, piece by piece. Eventually, the wall is down. Working with the whole, with metaphors and reframing, is more like going in with a bulldozer—the wall falls away with one sweep (Atwood, 1993). Working with part of a frame might be more incremental because it means working through a problem entrenched in language. Working with the whole, with reframes or metaphors, bypasses the entrenched language system, and goes directly to right brain processes that give new definitions to whole frames (Watzlawick, 1978). In either case, new frames arise that contain emergent possibilities. The above methods primarily address meaning systems, but in addition the therapist can work at the level of action by prescribing tasks or rituals, thereby offering a framework at both the meaning and behavioral levels.

Therapeutic Frame: Working with the Whole

THE REFRAME. Watzlawick, P., Weakland, J., and Fisch, R. (1974) developed the constructivist concept of *reframing*. According to their definition, reframings "change the conceptual and or emotional setting or viewpoint in relation to which a situation is experienced and . . . place it in another frame which fits the 'facts' of the same situation equally well or even better and thereby changes its meaning" (p. 95). In order to reframe, the couple presents the story of the EMS issue to the therapist. The therapist, using the client's language, gives the story a new meaning, one which is equally believable to the couple. In the case of EMS, the spouse who had been previously labeled "unfaithful" might be relabeled as someone who was "fearful" of the closeness in the relationship. Similarly, the "jealous" spouse could be relabeled as one who is "consumed with love" for the partner.

THE METAPHOR. Our concepts of reality are influenced by our language and our language is grounded in metaphor. A metaphor can also be seen as a model for changing the way we look at the world. In therapy, metaphors are intended to help couples elicit an unconscious search for alternatives and new meanings.

Papp (1982) uses "couples choreography," a metaphor designed to get at the core of the couple's struggle. Using imagery, the couple is asked to visually depict themselves and the struggles of their relationship in a nonhuman form. The imagery they both generate describes the EMS struggle in a non-language-entrenched form. The language they typically use to describe the problem is replaced with images, allowing the couple to see the reciprocal relationship in a gentle way.

One man saw himself as a fly caught in two black widow spider webs. He had one foot caught in the home web and one foot caught in the work web. He wanted to put both feet in the home web but it was difficult because the work web was stickier. This metaphor is ripe with substance about core issues and provides the couple with new ideas for solutions. "When did you notice the home web wasn't as sticky as it used to be? Could you have told the home spider that the web needed to be more sticky? What could you have done to make the home web stickier? In the future, will you notice when the home web becomes less sticky? What will you do? What else will you do? And spider, what could you do to make the home web stickier? If the fly comes close to you, will you make it safe for him or will you bite off his head? How will you let him know he's safe? How else? Fly, when the spider lets you know it's safe, how will you move in closer? What will the spider notice when you're moving in closer?"

Using the metaphor, the individual and the couple meaning systems are explored in detail. Through the exploration, discussion, and the expansion and rewriting of the metaphor, the couple can begin to reconstruct a new metaphorical image of their relationship—one that does not have the EMS issue.

Therapeutic Frame: Working with a Part

Once the notion of a couple meaning system is accepted, and the individual and couple meaning systems are uncovered, a competing meaning system can be introduced. It is not apparent to most individuals that there are alternate ways of behaving in a given situation. Our meaning systems make areas outside the dominant ones appear invisible. This invisibility serves to maintain and foster adherence to the dominant definitions. In fact, the function of socialization and of the sanctions against moving outside the dominant scripts is to keep individuals within it (Gagnon, 1990). One way of finding, naming, focusing on, and helping couples experience alternative meanings is evident in the search for exceptions.

LOOKING FOR COMPETING MEANINGS (EXCEPTIONS). White's (1989) idea of subjugated knowledge was originally based on Bateson's ideas of restraint—those ideas, events, and experiences that are less likely to be noticed by people because they are dissonant with individuals' descriptions of their problems. White (1989) indicated that as a couple's view of reality is challenged through questioning, the partners ultimately recognize other aspects of their reality that indicate success with problems. In so doing they create another story (narrative) about their lives that does not focus on the problem.

DeShazer's (1991) invocation of exceptions is similar, and refers to times in the client's life when the problem is absent. The therapist "seeks to find the element in the system studied (their conversation about the client's complaint, goals, etc.) which is alogical, and the thread . . . which will unravel it all, or the loose stone which will pull down the whole building" (deShazer, 1991). The therapist reinforces exceptions to the dominant description of the problem, helping to make visible areas outside the dominant meaning system. The rationale that previously had been specifying and justifying the couple's reality begins to be undermined (Amundundson, 1990).

The therapist now begins to plant new seeds as the old frame begins to break up. The therapist might ask, "Are there ever times when you are not thinking about the EMS issue?" The receipt of news of difference (when something is happening other than problem) is essential for the revelation of new ideas and a triggering of new responses for the discovery of new solutions. Once an exception is found, it must be amplified.

V. Amplifying the New Meaning System

The amplification of the exception is essential for triggering the new construction that holds the possibility of new solutions (Bateson, 1972). "When you are not thinking about the affair, how is your relationship? If you were to enjoy your relationship more frequently, how would you notice? What would be different?" By helping the couple to deepen the experience of a more positive relationship, the therapist is fostering a new construction. This new construction holds new meaning for the couple.

Another amplification method is termed the *appreciation frame*. At the end of each session, the partners are asked to tell each other what they appreciated about one another that day. The therapist then helps the couple to deepen this experience by asking each partner, "Could you tell us when you appreciated your partner recently? Could you tell him [or her] what it was that he [or she] did that gave you the sense of appreciation? Next, could you tell how you felt when that happened? When did you feel that your partner appreciated you?" This helps the partners to re-image each other and their relationship in a more positive frame.

VI. Stabilizing the New Meaning System

At this point, alternative meaning systems are available to the couple and what was invisible now holds potential for new solutions. The original meaning system that contained the EMS issue as an important part of the couple relationship has been deconstructed and replaced by a new description. Next, a version of deShazer's (1991) Miracle Question can be asked: "If a miracle were to happen tonight while you were asleep and tomorrow you awoke to find that this problem were no longer a part of your life, what would be different? How would you know that this miracle had occurred? How would others know without your telling them?" By asking questions about future trends and choices, the therapist is making that future more real and more stable.

The couple now begins to focus on the future. Future focus enables the couple to visualize their relationship without the EMS issue. Questions can take the following form: "If you could stretch the rubber band three years into the future, and the EMS issue was no longer an issue, what would your relationship look like? How would your relationship be different? How else would it be different?" This lays the groundwork for the notion that the couple has some control over their problem and that therefore they have some control over its solution (Atwood & Dershowitz, 1992). Such questions also encourage couples to generate different scenarios for the future, but without the problem. They generate an assortment of possibilities—safely imaged in the present.

The End of Therapy

At the end of counseling, a ritual for a fresh start may be helpful. At this time, couples can choose a new anniversary date where they recommit to each other. Some couples choose to rewrite their marriage vows, signifying the beginning of a new marriage. Along with restating their commitment to each other and to the relationship, they can write down

JOINING THE COUPLE'S MEANING SYSTEMS

↓

PROPOSING THE NOTION OF COUPLE MEANING SYSTEMS

↓

INVITING THE COUPLE TO EXPLORE THEIR MEANING SYSTEMS

↓

INVITING THE COUPLE TO EXPAND THEIR MEANING SYSTEMS

↓

AMPLIFYING AND STABILIZING THE NEW MEANING SYSTEMS

FIGURE 2.2   The flow of social constructionist therapy.

their future relationship vision. This then becomes their future image, their template for their relationship. Intentionality has been introduced into their meaning systems and they have learned that they can write and rewrite their future story. Figure 2.2 depicts social constructionist therapy.

SUMMARY

Napier (1988) claims that marriage in this society is thought to be the cure of all life's problems, when actually it is the medium through which all of our problems can be expressed. This article discussed the marital problem of EMS. In so doing, it presented information on the incidences of EMS, along with a summary of the research and literature around this issue. Examining EMS from a social constructionist perspective allows one to see how the issue is affected by the sociocultural context. Seeing EMS as part of a marital meaning system, integral to marital scripts, gives the behavior the quality of a narrative in which the EMS behavior is comprised of events ordered in time. A six-stage social constructionist couple therapy model for working with EMS issues was presented. Changes in the narratives that clients tell about EMS can lead to changes in their meaning systems and reorganize the way they view and experience their individual realities about the EMS and their relationship in general. Ultimately, change in a meaning system can result in a new way of viewing the world.

REFERENCES

Amundson, J. (1990). In defense of minimalism: Making the least out of depression. *Family Therapy Case Studies 5*(1), 15–19.

Ables, B. S., & Brandsma, J. M. (1977). *Therapy for couples.* San Francisco: Jossey-Bass.

Athanasiou, R., Shaver, P., & Tavris, C. (1970, Summer). *Psychology Today,* pp. 37–52.

Atwater, L. (1979). Getting involved: Women's transition to first extramarital sex. *Alternative Lifestyles, 2,* 33–38.

Atwood, J. (1991). Killing two slumpos with one stone. *Family Therapy Case Studies, 5*(2), 43–50.

Atwood, J. (1993). Social constructionist couple therapy. *The Family Journal: Counseling and Therapy for Couples and Families, 1*(2), 116–130.

Atwood, J., & Dershowitz, S. (1992). Constructing a sex and marital therapy frame: Ways to help couples deconstruct sexual problems. *Journal of Sex and Marital Therapy, 18*(5), 196–216.

Bateson, G. (1972). *Steps to an ecology of mind.* New York: Ballantine.

Bell, R. R., Turner, S., & Rosen, L. (1975). A multivariate analysis of female extramarital coitus. *Journal of Marriage and the Family, 37,* 375–384.

Berger, P., & Kellner, H. (1979). Marriage and the social construction of reality. In H. Bobboy, S. Greenblatt, & C. Clark (Eds.), *Introductory sociology.* New York: St. Martins.

Berger, P., & Luckmann, T. (1966). *The social construction of reality.* New York: Ballantine.

Bernard. J. (1968). *The sex game.* New York: Prentice Hall.

Blumstein, P., & Schwartz, P. (1983). *American couples.* New York: Morrow.

Boscolo, L., Cecchin, G., Hoffman, L., & Penn, P. (1987). *Milan systemic family therapy.* New York: Basic Books.

Bowen, M. (1978). *Family therapy in clinical practice.* New York: Jason Aronson.

Boylan, B. (1971). *Infidelity.* Englewood Cliffs, NJ: Prentice Hall.

Buunk, B. (1980). Extramarital sex in the Netherlands: Motivation in social and marital context. *Alternative Lifestyles, 40,* 11–39.

Caprio, F. (1953). *Marital infidelity.* New York: Citadel.

Cimmarutsu, R., & Lappin, J.(1985). Beginning family therapy. *Family Therapy Collection, 14,* 16–25.

Constantine, L. L., & Constantine, J. M. (1972). Counseling implications of comarital and multilateral relations. *The Family Coordinator, 2*(3), 267–273.

Constantine, L. L. (1984). Dysfunction and failure in open family systems. II: Clinical implications. *Journal of Marital and Family Therapy, 10,* 1–17.

Crenshaw, T. (1985). The sexual aversion syndrome. *Journal of Sex and Marital Therapy, 11,* 285–292.

deShazer, S. (1991). *Putting difference to work.* New York: Norton.

Durrant, M. (1991). *Ideas for therapy with sexual abuse.* Sydney, Australia: Dulwich Center Publications.

Edwards, J. (1973). Extramarital involvement: Fact and theory. *The Journal of Sex Research, 9,* 210–224.

Edwards, J., & Booth, A. (1976). Sexual behavior in and out of marriage: An assessment of correlates. *Journal of Marriage and the Family, 38,* 73–81.

Ellis, A., & Harper, R. A. (1975). *A new guide to rational living.* North Hollywood, CA: Wilshire.

Gagnon, J. (1973). Scripts and the coordinators of sexual conduct. *Nebraska symposium on motivation, 21,* 27–59.

Gagnon, J. (1977). *Human sexualities.* New York: Scott, Foresman.

Gagnon, J. (1990). Scripting in sex research. *Annual Review of Sex Research, 3,* 1–39.

Gass, G. Z., & Nichols, W. C. (1988). Gaslighting: A marital syndrome. *Contemporary Family Therapy, 10*(1), 3–16.

Gergen, K. (1985). The social constructionist movement in modern psychology. *American Psychologist, 40,* 266–275.

Gergen, K. J., & Gergen, M. M. (1983). The social construction of narrative accounts. In K. J. Gergen and M. M. Gergen (Eds.), *Historical social psychology.* Hillsdale, NJ: Erlbaum.

Glass, S., & Wright, T. (1977). The relationship of extramarital sex, length of marriage and sex differences on marital satisfaction and romanticism: Athanasiou's data re-analyzed. *Journal of Marriage and the Family, 39,* 691–703.

Green, S., & Bobele, M. (1988). An interactional approach to marital infidelity:

Including the "other woman" in therapy. *Journal of Strategic and Systemic Therapy, 7*(4), 35–47.

Guerin, P., & Fay, L. (1992). Triangles in marital conflict. *The Best of the Family* [Compendium III]. Rye-Brook, NY: Center for Family Learning.

Guerin, P., Fay, L., Burden, S., & Kautto, J. (1987). *The evaluation and treatment of marital conflict.* New York: BasicBooks.

Haley, J. (1967). Toward a pathological system. In G. Zuk & I. Boszormenyi-Negy (Eds.), *Family therapy and disturbed families.* Palo Alto, CA: Science and Behavior Books.

Harre, R. (1984). *Personal being.* Cambridge: Harvard University Press.

Hendrix, H. (1988). *Getting the love you want: A guide for couples.* New York: Harper & Row.

Hite, S. (1981). *The Hite report on male sexuality.* New York: Knopf.

Humphrey, G. (1983). *Marital therapy.* Englewood Cliffs, NJ: Prentice-Hall.

Humphrey, F. G. (1985a). *Sexual dysfunction and/or enhancement interactions with extramarital affairs.* Paper presented at Yale University Sex Therapy Program, New Haven, CT. January 9.

Humphrey, F. G. (1985b). *Extramarital affairs and their treatment by AAMFT therapists.* Paper presented at American Association of Marriage and Family Therapy, New York. October 19.

Humphrey, F. G. (1986). *Extramarital affairs: History, etiology, and treatment.* Englewood Cliffs, NJ: Prentice Hall.

Humphrey, F. G. (1987). Treating extramarital sexual relationships. In G. R. Weeks, & L. Hof (Eds.), *Integrating sex and marital therapy.* New York: Brunner/Mazel.

Humphrey, F. G., & Strong, F. (1976, May 22). *Treatment of extramarital sexual relationships as reported by clinical members of AAMFC.* Paper presented at Northeastern American Association of Marriage and Family Counselors, Hartford, CT.

Hunt, M. (1974). *Sexual behavior in the 70's.* Chicago: Playboy.

Hurlbert, D. F. (1992). Factors influencing a woman's decision to end an extramarital sexual relationship. *Journal of Sex and Marital Therapy, 18*(2), 104–113.

Imber-Black, E., Roberts, J., & Whiting, R. (1988). *Rituals in families and family therapy.* New York: Norton.

Jacobson, N. S., & Margolin, G. (1979). *Marital therapy.* New York: Brunner/Mazel.

Johnson, R. E. (1970). Some correlations of extramarital coitus. *Journal of Marriage and the Family, 32,* 449–456.

Kaplan, H. S. (1983). *The evaluation of sexual disorders: Psychological and medical aspects.* New York: Brunner/Mazel.

Kinsey, A. C., Pomeroy, W. B., & Martin, C. E. (1948). *Sexual behavior in the human male.* Philadelphia: Saunders.

Kinsey, A. C. , Pomeroy, W. B., Martin, C. E., & Gebhard, P. H. (1953). *Sexual behavior in the human female.* Philadelphia: Saunders.

Kohler-Reissman, C. (1989). Life events, meaning and narrative: The case of infidelity and divorce. *Social Science Medicine, 29,* 743–751.

Lampe, P. E. (1987). *Adultery in the United States.* Buffalo, New York: Prometheus.

Lawson, A. (1988). *Adultery.* New York: BasicBooks.

Levin, R. J. (1975, October). The *Redbook* report on premarital and extramarital sex. *Redbook,* pp. 38, 40, 190, 192.

Libby, R., & Whitehurst, R. (1977). *Marriage and alternatives: Exploring intimate relationships.* Illinois: Scott Foresman.

Lo Piccolo, L. (1980). Low sexual desire. In S. Leiblum and L. Pervin (Eds.), *Principles and practice of sex therapy.* New York: Guilford.

Macklin, E. (1980). Nontraditional family forms: A decade of research. *Journal of Marriage and the Family, 42,* 905–920.

Marett, K. M. (1990). Extramarital affairs: A birelational model for their assessment. *Family Therapy, 17*(1), 22–28.

Masters, W. H., & Johnson, V. (1970). *Human sexual inadequacy.* Boston: Little, Brown.

Maykovich, M. D. (1976). Attitudes versus behavior in extramarital sexual relations. *Journal of Marriage and the Family, 38,* 633–699.

Minuchin, S., & Fishman, C. (1974). *Family therapy techniques.* Cambridge: Harvard University Press.

Moultrup, D. J. (1990). *Husbands, wives, and lovers: The emotional system of the extramarital affair.* New York: Guilford.

Napier, A. (1988). *The fragile bond.* New York: Harper and Row.

Nass, G. D., Libby, R. W., & Fisher, M. P. (1981). *Sexual choices.* Belmont, CA: Wadsworth.

Papp, P. (1982). Staging reciprocal metaphors in couples group. *Family Process, 21,* 453–467.

Pervin, L. A. (1993). *Personality: Theory and research.* New York: Wiley.

Pietropinto, A., & Simenauer, J. (1978). *Beyond the male myth.* New York: New American Library.

Pittman, F. (1989). *Private lies: Infidelity and the betrayal of intimacy.* New York: Norton.

Pittman, F. (1991). The secret passions of men. *Journal of Marital and Family Therapy, 17,* 17–23.

Prigogine, I., & Stengers, I. (1984). *Order out of chaos: Man's new dialogue with nature.* New York: Bantam.

Schutz, A. (1962). *Collected papers: Vol. I. The problem of social reality.* Martinus Nijhoff: The Hague.

Singh, B., Walton, B., & Williams, J. (1976). Extramarital sexual permissiveness: Conditions and contingencies. *Journal of Marriage and the Family, 3,* 701–712.

Sluski, C. (1992). Transformations: A blueprint for narrative changes in therapy. *Family Process, 3,* 217–230.

Smith, T. E. (1991). Lie to me no more: Believable stories and marital affairs. *Family Process, 30,* 215–225.

Spanier, G., & Margolis, R. (1983). Marital separation and extramarital sexual behavior. *Journal of Sex Research, 19*(1), 23–48.

Sprey, J. (1972). Extramarital relations. *Sexual Behavior, 2,* 34–40.

Strean, H. (1980). *The extramarital affair.* New York: Free Press.

Sullivan, H. S. (1953). *The interpersonal theory of psychiatry.* New York: Norton.

Tavris, C., & Sadd, S. (1977). The *Redbook* report on female sexuality. New York: Dell.

Taylor, C. J. (1986). Extramarital sex: Good for the goose? Good for the gander? *Women and Therapy, 5,* 289–295.

Teismann, M. (1979). Jealousy: Systemic problem-solving therapy with couples. *Family Process, 18,* 13–18.

Thompson, A. P. (1984). Emotional and sexual components of extramarital relations. *Journal of Marriage and the Family, 46,* 35–42.

Thompson, A. T. (1983). Extramarital sex: A review of research literature. *Journal of Sex Research, 19*(1), 1–22.

Tomm, K. (1987). Interventive interviewing: Part I. Strategizing as a fourth guideline for the therapist. *Family Process, 26,* 3–13.

vonGlaserfeld, E. (1984). An introduction to radical constructivism. In P. Watzlawick (Ed.), *The invented reality.* New York: Norton.

Watzlawick, P. (1978). *The language of change: Elements of therapeutic communication.* New York: BasicBooks.

Watzlawick, P., Weakland, J., & Fisch, R. (1974). *Change: Principles of problem formation and problem resolution.* New York: Norton.

Weeks, G. R., & Hof, L. (1987). *Integrating sex and marital therapy.* New York: Brunner/Mazel.

Weis, D., & Slosernick, M. (1981). Attitudes toward sexual and non-sexual extramarital involvements among a sample of college students. *Journal of Marriage and the Family, 18,* 349–357.

Weiss, R. (1975). *Marital separation.* New York: Basic Books.

White, M. (1989, Summer). The externalizing of the problem. *Dulwich Centre Newsletter,* pp. 14–16.

White, M., & Epston, D. (1990). *Narrative means to therapeutic ends.* New York: Norton.

Wolfe, L. (1980, September). The sexual profile of that *Cosmopolitan* girl. *Cosmopolitan,* pp. 254–265.

Wolfe, L., (1982). *The* Cosmo *report.* New York: Bantam.

CHAPTER 3

AIDS and the Family Narrative: Reconstructing a Story to Encompass an Illness

Nancy Cohan

As families construct their own narratives it is likely that today's co-created stories color and shade a family's remembrances of the past as well as alter their plans for the future. Yet, a diagnosis of acquired immune deficiency syndrome (AIDS) in a family member challenges the family's understanding of itself in the past and the present. It therefore can render their meaning systems inappropriate and life scripts inadequate for the future. Byng-Hall (1988) explains that the family script is "used to explain the mechanism that enables families to repeat particular family scenarios when similar contexts are encountered" (p. 130). However, learning that a partner, child, or sibling has AIDS may stop the automatic utilization of the family's script and necessitates the development of a new script at a time when the family, in many ways, is depleted and vulnerable.

Historically, there may be little or no correlation between longstanding family beliefs and the AIDS diagnosis; however, current events may alter or obscure the clarity of memories or beliefs about the past. Recollections may become confused or inappropriately poignant as the family tries to integrate the AIDS diagnosis into a coherent, cohesive self-understanding. Learning that a loved one has AIDS may prompt the family to question the validity of the life script on which it had previously relied and the credibility of the meaning system upon which that script was developed.

AIDS AND THE FAMILY'S FORMER LIFE SCRIPT

For many families, the revelation of an AIDS diagnosis in a family member is a dual one in that the disclosure of the illness may be the first time the family learns that an adult child is gay or has been involved in intravenous (IV) drug use (Dane, 1989, 1991; Garrett, 1988; Kelly & Skyes, 1989; Lamendola & Wells, 1991; Land & Harangody, 1990; Lovejoy, 1990; Stulberg & Buckingham, 1988; Weiss, 1989). Similar to other studies (Savin-Williams, 1989; Cramer & Roach, 1988), Cain (1991) found that half of the gay men in his sample had concealed their homosexuality from parents. However, for many of these men, an AIDS diagnosis necessitated disclosure to parents and other members of the family. Such a discovery may raise issues the family had previously avoided or denied, thereby forcing them to confront illusions they may have maintained about the individual with AIDS or the family as a whole (Dane, 1991). For those families with tacit agreements not to discuss or ask questions about a son's or daughter's sexuality, learning of the AIDS diagnosis may require that they relinquish that specific area of denial from their script. Similarly, a family's beliefs about their closeness, their cohesiveness, and the openness of their communication may be challenged by the knowledge that a significant part of a family member's life has been kept secret from them (Stulberg & Buckingham, 1988). This realization may bring into question the parent's beliefs about the nature of the parent-child relationship as it existed prior to the AIDS diagnosis and the child's coming out to the family.

Scripting the Homosexual

Despite the on-going debate among researchers concerning the origins of homosexuality, for many parents the culturally popular notion that the roots of homosexuality can be traced to an incorrect pattern of early parenting continues to prevail (Gelman, Foote, Barrett, & Talbot, 1992; Hersch, 1991). As Hersch (1991) reports, "Many young lesbians and gays are made to feel not only that they have failed their parents, but that they have also made their parents feel like failures" (pp. 41–42). Parents, therefore, may feel personally responsible for somehow influencing their child's initiation into a lifestyle which they believe resulted in his or her contracting a life-threatening disease (Dane, 1991; Lovejoy, 1990).

Families who thought they had fostered an atmosphere of honesty and open communication with their child may find that they review past interactions differently in light of the new information obtained via the AIDS diagnosis. Recollections of mundane discussions of possible marriage and potential grandchildren may be later recalled as incidents of evasiveness and deception (Cain, 1991). A brother or sister who had related to the sibling as a close friend and confidante (Cain, 1991) may find that the friendship has been compromised by the discovery that the sibling withheld the information that he or she is gay.

Issues of trust and loyalty often accompany the discovery that some members of the family had known of an individual's gay lifestyle or drug use and others had not (Stulberg & Buckingham, 1988; Tiblier, Walker, & Rolland, 1989). Longstanding covert alliances may become overt, indicating the inclusion of some siblings in the secret and the exclusion of others. Parents may be dismayed to find that not only is a son or daughter gay but that the gay offspring has shared this information with a sibling who, in turn, actively participated in keeping the secret (Cain, 1991; Tiblier, Walker, & Rolland, 1989). Cain (1991) found that the siblings of some gay men in his sample played roles "facilitating or impeding disclosure within the family. For instance, parents sometimes approached a brother or sister for 'inside information' on the respondents" (p. 348). For some of these parents learning a child is gay also implicates a second child in the deception and may be experienced as an additional betrayal. A sibling, whose customary role had been to protect parents from adverse information or to shield siblings from parental disapproval, may find that the AIDS diagnosis has altered or eradicated his or her role in the usual family drama. Similarly, other role assignments in the family may require change to accommodate AIDS. A son, who had previously held a distant position in the family's configuration may find that illness dictates he solicit caretaking from the family from which he was previously estranged. Or as Tiblier et al. (1989) report, "A person with AIDS, for instance may designate a sibling who seems more tolerant of his/her lifestyle to replace the mother as caregiver, thus upsetting the normal family hierarchy" (pp. 89–90).

Married siblings of people with AIDS may have difficulties reconciling loyalty to their family of origin with loyalty to their own nuclear
family. This can be particularly problematic if the family of origin's
script maintains that although they may marry and move on, the primary
allegiance of individual family members must remain with the family
of origin. Conflict and resentment from the spouse of the sibling of the
AIDS patient may arise if that spouse finds more and more of his or her
partner's time and energy redirected toward a sick in-law.

Similarly, the anticipation of the loss of a child or a close sibling may
precipitate a reexamination of a tenuous marital relationship and could
result in the family's reorganization (Walker, 1991). Walker (1991) cites
the example of a sister, who after the diagnosis of her brother, "realized
that her closeness to him had made staying in a loveless marriage for
the sake of her children bearable" (p. 180). After her divorce and a subsequent remarriage, "the longstanding coalition of brother and sister
against the rest of the family weakened. . . . The mother, who had
always felt herself to be in an outside position in the family, was able
to meet with her son in a therapy session and discuss her feelings about
his being gay" (Walker, 1991, p. 180).

A family may be gratified to find that their son has developed a close
network of friends but simultaneously disappointed to find that he has
come to consider these friends, and not the family, his primary system
of support (Lamendola & Wells, 1991; Levine, 1991a; Land & Harangody, 1990; Tiblier, Walker, & Rolland, 1989). Lamendola and Wells
(1991) cite for example, a couple who four days before their son's death
were met by his friend who "took them aside when they arrived at the
hospital and said, 'Jim is gay and he has AIDS. You need to go into his
room and tell him you know he is gay and has AIDS and that you love
him and you need to use all these words'" (p. 24). This type of scenario
could be particularly problematic to a family with tightly closed boundaries who believe that blood ties are the only connections to be relied
on in times of trouble.

A family whose script requires that they anticipate or mourn their
losses privately and who are acutely aware of any boundary encroach-
ments, might feel resentful or displaced to arrive at a hospital room and
find it overflowing with the patient's friends. These friends are likely to
be viewed by the family as intrusive, and in the case of a partner, may
be blamed for the illness (Dane, 1989; Land & Harangody, 1990; Tiblier
et al., 1989). If the family's previous experiences with life-threatening

illnesses have led them to construct a script which calls for bringing the patient home for care, they may be dismayed to hear he has made prior arrangements to be cared for by people they may not even know.

The scripts of some families do not recognize full adult status in any grown child unless he or she has married. As a result, the gay young adult may linger in a prolonged state of adolescence in the family system. To many gay men, a move away from home facilitates the establishment of a career, often coincides with involvement in the gay community, and helps to solidify a sense of adulthood (Walker, 1991). For the gay man who must leave his job and rely on parents for caretaking as his illness progresses, Walker (1991) comments that "as he returns home, it is as a son or sibling, with the makers of his adult gay identity left behind" (p. 14).

Conflicts between the script of the family and the script of the patient's partner can arise if the family's script invalidates or disqualifies the spousal role which the partner has assumed in the life of the person with AIDS (Dane, 1991; Levine, 1991; Lovejoy, 1990; Walker, 1991). Walker (1991) again, cites the difficulties some families may encounter accepting the role of the gay partner "without having had the ritual of a marriage to mark the transfer of power from the parents as principal caregivers and decision makers to a spouse" (p. 16). Similarly, the gay partner involved in a committed, long-term relationship and who has supported his partner with AIDS throughout the early and protracted stages of the illness, may be disheartened to find that the biological family intends to now assume total responsibility for his partner's care (Lamendola & Wells, 1991; Stulberg & Buckingham, 1988; Tiblier, 1987; Tiblier et al., 1989). As there exists little or no legal consideration for the role played by the gay life partner, disputes between the parents and partner may persist after the patient's death to become vehicles for unresolved anger over the common loss (Lamendola & Wells, 1991; Levine, 1991a; Lovejoy, 1990; Nungesser, 1986; Weiss, 1989).

In many ways AIDS has brought into question the traditional definition of family and, quite often, the constructs of biological families and larger social system differ from those of the AIDS patient, his partner, and others in the gay community (Levine, 1991a). A family of origin, after losing their son to AIDS, may attempt to claim property and belongings acquired by their son and his partner despite the many years the couple lived together. Levine (1991a) discusses the difficulty a partner living in a city may encounter when a person named on a lease dies and both the surviving partner and the family claim the right to remain as a tenant in a rent-controlled or rent-stabilized apartment (p. 60). Lamendola and Wells (1991) offer the example of a man with AIDS whose prearrangement for cremation and a nonreligious funeral were overturned by his parents who, after his death, opted for a funeral Mass and excluded his gay friends from attending. In these cases, the functional construction of family was superseded by the more traditional definition which tends to define the family in terms of biological connections (Levine, 1991).

For families who have derived their life scripts from scripture, an AIDS diagnosis may compel either the reassessment of one or more religious doctrines or the abandonment of the person with AIDS. As Moynihan, Christ, and Silver (1988) have reported, "Although many clergy and religious groups have responded with compassion to AIDS patients, others feel they are limited by strict interpretation of religious law" (p. 386). Some families may experience difficulty reconciling their feelings of love for the member with AIDS with the tenets of a church that adheres to a strict or literal interpretation of biblical doctrine (Lovejoy, 1990; Moynihan, Christ, & Silver, 1988; Round, 1988; Schaper, 1987; Urwin, 1988). Families who have depended on what Urwin describes as "the rules of religion in living and dying" (p. 157) may find these rules inappropriate to their experience of coping with AIDS, particularly if these rules depict a dying son as a recipient of God's wrath against homosexuals (Schaper, 1987; Urwin, 1988). Or an individual who has witnessed a loved one undergo extensive physical and psychological suffering may find that the AIDS experience has precipitated a questioning, or in some cases, a loss, of faith. Compounding the potential pain of a spiritual severance from the church is the lack of social support a family may encounter if they abruptly leave the church community (Round, 1988). The church can be a predominant support system in times of crisis for many families, particularly those in rural or African-American communities (Round, 1988; Walker, 1991). For these families alienation from the church can result in feelings of isolation and inadequacy when facing the innumerable stresses accompanying AIDS.

The Drug-User's Family

The family of an HIV-infected drug abuser may also need to revise their life script when AIDS is diagnosed. For some families, the inability to reconnect with the AIDS patient may be related not to the illness, but to the drug-abusing behaviors which preceded it (Walker, 1991; Drucker,

1991). As Walker (1991) states, "families of drug users share community anger at their deviant members" (p. 280). Longstanding family conflicts such as difficulty with separation, problems establishing boundaries, and a history of unresolved loss often predate the AIDS diagnosis in the substance abuser's family of origin (Coleman, 1991; Drucker, 1991; Walker, 1991). Families may continue to harbor deep-seated resentments resulting from the adverse effects the drug abuse has had on their lives and, therefore, are reluctant to care for the drug abuser with AIDS. Those families resolved to no longer offering assistance to the child who continues to abuse drugs may have difficulty maintaining this stance if that individual becomes hospitalized with an opportunistic infection (Bartlett & Finkbeiner, 1991).

Coleman (1991) has found that issues of unresolved loss abound in the meaning systems and the scripts of many of the families of drug abusers. She reports that as a result, "any type of separation is particularly difficult for addict families (Coleman, 1991, p. 265). Families scripted to continuously rescue the drug abuser may feel guilty for not preventing that individual from engaging in the behaviors which resulted in his or her contracting the AIDS virus (Tiblier, 1987; Walker, 1991). A family which had utilized a cutoff as a means of coping with the individual's drug abuse, when faced with his or her impending death, may feel guilty over the estrangement, or regret the time together which was lost.

Similar conflicts to those which may occur within the families of gay men with AIDS may lead the drug abuser's family to blame a partner for the family member's continued substance abuse (Walker, 1991). Or the partner or spouse of the drug user may assert that the parents or siblings are in some ways responsible for the addiction (Walker, 1991). Conflict between partner and parents may result in care being contingent upon a promise to have no further contact with a spouse who may also be dying of AIDS (Walker, 1991). And, as it is less likely for the drug abuser with AIDS to have access to the level of community support that the gay man with AIDS may find available, the drug abusing AIDS patient is, therefore, more apt to look to family for caretaking and support throughout the course of the illness.

The Bisexual with AIDS

A spouse in a bisexual couple whose partner becomes infected with the AIDS virus as a result of sexual contact outside the marriage must reexamine her beliefs and re-evaluate her script of the couple relationship. For some couples a husband's bisexuality is framed as an event of the past, having occurred prior to the couple relationship, and has not been considered part of the marital script (Maloney, 1988; Walker, 1991). Maloney suggests, however, that when a husband is diagnosed with AIDS, "the wife, after the initial crisis, begins to wonder about her husband's former lifestyle; knowing he was bisexual does not necessarily indicate sophistication about gay sexual practices. Did he frequent bathhouses? Was he promiscuous aside from the lovers she knew about?" (p. 146).

In other couples, a wife might suspect that her husband had or is having a sexual relationship with another man but believes that a pursuit of her suspicion could compromise her marriage or, at least, her beliefs about that marriage (Walker, 1991). Some women construe a husband's bisexual behavior as their own personal failure (Walker, 1991). Some couples are likely to try to utilize scripts which dictate that sexual secrets must be protected and a husband's bisexuality is tolerated by his wife only within the context of the appearance of a traditional marriage. Lastly, there are some women who, prior to learning of their husbands' diagnoses of AIDS, were completely unaware that they had had any sexual involvement with men (Walker, 1991; Maloney, 1988).

Often the couple will avoid sharing information concerning the husband's illness with friends or extended family because disclosing the illness may jeopardize the couple's public persona of the "typical American family" (Maloney, 1988; Walker, 1991). Maloney (1988) has found, however, that "when AIDS families lie, vaguely implying they have cancer, they do not get the support they need. People respond to a definite reality, but they do not respond well to an anonymous illness with no predictable course, specific therapy, or clearcut symptoms. Some people, friends as well as family, are lost along the way" (p. 146). The family of the bisexual person with AIDS, therefore, is apt to be more isolated by the illness than families of homosexuals.

AIDS and Hemophilia

Hemophiliacs and other blood product recipients must reorganize their life scripts to accommodate the realization that they have contracted the AIDS virus from the miracle of modern medicine which they previously held responsible for their survival (Bayer, 1989; DiMarzo, 1989; Tiblier et al., 1989; Walker, 1991). "Because the management of hemophilia has been achieved by carefully controlling much of their environment, infection with HIV may destroy the hemophiliacs' fundamental trust in their ability to control their fate" (Tiblier et al., 1989, p. 100). As Bayer (1989), a hemophiliac infected with the virus, has said, "After more than 30 years of enduring one miserable disease, hemophilia, my life now was shaken by another. More than that, the very treatment that had at last given me an almost normal life was responsible for infecting me with the most dreaded and despised affliction of the century" (p. 50). Families often utilize denial as a means of managing hemophilia. Somewhat based in this denial, a reality is constructed by the families which, when augmented by the use of the clotting factor, offers the hemophiliac the opportunity to lead a normal life and develop a positive script for the future (Bayer, 1989; DiMarzo, 1989; Walker, 1991). However, when faced with the spectre of HIV infection, a script based on denial can result in not seeking early treatment for the HIV infection and potentially infecting others with the virus. Seroconversion may also alter the hemophiliac and his partner's scripts for intimacy. Bayer (1989) states that as a result of testing positive for the HIV virus, he has come to believe that "a virus has assumed primary control of my romantic life" (p. 55).

For families who had once emphasized the importance of leading a "normal life," the stress of the AIDS diagnosis may be compounded by the stigmatization of the groups the disease has been associated with. Bosk and Frader (1991) report hemophiliac patients in hospitals often emphasize how they contracted the disease. They found that "these patients 'display' wives and children to differentiate themselves from homosexual patients," believing they would be afforded better treatment by the hospital staff than gay or drug-abusing patients infected with the virus (Bosk & Frader, 1991, p. 164). Their perception was validated in some hospitals, where staff members designated AIDS patients exposed to the virus through blood products the "innocent victims" of the disease (Bosk & Frader, 1991).

FAMILIES AND AIDS: LIFE SCRIPTS FOR LIVING WITH THE DISEASE

Although family scripts rely on the family's past behaviors as guidelines for dealing with new experience, it is unlikely that they have had many previous experiences which will prepare them for the many challenges of living with AIDS. Walker (1991) states that "the combination of illness, actual or potential loss of family members, and the powerful stigma of AIDS creates an AIDS family, with new coalitions, structures, secrets, and boundaries" (p. 179). The family must compose a life script which incorporates AIDS into their lives without permitting the prevailing negative social constructions to permeate their meaning systems and hinder their ability to cope with the disease (Tiblier et al., 1989). The adequacy of the family's revised script as well as their ability to meet the needs of the person with AIDS and other members of the family may be contingent upon the rigidity of the former life script and the course taken by the illness itself.

The family who are aware that their son is gay and that he has tested positive for the AIDS virus before he becomes symptomatic is likely to find more latitude for revising their life script than the family who rushes to the hospital when notified their son is critically ill with an opportunistic infection such as *pneumocystis carinii* pneumonia. For this family the demands of the medical crisis combined with their reactions to the startling, often unsolicited news about the patient's sexuality or drug use, may diminish their ability to competently meet the demands of the disease (Walker, 1991).

The family's attempt to equip themselves to cope with a chronic, life-threatening disease can be further complicated by the roller-coaster-like nature of AIDS (Dane, 1991; Stulberg & Buckingham, 1988; Tiblier, 1987; Walker, 1991). Frequently there are alternating periods of acute illness and times when the person with AIDS appears to have improved (Dane, 1991; Moynihan et al., 1988; Walker, 1991). The family may need not only to abandon its pre-illness script but, at times, to rewrite the recently constructed one as well.

The family may find that they must repeatedly shift from a primarily caretaking role to one in which they permit the individual with AIDS an opportunity to partially return to a level of pre-illness functioning (Moynihan et al., 1988; Walker, 1991). Partners and family members, prepared to care for a dying patient, may have difficulty accepting the patient's decision to return to work or to participate in other activities which do not fit the family frame for serious illness (Moynihan et al., 1988). Equally problematic, however, is the family whose denial of the illness leads them to place "unrealistic demands on the patient to function independently and fail to provide comfort, support, and practical help" (Moynihan et al., 1988, p. 382). Tiblier, Rolland, and Walker

(1989) write that "family identity following an AIDS diagnosis will never be the same" (p. 118). As a result, the person with AIDS, his or her partner, family, and friends will be required to compose life scripts based on those meaning systems and identities irrevocably altered by AIDS (Walker, 1991).

The newly constructed script of the individual infected with the AIDS virus, however, may not necessarily replicate the scripts created by the people who love him. A similarity of scripts for the AIDS experience is somewhat contingent upon a concurrence of the meanings the individual family members ascribe to AIDS. This can include how the individual defines the illness, his or her pre-illness relationship with the person with AIDS, the extent to which the illness impinges upon his life, as well as the influence of the individual's sociocultural milieu.

The person with AIDS might wish to frame the disease as a chronic condition and concentrate on the unpredictability of his life expectancy in lieu of focusing on the inevitability of an early death. Nevertheless, he or she will still reconsider former life goals and need to make adjustments for the disease. "The fact that individuals are likely to become HIV infected at an early age in the lifecycle has important implications. A young man of 25, recently diagnosed with HIV, who is now drug free after an adolescent phase of drug abuse, suddenly finds that such normal life goals as marriage and children are closed to him. The life decisions he must now make are distinctly different than if he were to become ill at a later stage in life after he had accomplished more of his life goals" (Tiblier et al., 1989, p. 118).

The individual who tests positive for the HIV virus but whose symptoms remain manageable may be more prone to addressing the ways in which he can continue to enhance the quality of his life than he will be to planning for his death from the disease. However as he attempts to manage the progression of the disease and to lead a meaningful life he may find his endeavors undermined by continuous media attention emphasizing the rise in AIDS mortality or, perhaps, by those losses from AIDS he has personally experienced (Moynihan et al., 1988). Sustaining a balance between hope and a realistic appraisal of the AIDS crisis may be difficult for a person with AIDS in the gay community. Helquist (1989) suggests that "with so much uncertainty and fear overshadowing their days, gay men must find their own ways to cope, to not sink into a constant demoralized state that robs them of a present as well as a future" (p. 292). A similar, albeit less optimistic script for balancing an AIDS diagnosis and hope is offered by Holleran (1989) who writes that, "One has to have two programs, two set of responses, ready at all times: (a) Life, (b) Death. The switch from one category to the other can come at any moment, in the most casual way" (p. 42).

Walker (1991) has found that the "initial experience of hospitalization can be a framing event for the family"(p. 162). The first, and subsequent, hospitalizations of the person with AIDS may require that the individual and other members of the family become quickly accustomed to dealing with the health care system. As the immune system becomes increasingly compromised, AIDS patients become susceptible to different opportunistic infections which assault various parts of the body and which require various types of treatment (Walker, 1991). A patient's hospital stay may last for many weeks and involve a seemingly neverending parade of medical professionals. As Lovejoy (1990) has found, "Family members who have not dealt with the health care system since, 'my son was born'or 'I needed shots for school' find medical terminology, cost of care, and the complex health care system shocking" (p. 288). Ironically, health care providers, particularly in hospitals which are short-staffed and strained by the demands of the AIDS crisis, may look to the families of patients as auxiliary resources of care for the patient within and outside of the hospital. It is not unusual for a person with AIDS to receive a significant percentage of his care outside of the hospital (Walker, 1991). Very often, the family of the AIDS patient find they must revise their script to accommodate the need for home care.

AIDS is incongruent with the lifecycle—aging parents are asked to tend to the health care, and ultimately the death, of an adult child. Carter (1989) writes that, "Given that persons with AIDS are likely to be adults, a variety of outcomes are foreseeable. Adult parents of persons with AIDS may find income saved for retirement spent on their ill children, families and couples may lose their primary breadwinner or may devote all their available funds to care for the ill family member, and single individuals may find themselves financially devastated as a result of the cost of treating AIDS" (p. 166). Older parents who had developed a life script which organized their lives in such a way that they worked hard and saved throughout their lives so that they could comfortably enjoy their later years, may experience difficulty adjusting to the many requirements of their adult child's illness. They may have further difficulties if they view the disease as a result of behaviors they do not condone. The strain of caring for the AIDS patient may compound pre-existing stresses; conceivably the parents of the AIDS patient who returns home for care may already be responsible for the care of their own elderly or infirm parent. Dissension among family members can result from conflicting individual scripts concerning the extent to which the family is responsible for caring for the individual with AIDS (Kelly & Skyes, 1989). Family members directly involved in daily patient caretaking may become resentful of others who, they believe, have reneged on a family responsibility. For many patients and their families, revising a script to contend with AIDS may mean relinquishing a sense of control (Bartlett & Finkbeiner, 1991; Stulberg & Buckingham, 1988). Families will find that AIDS is a formidable opponent to a script which insists on order and stability; the course of the illness is unpredictable and medical treatment can be, essentially, one crisis intervention after another.

The person with AIDS and the parents, who may have instilled in their children a strong sense of self-reliance, might have difficulty adjusting to increasing dependence as the illness progresses (Bartlett & Finkbeiner, 1991). Couples may lose equilibrium as the well partner is asked to assume more and more caretaking responsibilities (Bartlett & Finkbeiner, 1991; Walker, 1991). For some couples, when the individual who before his illness was the predominate caretaker comes to require nursing and nurturing from a partner, AIDS can precipitate a major role shift in the relationship (Walker, 1991). One wife of a person with AIDS said, "that the more she took out the garbage, paid the bills, and mowed the lawn, the more her husband felt he was losing control, and the unhappier he became; sometimes he was grateful, she said, and sometimes he just screamed" (Bartlett & Finkbeiner, 1991, p. 93).

Levine (1991) states, "Traditional families that have already developed internal ways of coping may be totally unprepared for the stress created by external pressures such as stigma" (p. 52). The stigmatization of many of the groups associated with AIDS and the constructs society has adopted for HIV disease may hinder the family's ability to develop an acceptable script for the illness (Tiblier et al., 1989). Stigmatization, be it actual or perceived by the family, challenges the family's constructs about the external world and brings into question how they should operate in relation to that world. For many traditional families, instantaneous admittance into a community which their friends, relatives and clergy have designated as immoral and deviant can be disconcerting and unsettling.

The approach of some families to disclosure of their son's AIDS diagnosis is often not dissimilar to his secrecy or openness about being gay, as they are likely to have adhered to relatively similar scripts. The family may replicate his coming out process or choose to continue preserving the secret. As one mother explained, "When your child comes out, the family goes into the closet" (Hersch, 1991, pp. 41–42). Opting to contain information concerning the AIDS diagnosis within the nuclear family may lead to a new family script developed specifically to protect the secret. The stress of coping with the illness then becomes further compounded by the additional stress of maintaining the secret.

Conflict between family members occasionally will arise if some members, particularly the individual with AIDS, do not agree to operate within the auspices of a secrecy script and wish to be more candid about the diagnosis (Stulberg & Buckingham, 1988). Those family members who fear rejection and insist on secrecy must worry over whom to tell and who does or does not know about the AIDS diagnosis, as well as maintain a consistent, plausible story which will explain changes in their behavior (Kelly & Skyes, 1989; Stulberg & Buckingham, 1988). As secrecy and deception become more and more embedded in the family's illness script, the family is apt to feel alienated from friends, neighbors, and co-workers (Kelly & Skyes, 1989). The individual who begins to fear ostracization by friends and associates who learn that a family member has AIDS may begin to reevaluate the nature of those relationships and question the validity of those friendships. They may begin to systematically isolate themselves, thereby diminishing potential sources of support (Dane, 1991).

Byng-Hall (1991) states that, "the most powerful way to maintain self-deception is to remain surrounded by those who see things in a similar light" (p. 16). As the family systematically severs community ties to hide the AIDS diagnosis, the ensuing isolation places additional pressure on the family system. As extrafamilial influences on the family's developing AIDS script decreases, the likelihood of problematic interaction within the nuclear family may increase. As Tiblier et al. (1989) found, "the smaller the relationship arena, the more intense the pressure on that system" (p. 105). The many stresses resulting from the day-to-day management of AIDS may reactivate longstanding family difficulties and conflicts (Kelly & Skyes, 1989). Individuals may return to the family and reassume roles they had abandoned while living on their own or reenter triangles with parents or siblings. If the secrecy surrounding the diagnosis has sufficiently isolated the family, they may find little respite from the physical or psychological strains of caring for a person living with AIDS.

Gay and heterosexual couples with an infected partner may need to reevaluate their scripts to successfully accommodate intimacy and the AIDS virus. Developing an intimacy script appropriate to AIDS may lead to a reappraisal of current or future relationships and encounters. As Kantrowitz (1986) stated, "I stopped partying as soon as I realized that my survival was at stake, and I settled down in a relationship" (p. 16). Couples living with AIDS may find that they are unable to differentiate their feelings about sexuality from their adverse feelings about the virus. As Bartlett and Finkbeiner (1991) have found, "some people equate making love with getting sick" (p. 97).

A family member with AIDS can directly challenge the family's notion that the future can be even marginally predictable. For those families who have been overly reliant on a life script as a means of mastering fear or as an attempt at gaining some control over the future, this lack of predictability can be overwhelming. Families may become frustrated when unable to receive definitive answers from medical professionals about what to expect from the illness, or discouraged to find that overcoming one life-threatening opportunistic infection does not preclude the immediate development of a second one. Lovejoy (1990) has found that, "Occasionally, a family member may adapt the actress or actor role, pretending that the patient will get well or that a vaccine will be developed in time to save the patient's life. The pretense is difficult to maintain and inhibits the patient from discussing death-related concerns" (p. 303). The timetables of individual family members are no longer coordinated when one individual is undergoing anticipatory bereavement and another is frantically searching for a new drug protocol with the hope of extending the patient's life.

As the illness progresses, the family integrates the demands of the illness into their script so that they can adequately provide care for the person with AIDS. In addition, they must also continue fulfilling many of the basic requirements of their own lives. They must simultaneously work toward the development of a future script which will take into account the loss of the AIDS patient and still be appropriate for the surviving family members (Tiblier et al., 1989). Given that there is no absolute schedule for the progression of AIDS and that many families are unaware that an individual is ill until the last stages of the disease, some families may find that the separate scripts for past, present, and future converge throughout the course of the illness. For example, a wife may find that she must combine the tasks of caring for a terminally ill husband with those of working, maintaining a home, and raising children. While continuing to perform many of the functions of her previous roles, it is likely that during her husband's illness, she has assumed many of his as well. And, if she has resisted sharing her husband's condition with others, she may not have an adequate support system. Concurrent with her attempts to manage the constant stresses of living with AIDS, is the necessity that she begin to make appropriate plans for her children and herself in anticipation of the impending death of her spouse.

Tiblier et al. (1989) has found that in "a couple where one person is seropositive and the other is not, each person may have a different time frame for life" (p. 108). Whereas the partner with AIDS may feel a need to address unresolved issues or reconcile with the family of origin, the other may not experience the same sense of immediacy. The pressing needs of a medical crisis or the awareness of AIDS-related mortality rates can result in the family's belief that there is insufficient time to complete unfinished business with the AIDS patient. However, families may be leery of addressing negative feelings or expressing anger at the patient, as they believe the person with AIDS has already experienced excessive suffering as a result of the disease. Often the family's AIDS script will lag behind the progressive stages of the illness and compromise the patient's ability to manage the later stage of the illness and anticipate or plan for death.

Families with rules against discussing painful topics such as death, much like those families that prohibit discussions of homosexuality or drug use, may find that their prohibitions compel them to relinquish the opportunity to repair or restore relationships with the family member who is dying of AIDS. Terminal patients may find that their families attempt to prevent or discourage conversations concerning the extent of the disease or certain medical interventions and insist on proceeding as if the patient will soon recover. Denial utilized by the family before AIDS in reference to lifestyle or sexuality, may, with the onset of the illness be reworked into a script that avoids the issue of an anticipated death.

SETTING THE STAGE: AIDS AND THE FAMILY'S LIFE SCRIPT FOR THE FUTURE

Rolland (1989) writes that patients with a disease such as AIDS and their families experience "an undercurrent of anticipatory grief and separation that permeates all phases of adaptation. Families are often caught between a desire for intimacy and a pull to let go, emotionally, of the ill member. The future expectation of loss can make it extremely difficult for a family to maintain a balanced perspective" (p. 463). As the expectation of the loss expands into the family's illness script, they begin to revise that script for the future, making adjustments for the eventual loss of the person with AIDS.

The individual patient with AIDS may require a reconnection to key relationships, as well as a reconciliation of his self-definition and self-esteem with the suffering incurred as a result of the illness (Walker, 1991; Moynihan et al., 1988). The patient may want to make explicit plans or hopes for the futures of the survivors, to fulfill obligations or tend to anticipated responsibilities that will not arise until after death (Moynihan et al., 1988). Adequate provisions for the custody of children, for example, will be crucial for parents with AIDS (Bartlett & Finkbeiner, 1991; Drucker, 1991; Walker, 1991). Unable to sufficiently complete the tasks of parenting, the parent with AIDS may wish to structure a script which secures a future for his or her children.

Lovejoy (1990) states that the anticipatory grief of the families of terminally ill patients "begins when the patient begins to withdraw his emotional investment in others" (p. 307). For some AIDS patients, this withdrawal may coincide with the completion of unfinished business or may be related to progressive neurological impairment resulting from the illness itself. The patient may retreat from the family, turning instead to the medical professionals for palliative care and the management of increased pain (Walker, 1991; Reiss, Gonzalez, & Kramer et al., 1986). The family's response to this initial separation from the dying patient can be a precursor of the ways in which they will integrate loss and bereavement into the script they are currently constructing for use after the death of the person with AIDS.

Dane (1991) discusses the detachment process which the family of the AIDS patient may undergo during the later stages of the illness, as the limitations for treatment of the illness become increasingly apparent.

Caregivers begin to anticipate, and perhaps hope for, the end of the illness nightmare (Land & Harangody, 1990). Dane (1991) reports that during this process, "Hospital personnel sometimes complain about families' callous behavior or lack of interest in the PWA [patient with AIDS]" (p. 114). However, this stage may actually be a rehearsal of the script which the family will soon find they must reenact. They therefore begin to partially reinvest in their relationships with each other and begin the reassignment of roles and functions to compensate for the decreasing involvement of the terminally ill patient (Dane, 1991; Greif & Porembski, 1988; Macklin, 1988). Yet this initial period of detachment does not guarantee the family's transition to a future-oriented script or eradicate the influences of the scripts which were utilized before the family experienced the loss of a loved one to AIDS.

Walker (1991) states that "the meanings that family members give to AIDS will define their participation with the patient and the healing of their own system throughout illness after the patient dies" (p. 10). It is unlikely that any family's script can sufficiently prepare them for the devastation presented by the death of a family member from AIDS. However, it would seem that those families who insist on a rigid adherence to the pre-illness script, or whose belief systems deny inclusion to the AIDS experience, will have greater difficulty integrating that experience into the family's narrative.

Byng-Hall (1991) states: "Coping with threatened loss for any indeterminate period makes it much harder for a family to define present and future structural and emotional boundaries" (p. 149). Although this is apt to hold true in the case of any chronic, terminal illness, there are restructuring dilemmas which in some ways are unique to a loss from AIDS (Tiblier, Walker, & Rollands, 1989; Walker, 1991; Weiss, 1989). As families confront AIDS bereavement, they may find that reorganizing after the loss is hindered by many of the same obstacles they faced during the patient's illness.

Families of people who have died from AIDS embark upon the bereavement process depleted, and in some ways, diminished by the experience of having cared for someone dying of the disease. Long-term vigilance to the needs of the patient, and for many families, the relentless requirements of caring for a dying person at home, combine physical exhaustion with emotional fatigue (Kelly & Skyes, 1989). The death of the patient, however, does not offer the family respite as they must then meet the adjustment demands of bereavement. This can be especially difficult for the partner or other family member who, once directly involved in the patient's care, must, after the death, relinquish the caretaking role assumed during the stages of illness. This caretaking role may have served as a buffer to many of the stresses associated with anticipating a life devoid of the person with AIDS, and the loss of that person constitutes the ensuing loss of that role. Compounding the loss of the person with AIDS, bereaved spouses or partners contend with what Lovejoy (1990) describes as "secondary losses" (p. 308). These losses include a withdrawal of social support, the loss of the couple identity, a possible decrease in economic stability, and the loss of a sexual relationship (Lovejoy, 1990).

The loss of a partner may bring forth previously unaddressed concerns about the status of one's own health or that of a child (Land & Harangody, 1990; Oerlemans-Bunn, 1988; Walker, 1991; Weiss, 1989). Many of the somatic responses to bereavement, such as chills, shortness of breath, and muscle weakness, may appear to the survivor to be the harbingers of early HIV disease, and the individual, whose caretaking of the partner has left him attuned to noticing any minute physical changes, may begin to anticipate undergoing a similar medical crisis and an equally untimely death (Weiss, 1989). As Oerlemans-Bunn (1988) has found, "Among bereaved lovers of men who have died from AIDS, the fear of developing the disease is both acute and very painful. And, in view of our current knowledge of transmission, it is painfully realistic" (p. 474). The bereaved partner who is infected with the AIDS virus may face the prospect of his own declining health without the same level of support he was able to provide to his deceased mate; worrying that "there will be no one to take care of me when I need it" (Land & Harangody, 1990, p. 477). The surviving partner may feel guilty for not having saved the patient, or for subjecting him to what was often painful and ultimately ineffective medical procedures (Oerlemans-Bunn, 1988). If both members of the couple were seropositive for the HIV virus, the remaining partner may be concerned that he brought the virus into the relationship and feel culpability for the death of his mate (Lamendola & Wells, 1991; Land & Harangody, 1990; Oerlemans-Bunn, 1988; Walker, 1991). The seropositive individual will also become susceptible to the taxing effects which the psychological strain of bereavement may place upon his or her health (Walker, 1991; Oerlemans-Bunn, 1988). Walker (1991) reports that the stress accompanying loss and grief can compromise the immune functioning of the bereaved, noting that "to a person who is immuno-compromised or already ill with AIDS, the death of a partner constitutes a serious threat" (p. 250).

Single women with children may find that the impact of losing their spouse is obscured by overwhelming economic, housing, and childcare issues, as well as their own infection with the virus (Levine, 1991). These substantial issues, which may need to be addressed with immediacy in the midst of mourning, can divert the family's focus from constructing a script that adequately incorporates the loss of the husband or father.

Many gay and heterosexual families experience AIDS loss devoid of their accustomed support systems. As the result of self-imposed isolation or fear of stigmatization, they may not look to extended family, their church or friends for assistance in navigating the bereavement process (Lovejoy, 1990; Oerlemans-Bunn, 1988; Walker, 1991; Weiss, 1990).

If the family devised a secrecy script at the onset of the AIDS experience, this secrecy may permeate the script that the family adopts for mourning and reorganization after death. Families who were unable to differentiate their negative feelings about the AIDS-inducing behaviors from their feelings of love for the person with AIDS while he or she was ill, may find that disclosure impinges upon their ability to retain the memory of their loved one in a positive frame or that disclosure feels like posthumous disloyalty to the deceased.

Bereaved gay life partners may have already experienced multiple losses to AIDS and may find their support system depleted by the epidemic. This problem may be particularly aggravated for the gay partner who is also cut off from his own family of origin and unwilling or unable to elicit their support (Oerlemans-Bunn, 1988). Reluctant to open up discussions of his own sexuality, the bereaved gay lover may return to work and refrain from discussing his experience with co-workers or colleagues. Or, as Oerlemans-Bunn (1988) reports, many gay men "only publicly demonstrate grief appropriate to the death of a good friend, but not to the loss of a long-term partner" (p. 474).

Future-oriented scripts founded in shame and secrecy surrounding the AIDS death may present special difficulties for children in families with AIDS (Walker, 1991; Tiblier et al., 1989). Denial and confusion concerning the death of a parent may permeate the scripts of these children beyond the bereavement stage, for "it is hard to grieve when one cannot openly discuss the cause of death" (Tiblier et al., 1989, p. 114). Issues of trust and/or deception may become predominant themes for children who have been prohibited from understanding the nature of a parent's death. These issues may remain an influential part of their meaning system and the development of their own scripts for years after the death of the parent.

Byng-Hall (1991) states that at a "fundamental level, the way that the members of the family normally manage all their separations and losses determines the way that the distress of grieving is handled" (p. 131). However, for some AIDS families, there may be a history of an inability to contend with losses in previous generations, as is often the case in the families of substance abusers (Stanton & Todd, 1992). Or, there may be an aversion by the family to acknowledging differences, as in the case of those families who disown a gay son or a drug-abusing daughter. For these families to integrate the loss of a member from AIDS, it would seem that their former life scripts would require revision so that the AIDS death would not become another unacceptable difference or unresolved loss. Difficulty developing a post-AIDS narrative may arise precisely because the family has experienced an enormous shift and yet continues to try to perceive itself as if the shift has not occurred. Because of the negative cultural implications of AIDS, the family may remain reluctant to identify with the disease or the ensuing AIDS death. This reluctance, coupled with an attempt to diminish the pain of the loss, may encourage mourners to identify instead with distorted roles from the illness and dying script. Byng-Hall (1991) categorizes these distorted roles as "the dying person, good caregivers who attempt to help, or in the imagination, may even manage to prevent death; failed caregivers who are often held responsible for deaths; or killers who take an active role in promoting the death" (1991, pp. 132–133). The opportunity for over-identification with the deceased permeates the mourning stage of the gay partner, who may be infected with the same virus as the lover who died (Byng-Hall, 1991; Oerlemans-Bunn, 1988; Walker, 1991). However, this identification is not necessarily limited to the partners of the person who died. Members of the family, perhaps as a function of a shared sense of difference from the others in the family system, may incorporate this particular feeling of camaraderie into a "replicative script" (Byng-Hall, 1991, p. 133). This script can be potentially dangerous if it precludes the seropositive partner from attending to his own medical care; if it is motivation for a family member to engage in self-destructive activities, such as drug use; or if it results in the individual phobically curtailing his or her life to avoid "all contexts similar to that in which the death occurred" (Byng-Hall, 1991, p. 133).

The permanent stance of either a successful or thwarted caregiver may be a natural post-AIDS script for the individual who may have already participated as a caregiver to the deceased for years. And, as previously noted, the role of the ineffective rescuer may have been operable in the drug abusing family before the introduction of AIDS into the family script (Byng-Hall, 1991; Tiblier et al., 1987). Discouragement caused by the caregiver's inability to save the person who died of AIDS may result in the composing of a script in which the surviving individual seeks out those circumstances in which to prevail at the successful intervention, or conversely, the repeated failure to save others (Byng-Hall, 1991).

Identifying with a perpetrating role can be harmful to others besides the survivor if the individual engages in harmful behaviors as a result of the role assumption (Byng-Hall, 1991). This danger is especially salient in the case of survivors infected with the virus whose sexual behavior in the role may be potentially fatal to new partners. An overly corrective adaptation of this role, designed to manage fears about death's unpredictability, may result in a script which calls for the individual excessively restricting or curtailing any activity perceived as dangerous (Byng-Hall, 1991).

COSCRIPTING AN AFTERLIFE: IMPLICATIONS FOR INTERVENTION FOR FAMILIES WITH AIDS

Bereavement offers a family an opportunity for change. Byng-Hall notes: "One of the advantages of grieving work is that the intensity and urgency of the emotions that are generated can be used to get people together and to alter the family structure" (p. 135). If bereavement offers the chance to alter family structure, it follows that it will also be a time when the family's script will be readjusted as well. Intervention, therefore, should be aimed at assisting the family as they integrate the AIDS diagnosis, the stages of the illness, and ultimately, the death, into the family's meaning system not only so that they can competently manage the health care requirements presented by AIDS, but also so that they can eventually redirect their energies to new experiences and relationships after the person with AIDS has died (Walsh & McGoldrick, 1991; Walker, 1991).

Families can be encouraged to reconnect by exploring shared experience or by focusing on those aspects of the person with AIDS that do not reflect the virus-contracting behaviors (Walker, 1991). Meeting on common ground can be the impetus the family requires to eventually address and accept differences. For example, a family's constructions about homosexuality can be revised to accommodate new information. Describing a "template for recognition and growth," Walker (1991) states that "the experience of learning about their child's life, his friendship network, the meaning that being gay has had for him, and of caring for him within this context can be transformative, deeply enriching their lives, their sense of themselves as a family. It may even transform their politics" (Walker, 1991, p. 17).

To counteract feelings of stigmatization and isolation, patients and their families can access services or support from organizations such as the Gay Men's Health Crisis or local peer support groups (e.g., People with AIDS and the Families of People with AIDS) (Walker, 1991). Bereavement groups, specifically designed for those who have lost loved ones to AIDS, can present families with a safe, nonjudgmental environment in which they can address the loss without fears of rejection or reprisal.

Families can be directed toward developing new rituals which will serve to memorialize the person who died with AIDS and which add to their comfort. One family, in memory of their son, joins his friends in a yearly march to raise money for research directed at finding a cure for the AIDS virus. Therapeutic intervention can assist the family who rejects sharing their grief publicly by helping them develop memorial practices or rituals that are better tailored to fit the particular family's needs (Walker, 1991). Or, surviving family members may choose to participate in rituals specifically related to AIDS, such as the Names Project, which coordinates the AIDS quilt. As family members and friends work together to create a panel honoring the person who died, they begin to reflect on aspects of his life not connected to the disease while continuing to acknowledge the enormity of their loss. The Names Project, in particular, is an AIDS ritual which disputes the family's isolation. As the quilt progresses, each individual panel becomes one of many thousands (Imber-Black, 1991).

Byng-Hall (1991) comments that, "A family death teaches individuals not only how to mourn but also how to die" (p. 131). Clinical intervention after an AIDS death can help families develop ways to cope with the loss which will become part of the family's post-AIDS script, but not necessarily be limited to AIDS. Coming to terms with the loss of the family member by finding value and significance in the years of life can be expansive and retained by the family to assist with losses they may encounter in the future.

Interventions which facilitate self-acceptance by the person with AIDS aid in resolving outstanding family conflicts, and which help the patient achieve a dignified death will also become an integral part of the surviving family's life script (Walker, 1991). Clinicians who are able to help the patient accomplish these goals serve as deliverers of his or her gift to the family members left behind; as the surviving friends and family will have the legacy of the quality of the AIDS patient's death, as well as his life, to include in a later death script of their own (Walker, 1991).

REFERENCES

Bartlett, J. G., & Finkbeiner, A. K. (1991). *The guide to living with HIV infection.* Baltimore: Johns Hopkins University Press.

Bayer, P. B. (1989, April 2). A Life In Limbo. *New York Times Magazine,* pp. 9–13.

Bosk, C. L., & Frader, J. E. (1991). AIDS and its impact on medical work: The culture and politics of the shop floor. In D. Nelkin, D. P. Willis, & S. V. Parris (Eds.), *A disease of society: Cultural and institutional responses to AIDS* (pp. 150–171). Cambridge: Cambridge University Press.

Byng-Hall, J. (1991). Family scripts and loss. In F. Walsh, & M. McGoldrick (Eds.), *Living beyond loss: Death in the family.* New York: Norton.

Byng-Hall, J. (1988). Scripts and legends in families and family therapy. *Family Process, 27*(2), 167–180.

Cain, R. (1991, June). Relational contexts and information management among gay men. *Families In Society: The Journal of Contemporary Human Services,* pp. 344–352.

Carter, B. (1989). Societal implications of AIDS and HIV infection: HIV antibody testing, health care and AIDS education. In E. Macklin (Ed.), *AIDS and families* (pp. 129–185). New York: Harrington Park.

Coleman, S. B. (1991). Intergenerational patterns of traumatic loss: Death and despair in addict families. In F. Walsh & M. McGoldrick (Eds.), *Living beyond loss: Death in the family* (pp. 260–272). New York: Norton.

Cramer, D., & Roach, A. (1988). Coming out to mom and dad: A study of gay males and their relationships with their parents. *Journal of Homosexuality, 15*(3/4), 79–92.

Dane, B. O. (1989). Time of ending: New beginnings for AIDS patients. *Social Casework, 70,* 305–309.

Dane, B. O. (1991, February). Anticipatory mourning of middle-aged parents of adult children with AIDS. *Families in Society: The Journal of Contemporary Human Services,* pp. 108–115.

DiMarzo, D. (1989). Double jeopardy: Hemophilia and HIV disease. In J. W. Dilley, C. Pies, & M. Helquist (Eds.), *Face to face: A guide to AIDS counseling* (pp. 260–266). Berkeley: Celestial Arts.

Drucker, E. (1991). Drug AIDS in the city of New York: A study of dependent children, housing, and drug addiction treatment. In N. F. McKenzie (Ed.), *The AIDS reader: Social, political, ethical issues* (pp. 144–176). New York: Meridian.

Garrett, J. E. (1988). The AIDS patient: Helping him and his parents cope. *Nursing88,* pp. 50–52.

Gelman, D., Foote, D., Barrett, T., & Talbot, M. (1992). Born or Bred? *Newsweek,* pp. 46–52.

Greif, G. L. & Porembski, E. (1988). Implications for therapy with significant others of persons with AIDS. *Journal of Gay and Lesbian Psychotherapy, 1*(1), 60–66.

Helquist, M. (1989). Too many casualties: HIV disease in gay men. In J. W. Dilley, C. Pies, & M. Helquist (Eds.), *Face to face: A guide to AIDS counseling* (pp. 289–295). Berkeley: Celestial Arts.

Hersch, P. (1991). Secret lives. *The Family Therapy Networker, 15*(1), 36–43.

Holleran, A. (1989). The Fear. In J. Preston (Ed.), *Personal dispatches: Writers confront AIDS.* New York: St. Martin's.

Imber-Black, E. (1991). Rituals and the Healing Process. In F. Walsh & M. McGoldrick (Eds.), *Living beyond loss: Death in the family* (pp. 207–223). New York: Norton.

Kantrowitz, A. (1986, September). Friends gone with the wind. *The Advocate,* pp. 14–22.

Kelly, J., & Skyes, P. (1989, May). Helping the helpers: A support group for family members of persons with AIDS. *Social Work,* 454.

Lamendola, F., & Wells, M. (1991, May). Letting grief out of the closet. *RN,* 23–25.

Land, H., & Harangody, G. (1990, October). A support group for partners of persons with AIDS. *Families In Society: The Journal of Contemporary Human Services,* 471–480.

Levine, C. (1991a). AIDS and changing concepts of family. In D. Nelkin, D. P. Willis, & S. V. Parris (Eds.), *A disease of society: Cultural and institutional responses to AIDS.* Cambridge: Cambridge University Press.

Levine, C. (1991b). The special needs of women, children and adolescents. In

N. F. McKenzie (Ed.), *The AIDS reader: Social, political, ethical issues* (pp. 200–214). New York: Meridian.

Lovejoy, N. C. (1990). AIDS: Impact on the gay man's homosexual and heterosexual families. *Marriage & Family Review, 14,* 285–316.

Macklin, E. (1988). AIDS: Implications for families. *Family Relations, 37,* 141–149.

Maloney, B. D. (1988). The legacy of AIDS: Challenge for the next century. *Journal of Marital and Family Therapy, 14*(2), 143–150.

Monette, P. (1988). *Love alone: Eighteen elegies for rog.* New York: St. Martin's.

Moynihan, R., Christ, G., & Silver, L. G. (1988). AIDS and terminal illness. *Social Casework, 69,* 380–387.

Nungesser, L. G. (1986). *Epidemic of courage: Facing AIDS in America.* New York: St. Martin's.

Oerlemans-Bunn, M. (1988, April). On being gay, single, and bereaved. *American Journal of Nursing,* 472–476.

Reiss, D., Gonzalez, S., & Kramer, N. (1986). Family process, chronic illness and death: On the weakness of strong bonds. *Archives of General Psychiatry, 43,* 795–804.

Rolland, J. S. (1989). Chronic illness and the family life cycle. In B. Carter & M. McGoldrick (Eds.), *The changing family life cycle: A framework for family therapy* (pp. 433–456). Needham Heights, MA: Allyn and Bacon.

Round, K. A. (1988, May). AIDS in rural areas: Challenges to providing care. *Social Work,* 257–261.

Savin-Williams, R. (1989). Coming out to parents and self-esteem among gay and lesbian youths. *Journal of Homosexuality, 18*(1/2), 1–35.

Schaper, R. L. (1987, August 12). Pastoral care for persons with AIDS and for their families. *The Christian Century,* 1–4.

Stanton, M. D., & Todd, T. (1992). *The family therapy of drug abuse and addiction.* New York: Guilford.

Stulberg, I., & Buckingham, S. (1988, June). Parallel issues for AIDS patients, families, and others. *Social Casework, 69,* 355–359.

Tiblier, K., Walker, G., & Rolland, J. (1989). Therapeutic issues when working with families of persons with AIDS. In E. Macklin (Ed.), *AIDS and families* (pp. 46–71). New York: Harrington Park.

Tiblier, K. (1987). Intervening with families of young adults with AIDS. In M. Leahey & L. M. Wright (Eds.), *Families and life-threatening illness* (pp. 81–128). Springhouse, PA: Springhouse Corp.

Urwin, C. A. (1988). AIDS in children: A family concern. *Family Relations, 37,* 154–159.

Walker, G. (1988). An AIDS Journal. *Family Therapy Networker, 12*(1), 20–33.

Walker, G. (1991). *In the midst of winter: Systemic therapy with families, couples and individuals with AIDS infection.* New York: Norton.

Walsh, F., & McGoldrick, M. (1991). *Living beyond loss: Death in the family.* New York: Norton.

Weiss, A. (1989). The AIDS bereaved: Counseling strategies. In J. W. Dilley, C. Pies, & M. Helquist (Eds.), *Face to face: A guide to AIDS counseling* (pp. 267–275). Berkeley: Celestial Arts.

CHAPTER 4

Depression: Constructing the Flip Side of the Coin

Teri Pakula and Joan D. Atwood

INTRODUCTION

Depression is the most common of all the psychiatric symptoms. It has been estimated that 25% of the general public will experience at least one diagnosed episode of depression (Weissman, Myers, & Harding, 1978, cited in Gotlib & Colby, 1981) at some time in their lives. Weissman and Boyd (1983; cited in Gotlib & Colby, 1981) have shown that on average, 18% to 26% of females and 8% to 12% of males have, at some point in their life, experienced a major depressive episode and of those individuals, one third are hospitalized as a result. It has been estimated that 40% of the population (Bradburn, 1975; cited in Gotlib, 1981) will report feelings of depression in the course of a year. It has also been found that there is a higher risk for depression among individuals from lower socioeconomic backgrounds (Brown & Harris, 1978; cited in Gotlib, 1981) with the exception of the bipolar disorder which is more strongly associated with a higher socioeconomic status (Weissman, 1981; cited in Gotlib, 1981). Family studies cited in the *DSM III-R* have shown that major depression is 1.5 to 3 times more common among first-degree biological relatives than among the general population (American Psychiatric Association [APA], 1987).

It is important to note that there are many normal depressed moods which may be caused by grief, disappointment, and discouragement. However, in these cases, people recover from the depression alone or with brief therapeutic support. The major difference between a non-clinical depressed mood and a disorder is not the person's experience of the depression, but the lack of resilience to recover within a reasonable period of time (Flach & Draghi, 1975). The basic symptoms of clinical depression are summarized in Table 4.1.

Depression can be divided into two categories: exogenous depression and endogenous depression. *Exogenous depression* refers to factors outside of the individual which contribute to the individual's negative feelings and stress, and which contribute to the depressive state. Examples of such factors are marital stresses, the death of a loved one, unemployment, or any event which occurs outside of the individual (Atwood & Chester, 1987). Endogenous depression is a depression caused by factors within the individual, such as a biological or hormonal imbalance. In this type of depression, the physical dysfunction occurs first and is compounded by social stresses or losses. In these cases, psychopharmaceuticals are typically used in the intervention and treatment of endogenous depression (Atwood & Chester, 1987).

Depression is also categorized as being either primary or secondary (Atwood, 1987). *Primary depression* occurs when an individual who has no history of a physical or psychiatric disorder becomes depressed (Atwood, 1987). *Secondary depression* occurs when an individual already has a physical dysfunction, is anxious, or is an alcoholic, and then becomes depressed.

The depressive disorders fall under the classification of *mood syndrome,* a group of symptoms and moods which occur together lasting a specific duration of time (APA, 1987) (see Table 4.1). A *mood episode* is a type of mood syndrome which is not the result of a known organic factor. A *mood disorder* is determined by the character of the mood episodes. Mood disorders are either bipolar disorders, which have a history of manic or hypomanic episodes, or depressive disorders, which do not exhibit mania. The *DSM III-R* also provides a separate classification for major depressive episode (APA, 1987).

Dysthymia is similar to major depression but differs in duration and severity (APA, 1987). The impairments resulting from dysthymia in social and employment areas are less severe than those resulting from major depression. Unless there is a suicide attempt or a superimposed

TABLE 4.1   Basic Symptoms of Depression

- Depressed mood
- Loss of interest or pleasure in almost all activities
- Significant weight loss or gain
- Sleep disturbances—insomnia (difficulty sleeping or intermittent sleep patterns) or Hypersomnia (excessive sleep)
- Agitation or psychomotor retardation, such as slowed speech
- Loss of energy
- Inappropriate guilt or low self-esteem
- Difficulty in concentrating, easily distracted, indecisiveness
- Thoughts of death, and perhaps suicidal ideation

Source: American Psychiatric Association. (1987). *Diagnostic and Statistical Manual of Mental Disorders* (3rd ed., rev.). Washington, DC: Author.

major depression, hospitalization is rare (APA, 1987). In contrast, in major depression impairment in the same areas varies, but inability to function is frequent. The chronic nature of dysthymia, however, results in an increased tendency to develop substance abuse or dependence (APA, 1987).

The diagnostic signs for dysthymia are similar to those of major depression with the following exceptions: (a) the depressed mood must be in existence for at least 2 years, (b) during this time the person is not without the depressed mood for more than a 2-month period, and (c) there is also no evidence of major depression in the 2-year period, or if there is, it must have been in remission for at least 6 months (APA, 1987).

Epidemiology of Depression

A review of studies of depression spanning more than 40 years (Weissman & Klerman, 1977; cited in Paykel, 1982) indicated that differences in depressive symptoms are correlated with gender. The incidence of depression was higher in younger women and tended to decrease with age (Weissman & Myers, 1978; cited in Paykel, 1982). According to a study conducted by Mellinger and others (1974; as cited Paykel, 1982), the opposite situation was found in males. Depression increased as they got older. Divorced and separated individuals also showed an increase in depressive symptoms (Weissman & Myers, 1978; Hallstrom, 1973; Mellinger, Batter, Parry, Manheimer, & Coisin, 1974; Blumenthal, 1975; Comstock & Helsing, 1976; cited in Paykel, 1982). Hallstrom found that the rate was higher in single men than in single women (1973; cited in Paykel, 1982). Radloff (1975; cited in Paykel, 1982) found that the rate was higher in married women and single men.

As men reach their forties they match the rate of depression for women. Depression may be underdiagnosed in men, given the congruence of traditionally male characteristics with the symptoms or characteristics of a depressed person. Men's incidence of depression may also be underrepresented due to society's gender-based attitudes toward symptoms. A woman who rarely leaves the house, shows little interest in social activities, and is not particularly cheerful may receive cues from others that something is wrong with her. Similar habits in a man may be minimized with explanations like, "That's how men are," or "He doesn't need anything except his remote and his beer." In this way, a man's symptoms of depression may be framed within the context of independence, while a woman's independence may be framed as withdrawn and unhappy. This is not to say that depressed women are just independent or that independent men are depressed. However, therapists do need to consider the interfacing of gender role expectations and the perception of depression. Perceptions of the client, the client's interpersonal systems, and the therapist must all be considered.

SOME MAJOR THEORETICAL EXPLANATIONS OF DEPRESSION

The Psychoanalytic Explanation

An important contribution made by Freud was the comparison of depression to grief (Arieti & Bemporad, 1978). The psychoanalytic standpoint on depression is illustrated in Table 4.2. There is a lack of interest in activity and in the outside world, and there is a hindrance in the capacity to love. The difference between depression and grief is that in addition to grief symptoms, depressed persons also experience a vagueness about the loss. The individual also has an irrational expectation of punishment (Arieti & Bemporad, 1978). The unresolved feelings of loss can lead to

TABLE 4.2 Primary Assumptions Held by Psychoanalytical Theorists

- Depression is caused by a response to loss.
- The loss which evoked the depression may be real, fantasied or symbolic.
- Loss of physical or emotional contact between an infant and mother from the age of 6 months to thirty-six months can cause depression.
- A vulnerability to losses in life is caused by an earlier loss of contact with the mother at infancy or during early childhood. This loss could be emotional or physical.
- An early parental loss predisposes the person who experiences it to respond to later losses in life with more depression than does a person who has not suffered an earlier childhood loss.

Source: Fann, W., Karacan, I., Pokorny, A., & Williams, R. (1977). *Phenomenology and treatment of depression.* New York: Spectrum.

increased feelings of unconscious hostility and guilt, which, in turn, increase the dependency on the depriving or abandoning love object. The depriving object is primitively incapacitated and unconsciously fused to such an extent that the cruel and sadistic aspects of the love object become part of the ego and result in feelings of self-derogation and worthlessness. (Atwood & Chester, 1987, p. 10)

Therapy for depression within the psychoanalytic model has as its main goals: (a) bringing unconscious impulses, wishes, and desires to conscious awareness and (b) strengthening the ego so that behavior is modified (Corey, 1991). Specific therapeutic methods (free association, analysis of transference, analysis of dreams, analysis of resistance) are utilized so that the unconscious material can be brought out and worked through (Corey, 1991). Treatment using this model requires a long-term commitment.

Social Learning Theory

Social learning theorists assume that the cause of depression is in the person, the environment, or is a result of behavioral interaction. They assume that there is a relationship between depression and reinforcement (Lewinsohn & Shaw, 1969; Lewinsohn, Youngren, & Grosscup, 1979; cited in Clarkin & Glazer, 1981) in that they define depression as a lack of reinforcers in the person's environment. It is suggested that the low rate of reinforcers in an individual's behavior and the associated depression are elicited by a low rate of positive reinforcement or a by high rate of aversive experience (Grosscup & Lewinsohn, 1980; Lewinsohn, Youngren & Grosscup, 1979; as cited in Clarkin & Glazer, 1981). There are many reasons that these low rates of positive reinforcement or aversive experiences might occur in a person's environment: the environment itself may have few positive reinforcements or many aversive experiences, the person may lack the skills necessary to obtain positive reinforcers or to deal with aversive experiences, the positive reinforcers may be reduced, or the aversive experiences might be heightened (Grosscup & Lewinsohn, 1980; Lewinsohn, 1975; Lewinsohn & Amenson, 1978; Lewinsohn, Biglan & Zeiss, 1976; Lewinsohn & Talkington, 1979; Lewinsohn, Youngren & Grosscup, 1979; Clarkin & Glazer, 1981).

The Social Learning Model Applied to the Treatment of Depression

First the therapist and client must conceptualize the problem of depression. It is redefined in such a way that there is hope for change (Clarkin & Glazer, 1981). It is important for the client to see that specific problematic behavioral events are related to his or her depression. Many self-report questionnaires, daily monitoring, various activity schedules, and checklists are utilized. Person-specific interactions or environment-specific behaviors that contribute to the client's depression are identified and specific methods to enhance the quality and quantity of the client's reinforcement interactions are introduced. In using this model it is crucial that the client be an active participant in carrying out the assignments.

Cognitive/Behavioral Theories

Rational-emotive-therapy (RET) uses the three modalities of cognition, behavior (feelings) and action (activating event) in its model (Ellis, 1979a, 1979b, 1979c, 1987, 1989). This model is based on the theory that our emotions stem from our beliefs about, evaluations and interpretations of, and reactions to life situations (Corey, 1991). Through applying the model clients learn certain skills which enable them to identify and dispute irrational beliefs that they have acquired and maintained. As a result of learning how to replace these cognitions, their emotional reactions to situations also change.

Beck (1976) developed cognitive therapy, which is similar to RET in that it is also directive, active, structured, and time limited (Beck, Rush, Shaw, & Emery, 1979).

> The basic theory of Beck's cognitive model of emotional disorders holds that in order to understand the nature of an emotional episode or distur-bance, it is essential to focus on the cognitive content of an individual's reaction to the upsetting event or stream of thoughts. (DeRubeis & Beck, 1988, cited in Corey, 1991, p. 345).

Therapy involves an examination of the client's thought distortions. Eventually, clients learn to substitute other cognitions in place of the distorted ones. Beck devised cognitive therapy for the treatment of depression. He does not agree that depression is anger turned inward (Corey, 1991) as do the Freudians, nor does he believe that depression is caused by a lack of reinforcers. Instead, Beck focuses on the content of the client's negative thinking.

Biological Theories

Biological theories assert a number of different causes of depression. Too much or too little of the chemical serotonin might cause an individual to exhibit signs of depression (Barchas, Patrick, Raese, & Berger, 1977; Schildkraut, 1977, cited in Atwood & Chester, 1987). Other theorists report that women are more prone to depression as a result of the hormonal levels associated with the menstrual cycle (Weissman & Klerman, 1977; cited in Atwood, 1987). Twin and adoption studies support the theory that genetics are an important factor in some of the depressive disorders (Gershon, 1977; cited in Paykel, 1982). Thyroid pituitary imbalances and abnormal levels of dopamine and other chemicals of the brain have been found to be contributing factors in depression (Baldessarini, 1983). The most common form of drug treatment for depression involves the use of the tricyclics and monoamine oxidase inhibitors (Baldessarini, 1983). A physiological approach does not necessarily rule out psychological treatment. Frequently, neurological events will accompany psychological events in the experience of depression. In either event, the combined use of drugs and psychotherapy is the preferred method of treatment in many cases, especially if the depression is severe (Baldessarini, 1983).

TABLE 4.3 **Assumptions of the Interpersonal Model**

• Families and individuals will vary in their ability to deal with the stresses and demands of daily living and variability is based largely on the family's external support systems, the health of the family, and the individual's characteristics.

• Depression may develop from either interpersonal causes (social, familial, or marital) or from individual causes (cognitive or biological) Klerman, Weissman, Rounsaville, & Chevron, 1984).

Source: Adapted from *Interpersonal Psychotherapy of Depression* by G. Klerman, M. Weissman, B. Rounsaville, & E. Chevron, 1984. New York: Basic Books.

Interpersonal Theory

Interpersonal psychotherapy (IPT) arose as a therapy specifically for the treatment of depression (Klerman, Weissman, Rounsaville, & Chevron, 1984). It has evolved over the last 15 years from the experiences of the New Haven-Boston Collaborative Depression Research Project. This project involved the treatment of ambulatory depressed, nonpsychotic, and nonbipolar patients (Klerman et al., 1984). There are four studies in progress based on assumptions described in Table 4.3 that show the efficacy of IPT in ambulatory depressed patients (Weissman, 1984; as cited in Klerman et al., 1984).

According to Klerman and associates, the first stage of depression deals with an event or stressor (biological, physical, interpersonal or combination of both) which makes a demand on the individual for change. The depression is either maintained or increased as individuals in the person's environment respond to the depression and as the person develops cognitions based on their perceptions and interpretations of the reactions of others. Table 4.4 summarizes the practical and theoretical nature of IPT.

SOCIAL CONSTRUCTIONISM

Traditionally, thinkers such as Locke, Hume, and the Mills held an exogenic perspective which viewed knowledge as it represented the world. Others, such as the philosophers Kant and Nietzsche espoused the

TABLE 4.4   Summary of the Interpersonal Model

- Time-limited, short-term
- Problem-focused
- Here-and-now, although past interpersonal relationships might be assessed to better understand the present interactional patterns
- Client's are not encouraged to see their current situations as symptoms of internal conflict (i.e., intraspyshic) but are encouraged to explore their behavior in terms of interpersonal functioning.
- As cognitive distortions come up they are assessed in relation to significant others and to interpersonal relationships.

Source: Adapted from *Interpersonal Psychotherapy of Depression* by G. Klerman, M. Weissman, B. Rounsaville, & E. Chevron, 1984. New York: Basic Books.

endogenic stance, viewing knowledge as something innate to the organism. The German theorists played a major role in the development of psychology as they tried to blend both the endogenic and exogenic theories (knowledge as outside of the individual). As psychology developed in the United States, it was influenced by both theories, but was initially influenced more by the exogenic perspective. Behaviorism is an example of this greater influence. It appears though, that within the last two decades, there has been a reversal of this trend as the endogenic view has returned in the form of cognitive psychology (Gergen, 1985).

In addition, "The seeds for this evolution in social psychology were planted by Kurt Lewin, whose central concern with the psychological field was essentially a holdover from European endogenics" (Gergen, 1985, p. 8). This emphasis was furthered by such concepts as social reality as opposed to physical reality (Festinger, 1954, cited in Gergen, 1985), the social comparison process (Festinger, 1954, cited in Gergen 1985), motivated perception (Pepitone, 1949; cited in Gergen, 1985), emotions as perceived (Schachter, 1964; cited in Gergen, 1985), and cognitive dissonance (Festinger, 1957; cited in Gergen, 1985). Out of this background, social constructionism developed as a challenge to the concept of knowledge as a mental representation (Gergen, 1985). Bateson's work (Real, 1990) influenced the focus from the intrinsic quality of things to the surroundings which gave them their identity. For example, a chair cannot be described by an intrinsic quality of "chairness." Rather, it can be defined only by the things that are around it (the empty space, the floor, and the sofa). If everything which existed were one chair then we would have no way to describe it, nor to understand it. For Bateson, it is the pattern of relationships and the information which lies in *differences* which define things. This information, he believed, may be known objectively and described.

> "In the constructionist perspective, the idea of objectivity is given up altogether. Not only are 'things' not objectively knowable, but all descriptions, including descriptions of pattern, are seen as creations rather than discoveries. We do not live in a universe but in a 'multiversa' with as many descriptions as there are willing describers. Reality is not discovered through objective means but is agreed upon consensually through social interaction, through conversation." (*Real,* 1990, p. 258)

This shift reflects a move from "observed" to "observing" systems (Von Foerster, 1981, cited in Gilligan & Price, 1993). "The central metaphor for therapy is that of conversation" (Gilligan & Price, 1993, p. 110). The only truth or knowledge is that which evolves in the space between people, in the social interchange of language (Hoffman, 1991). It is important to understand the social constructionist view of the construct of emotions, especially since depression is an emotion, or feeling. The emotions are not viewed as pathologies nor are they attributed to interior states, as they are within the paradigms of biological and psychoanalytic thinking (Kippax, Crawford, Pam, Una, & Noesjirwan, 1988). Nor are they purely internal states; the cognitive approach fails to deal with emotions as they relate to social experience (Kippax et al., 1988).

As Coulter (1979, p. 133) notes, "the capacity to experience genuinely either shame, or guilt, or remorse, hinges upon a mastery of a natural language involving cultural knowledge and reasoning conventions" (Coulter in Kippax et al., 1988, p. 20). It is the contradictions that one encounters in society which force one to grow or change. As a result of the way an individual interacts with the environment, he or she constructs emotions in response to that responding. It is through the evaluation of what is happening or the appraisal of the situation that emotion is constructed. The anthropologist Levy (1984; cited in Kippax et al.) refers to this as primary and secondary appraisal. Psychologist Averill (1980, cited in Kippax et al.) refers to it as a first and second order monitoring. Basically, they suggest the same thing. First, there is the eliciting situation, perhaps the death of a friend. A feeling then enters into awareness as the result of the initial appraisal, perhaps a feeling of abandonment or loss. The second appraisal consists of interpreting the initial appraisal with its consequent feeling based on social or cultural understandings of loss and abandonment. The second appraisal is reflective and available to one's consciousness. This is the emotion of grief. With adults, the secondary appraisals frequently precede the primary appraisal (Kippax et al.). For example, the social context of a funeral produces the emotional response of crying or other expressions of grief which later evokes memories of loss (Kippax et al.). It is the contradictions and uncertainties which cause the person to search for some meaning, resulting in the constructing of emotions. In applying their constructionist model to the treatment of depression, these constructed emotions or meaning system of the client are explored, and then challenged.

In treating depression, the model of social constructionism does not attach the problem to the client. Traditional psychological approaches have as their goal changing the client's cognitions. The client will gain an inner awareness of past losses, or find evidence of when, where, and how often the depression occurred. The notion that language refers to an independent reality begins to suggest that problems and their causes are constructions. Directed by this view, one looks at what people are doing rather than being stuck on what they are (Gilligan & Price, 1993). For example, the following three statements imply very different possibilities:

- "You are a depressive."
- "You are under the influence of a depression."
- "You are doing depression" (Gilligan & Price, 1993, p. 278).

The first statement attaches the problem to the person. It gives credence to the notion that depression is an entity which one can have. This position is further supported in the classifications for depression in the *DSM III-R*. The second statement implies that depression is not something that is a part of the person. The third statement implies that depression is something that one does. Both the second and third statements create the possibility that the person may do something different in relation to the depression and that this choice and the power to accomplish it belong to the individual (Gilligan & Price, 1993).

There is a major difference between traditional therapy conversations and social constructionist therapy conversations. Traditional conversations focus on categorizing the client according to the *DSM III-R*. The problem with diagnosis is the pessimism that correlates with the labeling. Take, for example, the therapist's thought that depressed clients can take years to understand and work through their depression. Too often, this thought is communicated to the client, adding to the burden of hopelessness. In traditional conversation therapy, there are conversations for expressing emotion, for insight (based on the premise that insight has a curative effect as it helps promote change), conversations for inability (this is communicated to the clients and their families), for blame (frequently the client is blamed for manipulating others, or for not wanting to change), and adversarial conversations (therapist's are seen as the experts on what is "normal" and take the stance that they know what is occurring within their clients) (Gilligan & Price, 1993).

In social constructionist therapy, there are collaborative conversations: clients and therapists collaborate in deciding the focus of therapy and both are considered experts. The clients are the experts on their pain and experiences, and the therapist is an expert at creating the climate for change through conversation and safety. There are also conversations about change/difference, competence/abilities, possibilities, goals/results, and accountability (Gilligan & Price, 1993). Social constructionism is a possibility therapy. The social constructionist model attempts to externalize the problem in relation to the individual. Externalizing the problem is a technique devised by White (1989) which transforms the problem into an entity external to the person, thus allowing more fluidity and movement within the system. It enables a new perspective to emerge through language use, thus supporting the development of an alternate story for the client.

In order to externalize the problem, White uses "reflective influence questioning" (White, 1986, as cited in White, 1989, p. 8). This form of questioning asks people to track the problem's influence in their lives and relationships and also to see their own influence in the problem. By mapping the effects of the problem in their lives and relationships, clients are beginning to look at a relationship to the problem which moves through their experience, rather than being associated with a specific person or static situation (White, 1989). After the problem's influence is mapped, questions which address the influence of the client in the life of the problem are introduced (White, 1989). In using this technique, new information—significant facts which contradict the problem—are revealed. New pieces of information, referred to as exceptions, are amplified through questions, which then provide the opportunity for the incorporation of new meanings and new stories. By envisioning these exceptions and differences and what could lead to them, the client is beginning to write a future script. This creative act revises the client's relationship with the problem from cooperating with it to undermining it (White, 1989). The person also assumes some responsibility for the problem. The client can now start to investigate choices created as new possibilities emerge.

Other questions that generate alternative experience and knowledge explore other people's realities. Answering questions like What would your mother say about this situation? allow people to experience other points of view. Questions involving time (e.g., What are you doing now that is different from what you used to do?) elicit knowledge of past success and invite attention to improvement over time. Questions which explore hypothetical circumstances provide new ways for people to see their capabilities beyond the problem. Once the client is open to alternate possibilities through the questioning used throughout therapeutic possibility conversation, questions which build upon the initial possibility's becoming a story are asked, as are questions which explore the emerging story within the domain of the client's values and beliefs (Gilligan & Price, 1993).

The Therapeutic Stance

The therapist's stance of "not knowing" is also important in using the social constructionist model (Hoffman, 1991, p. 2). The therapist is not removed from the system, nor considered the expert, as in the psychoanalytic, behavioral, cognitive, and interpersonal models. Not knowing is in keeping with postmodern ideas of narrative theory. The attitudes that permit the therapist to adopt the necessary stance are exemplified in the quotations in Table 4.5. As Hoffman (1991) puts it:

> Knowledge, being socially arrived at, changes and renews itself in each moment of interaction. There are no prior meanings hiding in stories or texts. A therapist with this view will expect a new and hopefully more useful narrative to surface during the conversation, but sees this narrative as spontaneous rather than planned. The conversation, not the therapist, is its author. (p. 3)

In the social constructionist model, more than one story is encouraged and associative formats keep meanings unfixed (Hoffman, 1991). Through

TABLE 4.5   Social Constructionist Assumptions

- Understanding exists and is sustained by the changes or alternations of social processes. This cannot be measured by social research: ". . . the rules for 'what counts as what' are inherently ambiguous, continuously evolving, and free to vary with the predilections of those who use them" (Gergen, 1985, p. 266).
- "The terms in which the world is understood are social artifacts, products of historically situated interchanges among people" (Gergen, 1985, p. 266).
- "Forms of negotiated understanding are of critical significance in social life, as they are integrally connected with many other activities in which people engage" (Gergen, 1985, p. 267).
- "There are no absolute truths and there are no absolute realities" (Atwood, 1992, p. 199).
- Our inner world is a construct, colored by the past, and the past is a construction" (Atwood, 1992, p. 199).
- "We co-construct reality through language with another in a continual interaction with the sociocultural environment" (Atwood, 1992, p. 199).
- We recreate an image of our reality by seeking out behaviors in others which fit our perceptions (Atwood, 1992).

the use of dreams, ideas, images, metaphors, and stories, linguistic play constructs the possibilities for new realities.

Using Social Construction Therapy with Depression

Initially, a therapist joins with the client and the client's meaning systems. People construct perceptions based on the telling of stories about themselves and others. These stories help people to establish connections among life experiences (Atwood, 1992). Within this model, therapy is conducted through questioning people's processes and illuminating consequences of their constructions. People have certain emotional meaning systems which are created and maintained by interactions with others. A person who is feeling depressed and has low self-esteem will seek out events and persons that perpetuate this system. Meanings constructed in childhood are maintained by sociocultural influences. The individual will live out a meaning system through emotional scripts, which are acted out and developed from the meaning systems. It is

TABLE 4.6   Summary of Social Constructionist Therapy

- Join with the client's meaning system around depression through learning the client's language, listening, and creating a safe environment.
- Explore the past and how it contributed to the present meaning system.
- Put the past in perspective. This might be facilitated by using a ritual: ". . . Rituals are designed to express certain rites of redefinition of personhood and understanding" (Gilligan & Price, 1993, p. 254). Examples of ritual acts are burning (e.g., a letter or photographs), burying (lying to rest objects of the past), and declarations. In using rituals it is best to have the client, not the therapist, select symbols representing an old self and a new self. The therapist helps by offering suggestions, so that through conversation the ritual is created (Gilligan, 1993).
- Explore the current meaning system through reflective influence questioning.
- Invite clients to expand their meaning systems through reflective influence questioning and reframing.
- Amplify and stabilize the new meaning system through reflective influence questioning.

important for the therapist to construct a time line which introduces a beginning, a middle, and an end (Atwood, 1992).

Specific questions give information about the origins of the problem, a time when it did not exist, and help to externalize the problem. By going back and forth in time, one can also begin to realize that there was a time when depression did not occur. One begins to explore what was different then and begins to see how the future might be different (i.e., that there might be a time when the depression will not exist). In a safe environment, exceptions to the depression are explored and amplified in order to provide new possibilities for new solutions.

The therapy process outlined in Figure 1.7 is elaborated in Table 4.6 and in the case studies that follow.

Case Material

Slumpo

The social constructionist model was applied in a case of depression by Atwood (1990). Initially, a cognitive, behavioral approach was used by the therapist when she first saw Bob, a 41-year-old police officer who had a history of chronic depression. Bob was married to Laurie; they had a teenage daughter, Sara. Every couple of months Bob would isolate himself from his family by staying in his room and would barely be able to function at work. After engaging in therapy for approximately 8 months, Bob felt better and the therapy was terminated.

Two years later he returned with the same problem. Bob felt that he should have been able to handle his problems by utilizing the skills he had been taught previously. Although there were some behavioral improvements, he still held a view of himself as a depressed individual and as a failure who could not use his previous success to overcome the repeated depression. The approach the therapist used this time was a reframe, an attempt to provide the client with sources for new responses. The first phase was to explore the client's meaning system, which was based in his family of origin. Bob claimed he was always under the depression, as his father had been. Bob referred to his father's depressions as "slumps." By asking specific questions about Bob's relationship with his father, such as when the relationship was influenced by the slumps, and how Bob's family of origin responded to his slumps, the problem began to have a life of its own instead of belonging to the client. Through questioning, Bob learned that he wanted to be happy, but if he were different from his family (his depressed father) then he would be disloyal.

The term *slump* was gradually used as a substitute for depression and transformed to "slumpo" (Atwood, 1990, p. 46). The client's own language was utilized as a metaphor for the externalization of the depression. Learnings around the exceptions (when slumpo was not in control) were amplified. "Questioning about development over time was an effort not only to draw attention to the fact that the intensity had varied over time but also to identify that there had been times when the depression was absent" (Atwood, 1990, p. 47). Questions were carefully constructed to explore the family's relationship to the existence of slumpo and to highlight options.

Questions were also asked which led Bob to explore the possibilities if he did not allow slumpo to exist. "Would he allow slumpo to continue to control him more or less as time went by? If he allowed slumpo to control him, which direction would slumpo take him, in five years time? Would Laurie and Sara succumb more to supporting a slumpo lifestyle in their home or would they stage a war against further domination?" (Atwood, 1990, p. 47). The client was then asked if he was ready to take the responsibility and make a choice for lessening slumpo's hold on him. Bob was then asked to visualize slumpo in a nonhuman form. He saw slumpo as a dragon and found that the weapons he would need to defeat slumpo were stones, with which he would use to mentally shrink slumpo (Atwood, 1990). As Bob reported differences and improvements without slumpo, he was restrained from moving too quickly and warned not to underestimate slumpo's power. In helping Bob and Laurie prepare for the change, questions were asked regarding how things would be different once slumpo was dead. Also, in preparing for a relapse, questions were asked about what Bob would notice if slumpo returned. By asking questions built around the future, new possibilities and solutions were formulated and the client began to write and live his script.

One can see from this case study that in applying the social constructionist model, there is flexibility for movement. The problem is neither owned nor attached to the individual. The externalizing is done through questions, and through the utilization of the client's own metaphors as a foundation upon which to build. His family of origin and belief system were explored and worked with, especially as they applied to the present. By looking into the possibility of a future without the problem, new solutions began to arise.

Analysis of the difference between this model and the cognitive/ behavioral approach initially tried with this client, summarizes the social constructionist model: "In the second course of therapy, my role was much more one of working with Bob to build a frame that was meaningful to him, that challenged his persistent way of thinking, and which proposed, but sought not to prescribe, new possibilities for the future" (Atwood, 1990, p. 49).

The Medical Model Man

Epston (1993) also speaks of an interesting case on depression in Gilligan and Prices *Therapeutic Conversations*. A young couple, both in their mid-thirties, were referred to Epston by two psychiatrists in another country. The presenting problem was the husband, Rob, who referred to himself as the "Medical Model Man" (Gilligan & Price, 1993, p. 165). His wife, Sandy, had had enough of his depression and his staying in bed, his trying to out-doctor the doctors by reading psychiatric texts, by going to many different psychiatrists only to have them fail, ultimately resorting to electroconvulsive therapy (ECT), which did not fix his problem either.

After the meeting with the couple, Epston sent them a letter which summarized their session together. In the letter, he validated their situation and amplified the 7 years of their antidepressive relationship. Epston pointed out the things that they admired and appreciated in each other. He reframed Sandy's reactions to the recent stress as responding with all of her feelings and he told Rob that he had turned himself into a case study. How Rob's family responded to tragedy was explored in the letter. Epston commented that it was customary in Rob's family to go to bed with valium. His meaning system was explored through such questions as:

- Did your father treat himself to the same treatment?
- Do you think your father wanted you to grow up to be a Medical Model Man?"
- Do you feel indebted to psychiatrists?
- What do you think they thought about a person who supported questionable psychiatric practices more than they did? (Epston, 1993, p. 166).

These questions also suggest to Rob alternative views of the problem. These questions helped to loosen Bob's frame of reality. Epston then validated and reframed that Rob has been bedridden and a "good patient" (p. 166) since he "medical modelized" (Gilligan & Price, 1993, p. 166) himself and his feelings.

Epston also acknowledged that this process was beginning to hurt Rob, and his relationship with Sandy. He asked specific questions of Sandy, which amplified the extent to which the problem had affected their relationship. For example, he queried, "Do you get the impression that Rob is more attracted to the medical model than to you?" (p. 167). Epston put the responsibility for action into Rob's hands and challenged his present action by asking, "Rob, do you have any wish to take your life back from depression or is being a doctor to yourself more appealing?" (p. 167).

Questions which followed were constructed to explore what it was like before and how it might be different after the depression:

- How do you keep depression at bay?
- How did Rob specialize in being a person rather than a patient?
- Sandy, how did Rob make you respect and love him before depression first turned you into his nurse and then estranged you from him? (Gilligan & Price, 1993, pp. 167–168).

There were seven, one-hour sessions, over a span of 15 months in treating this case. Without focusing on the past, but by exploring it with thought provoking questions, Rob came to terms with the anger he felt toward his father, and the shame he felt about his father being a drunk.

Many of these questions were sent to the couple in letter form prior to a session, in order to provide the couple time to reflect and consider their responses. Toward the end of therapy, Epston asked Rob if he could share this case at conference. In putting closure to the process, clients are invited to share their stories at a future time in order to help others, or asked to summarize what their experience was like. Rob wrote a letter for Epston to share at the conference. The following excerpt highlights the difference between social constructionism and a more traditional model:

> I have been freed from the doubts and limitations imposed by the well-intentioned 'medical model.' As I once said to you, David, the medical school of mental diagnosis and treatment has several shortcomings. It turns acute conditions into chronic problems. It is problem-oriented, not solution-driven. You introduced me to the latter approach. Thanks! [The medical model's] pharmacological prescriptions become junk-mail subscriptions. Getting away from 'them' is like trying to convince American Express you don't want your card renewed. (Epston, 1993, p. 169)

REFERENCES

American Psychiatric Association. (1987). *Diagnostic and statistical manual of mental disorders* (3rd ed. rev.). Washington, DC: Author.

Amundson, J. (1990). In defense of minimalism: Making the least out of depression. *Family Therapy Case Studies, 5*(1), 15–19.

Arieti, S., & Bemporad, J. (1978). *Severe and mild depression.* New York: BasicBooks.

Atwood, J. (1993). Social constructionist couple therapy. *The Family Journal: Counseling and Therapy for Couples and Families, 1*(2), 116–130.

Atwood, J. (1992). Constructing a sex and marital therapy frame. *Journal of Sex and Marital Therapy, 18*(3), 196–218.

Atwood, J. (1990). Killing two slumpos with one stone: A man struggles with depression—and a therapist discovers new ways. *Family Therapy Case Studies, 5*(2), 43–49.

Atwood, J., & Chester, R. (1987). *Treatment techniques for common mental disorders.* New Jersey: Aronson.

Averill, J. (1980). A constructivist view of emotions. In R. Plutchik & H. Kellerman (Eds.), *Emotions: Theory research and experience* (Vol. 1). New York: Academic.

Baldessarini, R. (1983). *Biomedical aspects of depression and its treatment.* Washington, DC: American Psychiatric Press.

Barchas, J. D., Patrick, R. L., Raese, J., & Berger, P. A. (1977). Neuropharmacological aspects of affective disorders. In G. Usdin (Ed.), *Depression: Clinical, biological, and psychological perspectives.* New York: Brunner/ Mazel.

Beck, A. (1976). *Cognitive therapy of depression.* New York: Guilford.

Beck, A., Rush, A., Shaw, B., & Emery, G. (1979). *Cognitive therapy of depression.* New York: Guilford.

Blumenthal, M. D. (1975) Measuring depressive symptomatology in a general population. *Archives of General Psychiatry, 32,* 971–978.

Bradburn, N. M. (1975). The measurement of psychological well being. In J. Elinson (Ed.), *Health goals and health indicators.* Washington, DC: American Association for the Advancement of Science.

Brown, G. W., & Harris, T. (1978). *Social origins of depression.* New York: Free Press.

Clarkin, J., & Glazer, H. (1981). *Depression behavioral and directive intervention strategies.* New York: Garland Press.

Comstock, G. W., & Helsing, K. L. (1976). Symptoms of depression in two communities. *Psychological Medicine, 6,* 551–563.

Corey, G. (1991). *Theory and practice of counseling and psychotherapy.* Pacific Grove, CA: Brooks/Cole.

Cushman, P. (1987). History, psychology, and the abyss. *Psychohistory Review, 15*(3), 29–45.

Dell, P. F. (1985). Understanding Bateson and Maturana: Toward a biological foundation for the social sciences. *Journal of Marital and Family Therapy, 11,* 1–20.

DeRubeis, R. J., & Beck, A. T. (1988). Cognitive therapy. In K. S. Dobson (Ed.), *Handbook of cognitive-behavioral therapies* (pp. 273–306). New York: Guilford.

Elkaim, M. (1990). *If you love me don't love me: Constructions of reality and change in family therapy.* New York: BasicBooks.

Ellis, A. (1979a). The practice of rational-emotive therapy. In A. Ellis & J. Whiteley (Eds.), *Theoretical and empirical foundations of rational-emotive therapy* (pp. 66–100). Pacific Grove, CA: Brooks/Cole.

Ellis, A. (1979b). Rational-emotive therapy: Research data that support the clinical and personality hypotheses of RET and other modes of cognitive-behavioral therapy. In A. Ellis & J. M. Whiteley (Eds.), *Theoretical and empirical foundations of rational-emotive therapy* (pp. 101–173). Pacific Grove, CA: Brooks/Cole.

Ellis, A. (1979c). Toward a new theory of personality. In A. Ellis & J. Whiteley (Eds.), *Theoretical and empirical foundations of rational-emotive therapy* (pp. 7–32). Pacific Grove, CA: Brooks/Cole.

Ellis, A. (1987). The evolution of rational-emotive therapy (RET) and cognitive behavior therapy (CBT). In J. K. Zeig (Ed.), *The evolution of psychotherapy* (pp. 107-132). New York: Brunner/Mazel.

Ellis, A. (1989). Rational-emotive therapy. In R. J. Corsini & D. Wedding (Eds.), *Current psychotherapies* (4th ed., pp. 197–238). Itasca: F. E. Peacock.

Epston, D. (1993). Internalized other questioning with couples: The New Zealand version. In S. G. Gilligan & R. Price (Eds.), *Therapeutic conversations* (pp. 183–196). New York: Norton.

Festinger, L. (1954). A theory of social comparison processes. *Human Relations, 7*, 117–140.

Festinger, L. (1957). *A theory of cognitive dissonance.* Evanston, IL: Row, Peterson.

Flach, F., & Draghi, S. (1975). *The nature and treatment of depression.* New York: Wiley.

Gergen, K. (1982). *Toward transformation in social knowledge.* New York: Springer-Verlag.

Gergen, K., & Davis K. (1985). *The social construction of the person.* New York: Springer-Verlag.

Gergen, K. (1985, March). The social constructionist movement in modern psychology. *American Psychologist, 266*–273.

Gilligan, S., & Price, R. (1993). *Therapeutic conversations.* New York: Norton.

Gotlib, G. (1981) Self-reinforcement and recall: Differential deficits in depressed and nondepressed psychiatric inpatients. *Journal of Abnormal Psychology, 90*, 521–530.

Gotlib, I., & Colby, C. (1981). *Treatment of depression: An interpersonal systems approach.* New York: Pergamon.

Gotlib, I. H., Coyne, J. C., & Kahn, J. (1987). Depression. In T. Jacob (Ed.), *Family interaction and psychopathology: Theories, methods, and findings* (pp. 509–533). New York: Plenum.

Greist, J., & Jefferson, J. (1984). *Depression and its treatment.* Washington, DC: American Psychiatric Press.

Grosscup, S. J., & Lewinsohn, P. M. (1980). Unpleasant and pleasant events, and mood. *Journal of Clinical Psychology, 36*, 252–259.

Hallstrom, T. (1973). *Mental disorder and sexuality in the climacteric.* Goteborg, Sweden: Orstadius Boktryckeri.

Hoffman, L. (1991). A reflexive stance for family therapy. *Journal of Strategic and Systemic Therapies, 10*(3-4), 4–16.

Hoffman, L. (1990). Constructing realities: An art of lenses. *Family Process, 29*(1), 1–12.

Jacobson, E. (1971). *Depression: Comparative studies of normal, neurotic and psychotic conditions.* New York: International Universities Press.

Johnsgard, K. (1989). *The exercise prescription for depression and anxiety.* New York: Plenum.

Kippax, S., Crawford, J., Pam, B., Una, G., & Noesjirwan, J. (1988). Constructing emotions: Weaving meaning from memories. *British Journal of Social Psychology, 27,* 19–33.

Klerman, G., Weissman, M., Rounsaville, B., & Chevron, E. (1984). *Interpersonal psychotherapy of depression.* New York: BasicBooks.

Kukla, A. (1986, April). On social constructionism. *American Psychologist,* 480–481.

Levy, R. (1984). Emotion, knowing and culture. In R. A. Shweder & R. A. LeVine (Eds.), *Culture theory: Essays on mind, self and emotion.* Cambridge: Cambridge University Press.

Lewinsohn, P. M. (1975). The behavioral study and treatment of depression. In M. Hersen, R. M. Eisler, & P. M. Miller (Eds.), *Progress in behavior modification.* New York: Academic.

Lewinsohn, P. M., & Amenson, C. (1978). Some relations between pleasant and unpleasant mood related activities and depression. *Journal of Abnormal Psychology, 87,* 644–654.

Lewinsohn, P. M., Biglan, T., & Zeiss, A. (1976). Behavioral treatment of depression. In P. Davidson (Ed.), *Behavioral management of anxiety, depression, and pain* (pp. 118–151). New York: Brunner/Mazel.

Lewinsohn, P. M., & Shaw, D. (1969). Feedback about interpersonal behavior as an agent of behavior change: A case study in the treatment of depression. *Psychotherapy and Psychosomatics, 17,* 82–88.

Lewinsohn, P. M., & Talkington, J. (1979). Studies on the measurement of unpleasant events and relations with depression. *Applied Psychological Measurement, 3,* 83–101.

Lewinsohn, P. M., Youngren, M. A., & Grosscup, S. J. (1979). Reinforcement and depression. In R. A. Depue (Ed.), *The psychobiology of the depressive disorders.* New York: Academic.

Macphillamy, D., & Lewinsohn, P. (1974). Depression as a function of levels of desired and obtained pleasure. *Journal of Abnormal Psychology, 83,* 651–657.

Mellinger, G. D., Balter, M. B., Parry, H. J, Manheimer, D. I., & Coisin, I. H. (1974). An overview of psychotherapeutic drug use in the United States.

In E. Josephson & E. E. Carroll (Eds.), *Drug use: Epidemiological and sociological approaches* (pp. 333–366). New York: Hemisphere.

Mendez, C. L., Coddou, F., & Maturana, H. R. (1988). The bringing forth of pathology: An essay to be read aloud by two. *Irish Journal of Psychology, 9*, 144–172.

Paykel, E. (1982). *Handbook of affective disorders.* New York: Guilford.

Paykel, E. S. (1982). Psychopharmacology of suicide. *Journal of Affective Disorders, 4*, 271–273.

Penn, P. (1985). Feed-forward: Future questions, future maps. *Family Process, 24*, 299–310.

Pepitone, A. (1940). Motivation effects in social perception. *Human Relations, 3*, 57–76.

Radloff, L. S. (1975). Sex differences in depression: The effects of occupational and marital status. *Sex Roles, 1*, 249–265.

Real, T. (1990). The therapeutic use of self in constructionist/ systemic therapy. *Family Process, 29*, 255–271.

Rehm, L. (1981). *Behavior therapy for depression: Present status and future directions.* New York: Academic.

Rush, J., & Altshuler, K. (1986). *Depression: Basic mechanisms, diagnosis, and treatment.* New York: Guilford.

Schachter, S. (1964). The interaction of cognitive and physiological determinants of emotional state. In L. Berkowitz (Ed.), *Advances in experimental social psychology* (Vol. 1). New York: Academic.

Stroebe, W., & Kruglanski, A. (1989). Social psychology at epistemological cross-roads: On Gergen's choice. *European Journal of Social Psychology, 19*(5), 485–489.

Tomm, K. (1987). Fourth guideline for the therapist. *Family Process, 26*, 3–13.

Von Foerster, H. (1981). *Observing systems.* Seaside, CA: Intersystems.

Watzlawick, P. (1984). *The invented reality.* New York: Norton.

Watzlawick, P. (1990). *Munchhausen's pigtail or psychotherapy "reality."* New York: Norton.

Watzlawick, P., Weakland, J. H., & Fish, R. (1974). *Change principles of problem formation and problem resolution.* New York: Norton.

Weissman, M. M. (1984a). Onset of major depression in early adulthood: Increased familial loading and specificity. *Archives of General Psychiatry, 41*, 1136–1143.

Weissman, M. M., (1984b). The psychological treatment of depression: An update of clinical trials. In J. B. Williams & R. L. Spitzer (Eds.), *Psychotherapy research: Where are we and where should we go?* (pp. 141–154). New York: Guilford.

Weissman, M. M., & Boyd, J. H. (1983). The epidemiology of affective disorders: Rates and risk factors. *Psychiatry Update, 11*, 1039–1046.

Weissman, M. M., & Klerman, G. L. (1977). Sex differences in the epidemiology of depression. *Archives of General Psychiatry, 34,* 98–111.

Weissman, M. M., & Myers, J. K. (1978). Affective disorders in a U.S. urban community. *Archives of General Psychiatry, 35,* 1304–1311.

Weissman, M. M., Myers, J. K., & Thompson, W. D. (1981). Depression and its treatment in a U.S. urban community. *Archives of General Psychiatry, 38,* 417–421.

White, M. (1989). *Selected papers.* Adelaide, Australia: Dulwich Centre.

White, M., & Epston, D. (1990). *Narrative means to therapeutic ends.* New York: Norton.

White, M. (1986). Negative explanation, restraint and double description: A template for family therapy. *Family Process, 25*(2), 169–181.

CHAPTER 5

Suicide: Constructing Hope

Joan D. Atwood

SUICIDE AND SOCIETY

Each year between 240,000 and 600,000 people attempt suicide in the United States. As of 1990, it was estimated that five million living Americans have attempted to kill themselves (McIntosh, 1993). Leenaars et al. (1992) reported "that there are probably 8–10 suicide attempts for every completed suicide" (p. 332). The investigation and study of suicide has revealed distinctions previously unexplored; for example: "Clinicians now suggest . . . that attempters and completers form two different though overlapping groups, each with its own goals and motivations. Completers tend to be male: three times as many men as women kill themselves. Attempters tend to be female: three times as many women as men attempt suicide" (Colt, 1991, p. 96). Suicide does not exclusively affect those who attempt or complete. "The National Institute for Mental Health estimates on the average five survivors are intimately affected by each suicide" (Rosenthal, 1988, p. 121).

Although suicide is an unpleasant subject and the above-mentioned figures are alarming, there is some good news—suicide prevention, intervention, and elimination are not only possible but the odds for a positive outcome are high. This is because "no one is 100 percent suicidal . . . since the most ardent death wish is ambivalent, suicide is more preventable than any other cause of death" (Grollman, 1971, p. 87). The social constructionist model of therapy which will be discussed subsequently is an effective approach to addressing all the issues and circumstances which suicide, whether successful or unsuccessful, presents.

Myths About Suicide

Whenever phenomena cannot be fully comprehended or explained, people form myths or conceptions (which are often misconceptions) that seek to provide quick answers to complex questions. Often based on fear, these notions can be quite misleading and in the case of suicide, deadly. Listed below are a select handful of myths about suicide and their connective facts gathered from Lee (1989), Response of Suffolk County (1984), and Hankoff and Einsidler (1979):

Myth 1. *If a person talks about suicide, they will not attempt it.*

Fact 1. Talking about suicide has been identified as a warning signal that the person may be seriously thinking about taking his or her own life. Most suicidals will talk about their intention in some way beforehand.

Myth 2. *Talking about suicide with a suicidal person will make them commit suicide.*

Fact 2. You cannot give a person the idea of suicide since suicide is something that the individual concludes independently. Talking about suicide with a person contemplating it can be the first step to prevention.

Myth 3. *Suicidal people want to die.*

Fact 3. Suicidal people are unsure about the decision to live or die and they can be persuaded to live. More often than not a suicide attempt is a drastic and desperate cry for help and attention.

Myth 4. *Suicide is an impulsive act.*

Fact 4. Both successful and unsuccessful suicides are often precalculated and meticulously planned.

Myth 5. *Most suicides occur between Thanksgiving and New Years.*

Fact 5. The suicide rate increases at spring after a depression instigated at holiday time.

Myth 6. *Suicidal people are psychotic or mentally ill.*

Fact 6. Most suicides occur after a depression brought on by an actual or perceived loss and not as a result of mental illness.

Myth 7. *Successful suicides are the ones completed on the first try.*

Fact 7. A majority of successful suicides have been attempted several times before.

Myth 8. *An improvement in treatment after a long depression or suicidal crisis means the suicidal risk is over.*

Fact 8. Most suicides are attempted at "the end" of a depression or within a period of 3 months from a previous suicidal crisis.

It is crucial for clinicians to be aware of these myths, so that we use them in discussion and education of the suicidal's family and friends. If not addressed, the misunderstanding and ignorance of the suicidal may be at the expense of his or her life. For as condemnable an act as suicide is, its popularity and prominence in the arts and media throughout history has given this tragic end a shroud of romanticism which can make it compelling, attractive, and seductive to those who are vulnerable. "Suicide has historically been thought to be a romantic kind of death" (Hankoff & Einsidler, 1979, p. 158). Messages such as an exalted remembrance posthumously, a reunification with a loved one gone, or the attainment of eternal peace and love in a place called Heaven have been spread in written legend, song lyrics, works of art, and the themes of motion pictures. In particular, "the idea that women succumb to love, suicide, and suicide for love has a long tradition in Western culture. Depictions of betrayed and abandoned suicidal women are common in western art and literature" (Canetto, 1992–1993, p. 5).

Suicide, Art, and Artists

The legend of Lucretia has been characterized in many paintings since the end of the Tarquins' reign in Rome, and her suicide as a vow of vengeance became a symbol of virtue and heroism. Throughout time Lucretia has been as admired as the artworks created of her. A fictional character named Harlequin (whom many childhood dolls have been modeled after) was originally associated with death. "To be loved by

Harlequin was to be married to death. This is the idea of death as a lover; it relates to the romanticism of death itself" (Hankoff & Einsidler, 1979, p. 158).

In a song entitled "Don't Fear the Reaper" by the rock group Blue Oyster Cult, the lyric goes: "Romeo and Juliet are together in eternity/we can be like they are, come on baby, don't fear the reaper." These lyrics illustrate "the notion (or myth) 'that those with more life and passion go soon', that the best die young. It reminds one of those who have died 'too young'—Byron, Shelley, Keats, Mozart—and the particular poignancy of an untimely death of an especially beautiful or gifted person" (Hankoff & Einsidler, 1979, p. 158). Such is also the effect of musician Dan McLean's song, entitled "Vincent." In a tribute to artist Vincent VanGogh, a stanza sings, "And when no hope was left on that starry night you took your life as lovers often do, but I could have told you Vincent, this world was never meant for one as beautiful as you."

Hankoff and Einsidler (1979) noted that "one result of this mystique is a belief that especially sensitive people—artists, poets, painters, and writers—are unusually prone to commit suicide and, indeed, add to their reputations as artists by committing suicide" (p. 158). "Hemingway was a very intelligent, creative man. He had everything and he was very depressed, in fact, suicidal" (Madanes, 1990, p. 43). The connection between the artist and suicide did not come about unsubstantially. Against the countless, unnoticed deaths by suicide stand out some of the most celebrated and publicly acclaimed artists ever: VanGogh, Virginia Woolf, Hart Crane, Cesare Pavese, Randall Jarrell, Modigliani, Jackson Pollock, Mark Rothko, Ernest Hemingway, John Berryman, Sylvia Plath, Mishima, Kawabata Yasunari, and Thomas Chatterton. These people's lives made a statement and their deaths made a statement as well. In light of their careers, their suicides are not so much viewed as a final exit but as more of a grand finale.

Cutter (1983) traced the origins of suicide in art and found that six major themes evolved in painting, which coincided with specific ranges in time. The theme of the heroic suicide began in 1484, moving to themes of stigmatization, irrationality, depression, ambivalence and, by 1967, as a cry for help theme (pp. 111–127). Today Hollywood movies make use of all of these themes: suicide, if not an issue, is often a subliminal part of the movie's plot. Consider the following movies and their messages about suicide: *Dr. Strangelove, The Deer Hunter, The Omen, Lethal Weapon, Bachelor Party, An American Werewolf in London,*

Full Metal Jacket, The Dead Poet's Society, The Seventh Sign, Beetle-juice, The Hand that Rocks the Cradle, and *The Addams Family.* As Rosenthal noted, "approximately one out of every ten new movies currently features a suicide or a suicide attempt" (1988, p. 100). With all the glory, pomp, circumstance, and attention suicide receives though expression in the arts, it's no wonder that death by one's own hand is still revered as the most romanticized of all deaths, regardless of its taboo nature.

POSSIBLE CHARACTERISTICS OF SUICIDAL PERSONS

Because suicide is not an impulsive act for the most part, suicidal characteristics can be observed by the professional. While not everyone who possesses suicidal qualities will attempt suicide, it is beneficial for the clinician to be familiar with these cues in case of crisis. Rosenthal (1988) found that

> at the core of every suicidal individual's personality is a demanding per-fectionistic streak consumed with criticizing, cutting down, nit-picking, and downright tyrannizing every major, minor and even minuscule behavior . . . suicidal people have distinct difficulties expressing anger . . . The suicidal person saves up angry feelings in the same manner that other individuals collect trading stamps. Because they never fight with others (or at least wait until the last few days before the attempt), they generally end up fighting themselves . . . Every person who has killer instincts against self has a wish to become Superman (or in the case of a woman, Superwoman) . . . the suicidal often set extremely high standards for themselves which are at best unattainable. The suicidal individual's fantasy self is omnipotent and immortal. The poor owner of this fantasy does not see his or her conceptualization as impractical nor impossible. . . . Often one is accurate to say that they are masters of self-harm and live in a self-induced psychic prisons. In essence, they are serving emotional sentences for their self-proclaimed evil streak every day of the year (pp. 76–93).

"People who dislike themselves and are generally depressed may contemplate suicide, but the seriousness of such contemplation is greatly increased in people who also feel hopeless about the future" (Stillion & McDowell, 1991, p. 333). Other distinctions that are particular to suicidals include depression, feelings of hopelessness and helplessness, low self-esteem, and poor coping behaviors. . . . [S]uicidal individuals become more rigid and dichotomous in their thinking and narrow their cognitive focus to suicide as the best, and perhaps the only, answer to their problems . . . [T]he thoughts of depressed people (who are often also suicidal) are marked by four types of cognitive distortions: rigidity of thought, selective abstraction, overgeneralization, and inexact labeling. . . . [S]uicidal people tend to reinforce their misery by giving themselves continuous messages relating to their inferiority, their hopelessness, and their helplessness, thus using their cognitive gift of language to reinforce their suicidal state. (Stillion & McDowell, 1991, pp. 333–334)

From the suicidal's point of view, a different insight is gained. As noted by Gernsbacher (1985) "the suicide suffers from the pain of his anxiety. But he also suffers on many other accounts" (p. 164).

His rationalizations do sometimes seem to make sense, especially if they are not examined too closely. He lays the blame on coincidence, unavoidable circumstances, bad luck, poor health, etcetera. He may even admit to carelessness, rebelliousness, procrastination, or neglect. Such explanations convey an aura of general acceptance. Life does have its hazards, and he is, after all, only human. . . . It matters little whether his body lives or dies. In fact, the sooner he is rid of it, the better off he will be. (p. 159).

Suicide "is seen more often by attempters as an intelligent act, being a sound way to overcome their personal difficulties. It is functional" (Leenaars et al., 1992, p. 339).

Although attempters and completers of suicide may behave, feel and think similarly, there is a difference between the two. "Completers use more lethal methods—guns, hanging, and jumping—while 70 to 90 percent of all attempters swallow pills and about 10 percent cut their wrists, methods that also allow more time for rescue. Attempts are often made in settings that make survival not only possible but probable" (Colt, 1991, p. 96). Suicidals who have attempted suicide previously may have learned that "Parasuicide evokes response in others. Indeed, the act may well be undertaken with a general disregard for a beloved person, spouse, society, etc., to evoke a response in them" (Leenaars et al., 1992, p. 339). For attempters who desire to be saved by the one they love, their plans of suicide are frequently interrupted or conveniently discovered (as planned). The notion that being rescued from suicide by the one you love as an ultimate test of love can become a deadly game of Russian Roulette when the "knight in shining armor" or the "Florence Nightingale" is held up in traffic or delayed at the office.

Stillion and McDowell (1991), in their study of suicide, proposed that "suicidal behavior has at least four categories of causal factors: biological, psychological, cognitive, and environmental . . . each of them must be examined to understand any suicide completely" (p. 328). Biologically, they learned, "a deficiency of serotonin may be implicated in both depression and suicide attempts, especially impulsive suicide attempts . . . [and] the incidence of suicidal behavior among relatives of suicidal persons is higher than in the general population" (p. 330). Factors such as "turbulent home lives, the presence of child abuse, alcoholism, separation, and divorce are all correlated with increases in depression, self-destructive behavior, and suicide. . . . [L]oss is a clear factor increasing the risk of suicide" (pp. 334–335). Whether the loss be actual or perceived, for the suicidal unable to go beyond grief, life is unbearable. Prolonged physical and/or emotional pain may cause a person to consider suicide, especially if they feel surrounded by feelings of worthlessness, unlovability, inefficiency, lack of purpose or significance, and hopelessness. The feeling of facing a problem without an acceptable attainable answer can also provoke suicidal behavior.

Negative life events have "the power to make people examine their prior assumptions. Generally such examination leads individuals to lose some of their faith in a just world, their self-esteem, their basic sense of trust, and positive outlook" (Stillion & McDowell, 1991, p. 335). For the suicidal, cognitive processes are running on overload and can stymie physical action and emotional reaction. Physical maintenance and appearance become a burden and their emotional affect is flat and "burnt out."

Gernshacher (1985) holds that self-hatred, vindictiveness, and hopelessness motivate him towards suicide ". . . through a balance between them, however, the suicide can attain a certain degree of what we customarily call normalcy" (p. 151). Cutter (1983) asserts that "the motives for self-injury remain obscure, especially to the victim" (p. 11). However, as suicidal tendencies evolve, one universal decision that all suicidals will come to is the conclusion to commit: from out of the darkness comes a light. With the discovery of a "way out" one answer is found to solve all problems. Peace, freedom from pain, tears, and misery is now within reach. The decision to commit suicide may come as a sobering intelligent conclusion for some—in that they know now what they must do—or as a jubilant revelation and in the same spirit, as if planning a party, preparations are made for the big day.

Gender-Based Differences

"Traditionally, women are said to be suicidal for love; men, for pride and performance" (Canetto, 1992–1993, p. 1). Differences in gender have been recognized as having important implications with regard to suicidal behavior. Canetto remarked on a number of phenomena associated with male suicide:

> In western cultures, men are not supposed to fall to defeat; they are supposed to win and be in control of themselves and others. (p. 7) . . . [E]xplanations for men's suicides have focused on the dynamics of performance, pride, and independence. . . . [M]en are suicidal when their self-esteem and independence are threatened by difficult economic conditions, unemployment, or severe physical illness. . . . [S]uicidal men are often portrayed as victims of powerful social and/or physical calamities. Their suicidal act is construed as part of their resistance against such forces, not as defeat; as a triumph against the possibility of submission, not as submission. (p. 5) . . . men are suicidal as a result of trials of material order, such as misery, business embarrassment, losses, ungratified ambition, the abuse of alcohol, the desire to escape from justice and so on (p. 7) . . . [M]en's high rates of mortality by suicide may be influenced by cultural expectations about suicide and masculinity. (p. 12) . . . [T]he risk of suicide is higher in men who are unmarried (single, separated, divorced, or widowed), living alone, and socially isolated. (p. 10)

Research by Stillion and McDowell (1991) suggests that "given the facts that male aggression is greater then female aggression across species and from the very earliest ages at which it can be measured, the most logical inference is that there is a genetic or prenatal basis for heightened male aggression . . . [and that] such a tendency, when directed at the self, may help to explain the consistent sex difference in suicide rates" (p. 331).

Canetto's (1992–1993) findings report that

> women's suicidal behavior has traditionally been attributed to problems in their personal relationships . . . the disposition to suicide is the result

of excessive identification with, and dependence upon, a love-object. . . . Women's love and suicide are labeled neurotic. Motivations other than loss and dependence are typically not given prominence in studies of women's suicidal behavior. . . . Suicidal women are subject to moral influences, such as disappointed love, betrayal, desertion, jealousy, domestic trouble, and sentimental exaltation of every description. (p. 4–5) . . . the mechanisms leading to suicidal behavior in women may have less to do with women's neurotic attachments, and more with either the stresses of a dysfunctional intimate relationship (possibly including serious emotional neglect, infidelity, and physical abuse) or women's reduced access to the rewards of employment. (p. 9)

WARNING SIGNS

"Suicidal ideation, triggering events, and warning signs form an interrelated triad that is present in many suicides" (Stillion & McDowell, 1991, p. 335). While the friends and family of a presuicidal may not recognize or comprehend suicidal ideation or triggering events, one thing they may experience first hand are warning signs; however, they may not recognize them unless they have been educated to watch for the clues listed below:

- Suicidal references to death or talking directly about suicide.
- Taking a sudden interest in death-related items and matters such as funeral practices and costs, cemetery plots, locations or visitations, sad poetry, books, morbid art and music.
- Making farewell gestures or preparing others for an unspecified departure of unknown or vague destination/return.
- Giving away possessions, instructions for the care of pets, children and/or plants, discovery of a recent will.
- Lack of interest or motivation to previously pleasurable activities and relationships.
- A noticeable withdrawal from friends, family, activities.
- Carefree risk-taking or dangerous behaviors with a lack of concern for potential self-harm or harmful self-consequences. (If another is present, the suicidal will continue to exhibit safety care and concern for them.)
- Involvement with drugs and alcohol.

Aside from these signals the therapist may also notice other behaviors such as:

- A preoccupation or idealization of death.
- A minimization in definition or relevance of physical pain.
- A sudden "lift" from a long depression; presenting as relieved, happy, calm and resolved.
- A description of a detailed suicide plan and accessibility to the means described.
- Desire to terminate therapy without a previous discussion of this decision, to pay off outstanding balance in full and attempt to say something profound in parting as a remembrance.
- A sense of lost hopes, dreams, aspirations, isolation, devastation, unworthiness or despair, that "all is in vain"; inability to verbalize any kind of future forecast.

If these harbingers to suicide are missed, the consequences for all involved could become an inescapable nightmare. Regardless of the therapist's theoretical orientation or practice, an educational component to dealing with a suicidal client and the family is a must.

SURVIVORS

"Suicide is the cruelest death of all for those who remain. . . . a suicide leaves behind a great many victims—wife, husband, parents, children, friends—for whom the pain is just beginning" (Colt, 1991, p. 409). The immediate reactions to a suicide are the same as with any unexpected death: shock, grief, disbelief and pain from not having been able to say goodbye. As the survivors of a suicide begin to process what has occurred, they may often blame themselves for not having been able to foresee or prevent the suicide. It is not uncommon at this time for the survivor to "believe he sees or hears the person who committed suicide" (Rosenthal, 1988, p. 120). Self-blame then turns to anger, as Rosenthal notes: "Often the anger increases as one ponders the fact the individual gave him no chance to intervene. . . . [T]he anger may also be directed toward another individual such as a teacher, employer, friend, or relative who was intimately involved in a crisis situation which took place in close proximity to the suicide" (1988, p. 120). "The survivors are turned against themselves and sometimes against each other, pointing the finger of blame" (Victoroff, 1983, p. 205). With relation to others, Victoroff recorded that "there is intense guilt and shame as members of the family, particularly the surviving spouse, have stressful confrontations with the physician, the hospital authorities, neighbors, friends, employers, insurance agents, the police, and the coroner's or the medical examiner's office" (1983, p. 205).

Canetto (1992–1993) wrote that "a suicide always implies resignation and defeat" (p. 7). This inference is one of many which the survivors of suicide must face while at the same time seeking comfort in their time of loss. Death by suicide has an isolating effect on those left behind perhaps as a result of the many connotations that suicide imparts. Wagner and Calhoun (1991–1992) found that "although the survivor may experience a strong need for support, the support system's ability to fulfill this need adequately may be adversely affected by the suicide" (p. 62). "In contrast to the loving support that the community ordinarily gives the bereaved when there is death, neighbors and friends are ambiguous and try to avoid contact" (Victoroff, 1983, p. 205). Calhoun and Allen (1991) discussed survivors' problems:

> Spouses of suicide victims were perceived as being more to blame, more ashamed of the cause of death, and more able to have prevented the death than surviving spouses of victims of leukemia or of accidents . . . suicidal deaths were viewed as more difficult to cope with and interactions with the suicide survivors as more stressful for members of the social network. . . . '20/20 hindsight' essentially serves to make survivors feel more guilty and responsible and potential comforters more condemning and judgmental. . . . [S]uicide survivors seem to absorb the negative stigma attached to the suicidal act. In most of the studies, individuals bereaved by suicide tended to be viewed as more psychologically disturbed, less likable, more blameworthy, more ashamed, more in need of professional mental health care, and more likely to remain sad and depressed longer. (p. 97–100)

In particular, survivors have identified damaging elements: "Negative stigmatizing events that were reported included: gossip, negative reactions from officials, and being accused of having caused the suicide. . . . A client who is a survivor is quite likely to experience some degree of social distance and possible isolation from others, even from those who try to be supportive" (Calhoun & Allen, 1991, pp. 101–104).

Survivors of suicide endure a potpourri of tumultuous emotions which are unique to other survivors. "The bereaved said they felt isolated from family and friends; they described feeling deserted, stigmatized, and blamed by the social network" (Wagner & Calhoun, 1991–1992, p. 62).

Mothers who experienced the unexpected death of a child commonly experienced guilt because of perceived responsibility for the death; also, some mothers reported guilt as a result of their sense of relief at the ending of an ambivalent relationship. . . . During the search for answers, family members, including parents, often reviewed their roles with the deceased and felt guilty. Common sources of guilt included: being unaware of the family member's suicidal intent, feeling responsible for the death, and regretting past interactions with the deceased. (Miles & Demi, 1991–1992, p. 204). Rosenthal (1988) observed that "the guilt is often inseparable from the anger" (p. 121). One thing seems certain: "The suffering of survivors is acute after any death, but the grief inflicted by suicide may be the hardest of all to bear" (Colt, 1991, p. 409).

Due to the unpreparedness of the survivors for their loved one's suicide, internal manifestations designed to help the survivor cope may arise.

Psychological adaptive mechanisms include incorporation in which the dead person is imitated. His habits become adopted, his standards and esthetic taste replicated. Sometimes there is substitution. Members of the family will keep the artifacts of the dead person as symbols of his previous life. . . . Sometimes a loved object, a strain of music, a place to go, a passage in a book, a photograph may become a symbolization. Investing in objects is a way of postponing grief and refusing to admit the permanency and irrevocability of death. Mystification occurs when a strange horror is attributed to the dead and the act of suicide is assumed to have an occult purpose beyond the ken of the survivors . . . depersonalization may occur. They feel numb and withdraw to a point where they brood about the deceased in an obsessional exaggeration of normal mourning. . . . Such mysteries are usually entirely fantasized and represent psychological techniques of postponing the task of grief" (Victoroff, 1983, p. 206).

Therapy for Survivors

With so many issues being presented by survivors of suicide, where does a therapist begin? Victoroff (1983) suggests that the major immediate task of the therapist is to give hearing to the guilt, the grief, and the anger of the survivors. . . . When acceptable and solicited, the implication of the existence of an all-forgiving, all-knowing, loving God who is the ultimate spiritual resource may offer security and hope as well as strength to tolerate the painful affects that afflict the survivors of suicide for some time after the incident. (p. 209–210)

Smith, Range, and Ulmer (1991–1992) established that a

high belief in afterlife was associated with greater recovery from bereavement, regardless of the cause of death. . . . [R]elatively high purpose in life for bereaved individuals is associated with greater social support, less felt impact, and greater overall life satisfaction. . . . Accepting and finding meaning in the death are particularly difficult for those bereaved by suicide. . . . All those who reported having some type of therapy said they had found some meaning in the death, whereas less than half of those who reported no therapy experience said they had found some meaning. Professional therapists may be particularly helpful to those bereaved by suicide in their search for meaning in the death. (p. 222)

As recommended by Victoroff (1983), "the urgent message to give to survivors is that life is for the living" (1983, p. 209)—regardless of the therapist's choice of theoretical application.

THERAPY FOR SUICIDE ATTEMPTS

A double-edged sword awaits the suicidal who attempts and is unsuccessful. Colt (1991) points out that, "The suicide attempter was regarded as a double failure—not only at life but at death" (p. 96) and Canetto (1992–1993) echoes that for men "surviving a suicidal act is considered unmasculine" (p. 11). Messages such as these seem more like encouragement toward another suicide attempt; although not intended to be translated as such, they are most often the messages of shame, embarrassment, humiliation, and failure that an unsuccessful suicide faces almost immediately following a rescue. The love, care, concern, and promises of renewed, undivided attention that the suicidal may have hoped for as a result of their rescue very often wane and dissipate right before their eyes. For an instant they receive what they most wanted, but as they recover, survivors may become enraged by the attempt and view it as a manipulation or as a selfish act without regard for their feelings. If the suicidal genuinely intended to die, he or she may be devastated by the botched job and sink into depression once more. If the suicidal's intent was to get help or attention, there may be harsh and rude disillusionment as the romantic rescue does not produce magical changes in others as anticipated. While friends and family members may initially be consoling and attentive to the attempter as well as self-blaming, these feelings give way to contempt, anger, and blame of the attempter when they think How could they do this to me? A minimization of the attempt by the projected survivors is common not so much as a challenge for the attempter to do it right next time, but as a way for friends and family to alleviate their fright, feelings, and self-blame about the suicide attempt. As Calhoun and Allen (1991) wrote, "there are perceptions of family pathology, blame and prolonged grief when anyone engages in suicidal behavior of any level of lethality" (p. 98). These ideas may escape the attempter who may view circumstances as going from bad to worse once fully recovered from the suicidal incident.

Theoretical Background

There have been many approaches and treatment techniques developed to address the issue of suicide. Each approach contributes a unique view and understanding of the subject. Most familiar perhaps is the sociological explanation of Emile Durkheim. Durkheim categorized suicide into three distinct groupings: egoistic, altruistic and anomic. An egoistic suicide occurs when the individual has few connections to a community and has not adequately integrated into society. The altruistic suicide occurs when the individual sacrifices himself or herself for a cause or a greater good in martyr-like fashion. An anomic suicide occurs as the result of an individual not being able to have adapted to some sort of change in society. This type of suicide follows a crisis point or a failure in transition.

Psychoanalysis

Psychoanalytic schools of thought offer the perspectives of Freud, Adler, Horney, and Jung. Sigmund Freud represented two instincts: one for life, Eros, and one for death, Thanatos. Thanatos is described as a death wish or as the destructive, aggressive side of human beings. Suicide and homicide are both the translations and manifestations of Thanatos. Adler believed that "suicide signifies a veiled attack upon others. By an act of self-destruction, the suicide hopes to evoke sympathy for himself and cast reproach upon those responsible for his lack of self-esteem" (Grollman, 1971, p. 35). Analyst Karen Horney viewed suicidal individuals as suffering from feelings of inferiority and as having a child-like dependency on others. She held that suicide was the result of the combination of environment and personality traits. Carl Jung's perspective focuses around the idea of rebirth following suicide in both physical and spiritual realms. He explains that by the suicidal's death, the person can be resurrected and then reborn to start over again.

Behaviorism

"The behavioral viewpoint challenges the notion of a suicidal person and speaks instead of people as engaged in specific suicidal behaviors. Like all behavior, suicidal behaviors are learned and can be unlearned" (Hankoff & Einsidler, 1979, p. 184). From this approach, suicide is seen as an operant behavior and techniques associated with the behavioral school include desensitization, relaxation, and assertiveness training.

> Briefly, desensitization is suggested to reduce anxiety during an acute crisis in order to prevent depression. The relaxation response becomes an alternative to a suicidal response. Assertive training is considered to be especially useful when depression has set in, and it is recommended that family members become involved as reinforcement agents. (Hankoff & Einsidler, 1979, p. 184)

"The cognitive-behavioral model in general and the Rational-Emotive Therapy (RET) model in particular emphasize the role played by conscious or preconscious cortical processes (belief systems and evaluations) in determining inappropriate emotional reactions and self-defeating behavior" (Woods, Silverman, Gentilini, Cunningham, & Grieger, 1991, pp. 216–217). The cognitive-behavioral approach integrates and addresses the thinking and acting aspects of suicide. Research done by Woods et al., (1991) led to the development of two models utilizing RET techniques as applied to suicide: The first model considers suicidal contemplation as a consequence of a self-hatred or self-damning schema [and] the second model considers depression and suicidal contemplation as a consequence of thinking irrationally about one's own original feelings of depression or other emotional discomfort (p. 242).

Interpersonal Theory

Harry Stack Sullivan's interpersonal theory describes suicide as a transformational event within his conceptual frame of three personifications of "me." Sullivan postulated that individuals perceive themselves in terms of "good me," "bad me," or "not me." Suicide occurs at the point of "bad me" turning into "not me" when feelings of numbness and alienation take over.

Systems Theory

From systems theory the idea of suicide is presented as a transgenerational theme (i.e., "the history, traditions, myths, and values of the family are interjected and handed down from one generation to the next" [Richman, 1986, p. 31]). Perpetuated patterns such as loss, abandonment, despair, isolation, and unworthiness can be discovered while working with a suicidal individual or family through sessions or depiction on a genogram. A family myth might designate a family member for self-destruction, or rigid boundaries and inflexible roles can lead to suicide by not allowing for change. From a family life cycle perspective, failure at a transition point can also set the stage for a suicide attempt.

SOCIAL CONSTRUCTIONIST THERAPY INVOLVING SUICIDE

Before proceeding to the social constructionist approach to suicide, it is crucial to address therapists' self-issues in regard to this topic. Grollman (1971) summed the situation: "Suicide is ugly for onlookers, devastating for relatives, and harrowing even for those professionally involved. . . . [T]he entire subject is often studiously avoided, even when a person threatens to take his own life. Some just do not want to become entangled in the sordid predicament" (p. 87).

> In conducting therapy with the suicidal client, therapists must grapple with anxieties about their own competence and compassion in the face of

escalating client demands and intense emotional distress. . . . [S]uch situations may be especially difficult for therapists with elevated levels of personal death anxiety or threat, because client's struggles with loss or death may trigger fears about the therapists' own mortality. (Kirchberg & Neimeyer, 1991, p. 604)

Because of the life or death consequence before us in working with a suicidal, it is of critical importance for therapists to feel comfortable, confident, and competent in their abilities and approaches. Suicide must be dealt with directly, not danced around. If the therapist feels uncertain or excessively uncomfortable with the topic or the client, great benefit will be gained from realizing these limitations and referring clients to a therapist known for experience or specialization in suicide. Experimentation with suicide treatment should not be conducted in crisis in an independent office setting, but rather in workshops, seminars or in a supervised team framework. Suicides cannot be undone; don't let one unnecessarily happen to you.

The social constructionist approach to suicide is broken down and elaborated on in four parts: as applied to the suicidal individual, the surviving family and friends of a successful suicide, the failed attempter, and the failed attempter with family. The model for the following protocols is based on the work of Atwood (1993).

The Suicidal Individual

1. Join with the suicidal's meaning system and explore it.
2. Construct a story about the past of the suicidal which minimizes the overwhelming bad aspects and exemplifies the good and happy times. Find the exceptions in the negative narratives and amplify them.
3. Put the past into perspective and lay it to rest.
4. With a focus on the here and now, explore the suicidal's current meaning system and explore the effects of suicidal ideation on the person's outlook, view of the world, interactions, and relationships (or lack thereof) with others.
5. Amplify the suicidal's process through techniques such as tracking, exaggeration, instant replay, word imagery, sculpting, or through circular and reflexive questioning.
6. Loosen the self-destructive frame through metaphor or by reframing weaknesses as strengths (e.g., frailty as sensitivity). *Remember*

the romantic notion of suicide. Work with the reframe and meta-phor.

7. Look for exceptions and breaks from the gloom-and-doom sto-ries and amplify the exceptions when they occur. If an exception isn't given, ask for one—probe.

8. Co-construct an improved self-esteem through new meanings and reframes. In a failed love relationship, for example, ask "What positive, learning attributes can you walk away with from the break-up?" Advise a client to "think not that there is something wrong with me but rather that the combination of us wasn't exactly right." "Encourage perseverance and hopefulness: "Keep searching to find the right fit." "Quit now and you may be deny-ing someone who is looking for the right fit in you."

9. Create a frame of self-appreciation through self-affirmations (e.g., I am a survivor, everyday is a new day for me to learn; I have a right to be here same as anyone else).

10. Ask the client how he or she will recognize a slip-up (reverting back to suicide ideation). Review what they can do to get them-selves back on track when and if it occurs.

11. In tying up the therapeutic change (when ready), have the client recount and review what has occurred since the first day he or she walked in. Ask the client to describe thoughts, feelings, and outlooks then and now. If a marked change in description is not given, go back to Step 8.

12. Co-construct a frame for seeing the future without suicide attempts or ideations. Ask "How will it be? And how else? And how else?"

13. Help the client incorporate a view of life that's more positive, hopeful, and meaningful. Hope—above all else—is essential to impart with any suicidal situation. The conclusion to commit is arrived at after all hope is lost. At this point in therapy, if there is any spiritual belief or religious faith, now is a good time to plug it in.

14. A ritual for a fresh start could include disposing of the available suicidal means from the household (throw away razor blades, rat poison, tube for exhaust pipe on car, etc.); ripping up a written copy of suicide plans, a will composed for the occasion, or a suicide note; or holding a funeral for the source of pain by bury-ing someone's picture or putting mementos in a shoebox and entombing them in a basement, friend's house, or back closet.

The Surviving Family and Friends

1. Join with the surviving family's meaning system and listen. Having and employing bereavement skills is beneficial at this time. When the overpowering mourning has subsided, explore the family's meaning system in relation to the deceased.
2. Construct a story about the past that includes the deceased and that considers both pains and strengths of the relationship or relationships.
3. Put the past into perspective and allow the deceased to rest in peace. The amount of grief experienced by the friends/family will determine how quickly or slowly they will arrive at this step. It may take some time.
4. With a present focus, explore the survivor's meaning system which no longer includes the deceased. What effects did the suicide have on themselves, on their relationships with each other and outsiders? How does the suicide impact on their view of the world, of life, of death?
5. Amplify the survivors' processes through the techniques of tracking, exaggeration, word imagery, sculpting, circular and reflexive questioning.
6. Loosen the frame which will keep them stuck in time or in a state of anger and blame through the use of metaphor and reframe. Emphasize, for example, that the deceased carefully planned and executed his or her death, rather than that a friend or family member may have missed a sign which led to the death.
7. Look for examples of functioning that are independent of the deceased (not tied to him or her in memory) and amplify. Point out the exceptions to "life cannot go on without him or her."
8. Co-construct a sense of security in new meanings. The therapist may need to give the family permission to do so, because taking on new meanings may feel like betrayal to the deceased by the survivors. A useful reframe may clarify that their lives are not destroyed forever, but changed forever.
9. Create an appreciation frame among friends and family members which will give them support and a sense of unity with each other. This will come across as a compliment or as an admiration of a member's quality (e.g., "I appreciate your patience with me" or "I appreciate when you allow me uninterrupted time to myself").

10. Ask the survivors how they will recognize slip-ups (times when they begin to blame the deceased or each other for occurrences). Review what they can do to refocus themselves when or if slip-ups occur.
11. In tying it all up, have the family members recount the differences from their first day in therapy to now, encompassing their old views, attitudes, and feelings. Have them verbalize transitions in thinking and feeling from anger to acceptance.
12. Co-construct a frame for the future without the repercussions of suicide or with the absence of the deceased. Ask "How would this be? And how else?" Create a possible future frame which leaves the tragedy behind.
13. Assist the survivors to incorporate a view of their relationships as more positive and supportive. "What did sharing the experience mean to you as a family? How does it make your family stronger?"
14. A ritual for a fresh start could include visiting the gravesite of the deceased as a family with members taking turns saying good-bye, or each member of a group of survivors writing a letter saying what they wish for closure and then as a group burning the letters in one fire.

The Failed Attempter

The social constructionist approach with this individual is the same as with the suicidal individual cited previously. In this case, however, the issue of failure will be more pronounced. Since failed attempters generally will try again, approaching the failed attempter as a suicidal individual is the safest practice.

The Failed Attempter with Family

1. Join with the family's meaning system and explore it.
2. Construct a story of the past, including the suicide attempt, which considers both pains and strengths of their situations and relationships.
3. During narrative construction, the failed attempter and family should be seen separately. With the failed attempter, the past should be put into perspective and laid to rest. With the family,

however, the therapist should teach the family warning signs to suicide since another attempt is possible. Put the past into perspective, but do not lay it to rest just yet, since information from the past may be useful with regard to prevention. Employ an "as-if" perspective, in order to permit progress yet maintain a certain level of problem awareness simultaneously.

4. With a focus on the here and now, explore the attempter's and the family's meaning system and what the effects of the attempt have had on them and their relationships to each other.

5. Amplify the family's processes through the use of tracking, word imagery, exaggeration, sculpting, instant replay, circular and reflexive questioning.

6. Loosen the frame that will keep them angry and blaming through the use of metaphor and reframe (e.g., the suicide attempt was not an act of aggression against others but a cry for attention). Work with the reframe and metaphor.

7. Look for exceptions to the narratives of insecurity, fear, powerlessness, and anger over the situation, and each other. Point out when they have acted as a caretaking unit, a support system, source of love for each other.

8. Co-construct new meanings in situations, interactions, family definitions, and other circumstances. Create an environment that allows for individual differences and can be a sanctuary in bad times as well as a place to call home in good times.

9. Create an appreciation frame, especially focusing on the failed attempter. Teach family members how to use the appreciation frame when the situation is tense as well as when things are heading in the right direction.

10. Ask the failed attempter and family members to identify when slip-ups occur (suicidal ideation for attempter and blaming, angry behaviors, thoughts, feelings for the family). Have them review what they can do to stop the slip-up.

11. In tying it all up, have the attempter and family members report their progress from the day they came in until the present, citing differences in their thoughts and feelings.

12. Co-construct a frame for the future that leaves the suicidal crisis in the past. Ask how the future will look. "What would happen in a time of crisis without a fear of suicide? How would this be? And how else?"

13. Help the attempter and family incorporate a view of the world and each other as enduring, positive, and supportive. How has weathering the storm together without falling apart made them stronger as a unit?
14. A ritual for a fresh start may include reciting the marriage vows (if the attempter was a spouse), creating a family vow and ceremony in which all participate, or taking a family photograph and giving each member a copy.

The social constructionist therapeutic approach is creative, a free-flowing method that draws upon the courageous experiences of both the client and therapist. It is intended as the basis for a more positive approach to suicide treatment, one which gives the client the imagery of hope and change.

REFERENCES

Atwood, J. D. (1993). Social constructionist couple therapy. *The Family Journal: Therapy and Therapy for Couples and Families, 1*(2), 116–130.

Calhoun, L. G., & Allen, B. G. (1991). Social reactions to the survivor of a suicide in the family. *OMEGA Journal of Death and Dying, 23*(2), 95–107.

Canetto, S. S. (1992–1993). She died for love and he for glory: gender myths of suicidal behavior. *OMEGA Journal of Death and Dying, 26*(1), 1–17.

Colt, G. H. (1991). *The enigma of suicide.* New York: Summit.

Cutter, F. (1983). *Art and the wish to die.* Chicago, IL: Nelson-Hall.

Gernsbacher, L. M. (1985). *The suicide syndrome: Origins, manifestations, and alleviation of human self-destructiveness.* New York: Human Sciences Press.

Grollman, E. A. (1971). *Suicide: prevention, intervention, postvention.* Boston, MA: Beacon.

Hankoff, L. D., & Einsidler, B. (Eds.). (1979). *Suicide: Theory and clinical aspects.* Massachusetts: PSG.

Kirchberg, T. M., & Neimeyer, R. A. (1991). Reactions of beginning therapists to situations involving death and dying. *Death Studies, 15*(6), 603–610.

Lee, C. P. (Ed.). (1989). *Secrets you shouldn't keep: The teen survival booklet.* (Available from SCOPE, 810 Meadow Rd., Smithtown, NY 11787.)

Leenaars, A. A., Lester, D., Wenckstern, S., McMullin, C., Rudzinski, D., & Brevard, A. (1992). Comparison of suicide notes and parasuicide notes. *Death Studies, 16*(4), 331–342.

Madanes, C. (1990). *Sex, love and violence: Strategies for transformation.* New York: Norton.

McIntosh, J. L. (1993, February). *U.S.A. suicide: 1990 official final data.* (Available from American Association of Suicidology, 2459 S. Ash, Denver, Colorado 80222.)

Miles, M. S. & Demi, A. S. (1991–1992). A comparison of guilt in bereaved parents whose children died by suicide, accident, or chronic disease. *OMEGA Journal of Death and Dying, 24*(3), 203–215.

Response of Suffolk County. (1984). *Adolescent suicide and self-destructive behavior.* Stonybrook, NY: Author.

Richman, J. (1986). *Family therapy for suicidal people.* New York: Springer.

Rosenthal, H. (1988). *Not with my life I don't: Preventing your suicide and that of others.* Muncie, IN: Accelerated Development Inc.

Smith, P. C., Range, L. M., & Ulmer, A. (1991–1992). Belief in afterlife as a buffer in suicidal and other bereavement. *OMEGA Journal of Death and Dying, 24*(3), 217–225.

Stillion, J. M., & McDowell, E. E. (1991). Examining suicide from a life span perspective. *Death Studies, 15*(4), 327–354.

Victoroff, V. M. (1983). *The suicidal patient: Recognition, intervention, management.* Oradell, NJ: Medical Economics Books.

Wagner, K. G., & Calhoun, L. G. (1991–1992). Perceptions of social support by suicide survivors and their social networks. *OMEGA Journal of Death and Dying, 24*(1), 61–73.

Woods, P. J., Silverman, E. S., Gentilini, J. M., Cunningham, D. K., & Grieger, R. M. (1991). Cognitive variable related to suicidal contemplation in adolescents with implications for long-range prevention. *Journal of Rational-Emotive & Cognitive-Behavior Therapy, 9*(4), 215–245.

CHAPTER 6

Dueling Couples

George J. Meyer

INTRODUCTION

Definition of Marriage

Marriage is a cooperative venture, requiring a team effort in order to obtain mutual goals, such as parenting and financial stability. Two individuals who seek to share their lives together do not live by themselves: each individual brings his or her family history, a history of previous relationships or marriages, gender, cultural, and socioeconomic background into the marriage. Some of these may represent shared belief systems or expectations, while others may bring about conflict or misunderstandings.

Stressors

Change is inevitable in the life of a marriage. Changes are brought about by internal and external stressors. One source of *internal stress* is the developmental lifespan on the marriage itself, a natural progression of expected changes (e.g., having children) and unexpected changes (e.g., a spouse suffers from multiple sclerosis). These developmental changes either stimulate growth or cause conflicts for the couple or either spouse. For example, the couple decide to have children but then argue over methods of discipline or desired degree of involvement of each in the parenting process. A second form of internal stress is the ability of each spouse to effectively cope with his or her respective developmental lifespan issues, such as becoming professionally established, or coping with aging or failing health. The life experiences ("baggage") of each spouse either enrich or hamper the ability to effectively cope or make reasonable adaptations. These life experiences include but are not limited to: family of origin experiential history; previous marital experiences; gender, cultural, and socioeconomic differences; and generational gaps. These stressors bring about needs and perceptions within each partner that may challenge the other spouse's self-image, functioning, and adaptability, which in turn, threatens the adaptability of the marriage.

By contrast, *external stressors* create conflicts that are due to a rapidly changing world. An increasingly complex society places new demands on each person's ability to adapt, as well as a couple's ability to keep marital and family lives intact. For example, labor market "down-sizing," the emphasis on individual excellence, consumer demand for immediate gratification, and the need to develop highly specialized skills, all actively interfere with each person's ability to maintain satisfactory communications, social, and personal lives. Increased mobility and an emphasis on telecommunications have markedly affected the ways we interact, making it more difficult for us to maintain satisfactory marital and family relationships. Stressed relationships fail to offer spouses and children (a) appropriate psychosocial developmental and adaptive experiences, (b) a sense of belonging and identity, and (c) continuity. Diminished resources in turn mean that the family will lack alternate ways of coping with internal and external stressors.

Marital Conflict

Marital conflicts are due to the spouses' individual or joint inability to effectively cope with internal and/or external stressors. Marital relationships are a medium for emotional exchange, which creates a feedback loop for each spouse. This emotional exchange feedback loop provides each spouse with either a positive or negative experience, depending upon the other's reaction to his or her action. Such positive or negative psychological experiences produce corresponding physiological arousal states in each spouse. When negative emotional exchanges continue, unchecked, a predictable interactional pattern takes hold, consisting of automatic thoughts, feelings, and reactions. A "phobic response" to the other emerges which further narrows the interactional pattern.

Interactions begin to take the form of a self-defeating dance, mutually choreographed and justified by each spouse's feelings of being unappreciated, misunderstood, and unloved. At this point, the spouses are unable to use their adaptive cognitive and social skills to help them navigate through this tempest or to correct their course. Their reactions to each other are totally reflexive, and their perceptions of each other's and of their own behavior are blinded by automatic negative thoughts and feelings. These negative thoughts and feelings produce corresponding negative physiological changes, such as muscle tenseness, pounding heart, and an inability to breathe in the presence of the other. Each is drowning in a sea of failure, hopelessness, and alienation. A "dance of death" has begun.

INITIAL ASSESSMENT

How does the therapist make sense of, stop, and deal with the raging marital conflict appearing in the office? A sound diagnostic procedure will not only help identify and understand the way in which each spouse helps to create the mayhem, but also provide the therapist with a treatment plan. Assessment begins with the couple's presenting problem, which is best seen as two separate presenting problems. Three facets of the problem presented by each partner should be examined by the therapist. First, the presenting problem is a metaphor, which holds symbolic but different meaning for each of the spouses. Each perceives the actions of each partner differently from the way they were intended. This difference in perception is based upon the experiences of each in relation to gender, culture, family of origin, or previous relationships.

Second the therapist must ask why such perceptions, which are at variance with feedback or in contradiction to situational demands, are actively maintained and preserved. Their maintenance can be seen as a spouse's attempt to rectify a past experience, rooted in either his family of origin issue (a child who can do no wrong), a previous relationship (a failed previous marriage), or personal experience (being passed over for a promotion due to lack of training), that has unconsciously reemerged in the current spousal relationship.

The third facet is concerned with a spouse's unwillingness to give up a certain way of perceiving life or behaving, despite its self-induced pain and its failure to bring about corrective ends. The therapist needs to understand the purpose the idea or behavior serves. Does it provide the individual with a sense of valor or heroism? Does it provide for the continuous experience of martyrdom? Is it an attempt to avoid looking at one's role in maintaining painful relationships? Or does it challenge the very belief system that a spouse's belief system is based upon? Then there is the "what if" question, the possibility that the world is not as one believes it to be. Acknowledgement of such a possibility can threaten one's identity and way of relating to the world and others, exemplified in Tevye's dilemma when asked to bend too far from tradition in *Fiddler on the Roof*. Does it symbolize an ungratified need that is being vicariously gratified through the marriage, the method of satisfaction of which CANNOT ever prove acceptable or satisfactory? The reason for this last is that true acceptance of the method by which it was obtained can only be realized within the original and not a substituted relationship. If the original relationship is no longer available due to death or divorce, then satisfaction or at least resolution needs to be obtained within the spouse himself.

Collectively, a couple's presenting problems interface to both support their perceptions and deny their resolution. They have choreographed a destructive dance that each maintains and refuses to quit. The therapist must observe the couple's dance and each spouse's part in it. In this way, the therapist learns both the intended purpose and meaning attached to each part, and how each part triggers off the other.

Diagnosis

A complete diagnosis of the couple's presenting problem requires the therapist to assess the intrapsychic dynamics of each spouse in several areas of functioning: (a) life cycle stage of individual and marital development, (b) relational and intergenerational themes (Appendix A), (c) sexual behavior, anxiety, and tolerance levels (willingness, resistance, and resilience), and (d) willingness to disengage from the destructive interaction and engage the therapist. An assortment of diagnostic techniques can be used to ferret this information out (Appendix B). Once the data have been collected, a number of classification systems (e.g., those based upon discrete categories, dimensional ones without discrete categories, or both; Appendix C, styles of conflict) will help the therapist choose the most appropriate theoretical approach (e.g., structural, Bowenian, cognitive-behavioral) and treatment plan for this couple.

Classification

Tolsty wrote, "Happy families are all alike, but unhappy families are each unhappy in their own way." What originally drew each partner to the other now ironically divides them and sets them against one another in one of two ways. First, there are marriages comprised of individuals who are drawn together due to their similar patterns or experiences, "birds of a feather" who "flock together." For instance, a couple may seek from one another the comfort and understanding they were accustomed to receiving from their families of origin. This steady diet of sameness may yield a devitalized relationship that eventually dies, like nonyielding farm fields when crops are not rotated. These marriages lack the richness and diversity to keep them vital and adaptable. Some may continue as long as no major new stimuli impact on either spouse or the marriage. Second, there are marriages comprised of individuals who are drawn together by what they failed to get or feel in their families of origin but find they can receive in their marriage. This complementary arrangement of finding a wonderful source of need gratification carries them through the early stages of marriage. However, in the middle stages of marriage, it drives them apart for one of three reasons: (a) one spouse becomes tired of the endless responsibility of caring for the other's needs, (b) one spouse experiences need gratification as suffocation, or (c) one spouse becomes acutely aware that only one's self can truly gratify internal needs.

Marital conflict is based on negative patterns of interaction. If these are allowed to continue uninterrupted, then they will ultimately cause the demise of the marriage. There are four types of toxic interactions: criticism, defensiveness, contempt, and stonewalling (Gottman, 1994). These expressions prove to be most toxic when they are accompanied by the word *always*. Gottman (1994) identified gender differences in the usage and impact of these toxic expressions. For example, men tend to use stonewalling, rationalizations, withdrawal, and avoidance to ward off negative emotional and physiological feelings that they experience as a result of women's anger. Women, on the other hand, tend to pursue their spouses with complaints, criticisms, and demands in an attempt to obtain conflict resolution. In either case, constant repetition of these toxic interactions spreads like a cancer, destroying the relationship and producing a psychological climate of helpless misery, which in turn produces and maintains unhealthy levels of physical arousal in the body (Gottman, 1994; Selye, 1956). Gender differences regarding the physiological impact of these repeated toxic exchanges are reported by Gottman (1994). For example, the continual use of stonewalling or withdrawal causes men's heart rates and blood pressure to be higher and remain so for a longer period of time than for women's under the same circumstances. On the other hand, men's use of contempt has been positively correlated with the number of infectious diseases their wives will incur over the next 4 years.

A dance of death has begun: One spouse's negative behavior is met and matched by the other's. On and on they go, keeping in step to an increasingly constrictive and destructive tune. Thus a complex negative feedback loop is created that perpetuates a back-and-forth exchange of negative psychological feeling (e.g., misery, low self-esteem), destructive behaviors, and an abnormally high physiological arousal state (stress). This negative interactional pattern between the spouses becomes highly predictable; hearing a negative exchange, a listener can predict the next negative response. The couple's repetitive use of these negative exchanges, which evoke and sustain negative psychological and physiological reactions, becomes a formidable and permanent response style for each spouse in this relationship, waiting to be triggered by the other, highly resistant to change. The spouses become increasingly less able either to keep stress levels within acceptable limits, or to repair their mutual states of hurt, contempt, and defensiveness. They can no longer breathe and move naturally within each other's presence. Their muscles are tense, their hearts are pounding, they can hardly catch their breath. They are overwhelmed by a sense of failure, succumb to hopelessness, and accept mutual alienation. They no longer share a common ground and have exhausted their respective resources and coping strategies.

The Presenting Problem

The presenting problem, despite its destructiveness, does serve a purpose for both spouses, collectively and separately. Their continued participation in the dance is often seen as an attempt to rectify a past family of origin/relational/personal perception, which has reemerged unconsciously within the current relationship. Instead, their efforts serve only to further irritate ungratified needs and to give rise to negative psychological and physiological states.

When the couple engage, the therapist is observing how each spouse's anticipatory emotional reactivity is being triggered by the other's negative behavior (tracking the behavior). The therapist needs to identify and understand the type of pattern they are collectively creating as well as the behaviors each is performing. In this manner, he obtains a working hypothesis as to what actually is being transacted. Certain diagnostic techniques are useful in gathering information about family and spousal relationships, intrapsychic dynamics, life cycle issues, and major areas of concern (e.g., sex and childrearing issues, Appendix B). It is also important to gauge two other facets of each spouse's character. The first is anxiety or tolerance level, which will indicate how much and in what areas it is possible to probe for change. This factor can be determined by the level of willingness, resistance, or reactivity exhibited when discussing certain issues. The second trait is receptivity to change, determined by the willingness to disengage momentarily and accept the therapist's suggestion to do or not do something.

Diagnostically, the toxic interaction symbolizes an ungratified need that has been vicariously gratified through marriage. This method of gratification inevitably proves unsatisfactory, as true need gratification is best achieved mainly through one's own efforts and not by relying primarily on those of another. Persons in this type of marriage have avoided developing ways of more appropriately gratifying their own needs for any one of three reasons. First, they would be compelled to revisit old relational business with its coauthors. But there are strong inhibitions to revisiting old business because limitless pain has been a consequence of repetitive and futile attempts to correct it in the past. Second, they would have to give up a way of life that has served them well in the painful relationship, even though it no longer serves any other useful purpose than to provide them with a sense of valor and identity, like a war veteran living on his war stories of heroism and sufferings. The third rationale for avoidance of change is the challenge of reorganizing their personal belief systems about themselves, the world, and others. Remember the story of the four blind men trying to determine what an elephant is, when one is only exploring only the tail, another the leg, another the trunk, and one exploring the ear? Now imagine them actually seeing the whole elephant. This new experience would change the world picture for them, as surely as Columbus changed history.

IMPACT OF MARITAL CONFLICT ON CHILDREN

Marital conflict promotes mutual dependence and hostility among family members, especially children. It destroys psychological stability and identity, the opportunity for new learning and development, and role adaptation. Instead, marital conflict increases internal conflict. Pathological defenses take over to assuage anxiety, which is directed outward, through projection, scapegoating, and delinquency (Robinson, 1994). These spousal pathological defenses not only destroy the marital relationship but also transcend their parenting roles, effecting their children's psychological development. Robinson (1994) reports that researchers have found that parental depression, marital conflict, and emotional distance can have detrimental effects upon children. Children are at risk when the father is angry and withdrawn. Under these conditions, the children often develop internalizing disorders, such as anxiety, peer withdrawal, and depression.

Children are at risk when they live with a loveless marriage or in a "noisy marriage" in which one parent turns to the children for emotional need gratification. In this case, the children have become part of the unhappy marriage. In either scenario, children may grow up suffering from developmental issues of separation, intimacy, trust, and commitment. Pittman (cited in Robinson, 1994) disagrees that divorce is the answer for conflictual marriages with children. Like amputation, he says, it should be avoided unless the damage is life threatening. He believes that it is not detrimental to children's well-being to be raised in unfulfilling marriage or with bored parents, since a stable relationship is a far more important contextual value than parental fulfillment.

TREATMENT PLANNING

A variety of therapeutic approaches have been used with conflictual couples: Bowenian therapy (Nichols, 1984), Minuchin's (1974) structural therapy, Fogarty's (1976) pursuant-distancer paradigm, Haley's (1976) strategic therapy, a Jacobsonian collaborative behavioral exchange (Jacobson & Margolin, 1979), Dattilio and Padesky's (1990) cognitive-behavioral approach, Scharffs' internalized object-relations approach

(Scharff & Scharff, 1987), O'Hanlon's and deShazer's solution-oriented approach (O'Hanlon & Weiner-Davis, 1989; deShazer, 1982). Each has both value and limitations in treating conflictual couples.

Most therapists find a multimodal approach, combining two or more methods most successful in working with conflictual couples. I prefer one that integrates intrapsychic, cognitive-behavioral, and systems approaches, and have devised a decision tree to illustrate the progression of steps (see Figure 6.1). The decision tree works very much like an "if-then" branching program in a computer, or the elimination series used in sports tournaments.

Decision Tree

1. Can the couple disengage from their toxic interactional pattern?
    a. If not, then help them separate or get divorced.
    b. If they can, then assess their situation.
        (1) If they cannot allow each other to tell their tale of woe, then return to #1.a.
        (2) If they can, then identify the couple's operative baseline, through Care Days.
            (a) If they cannot do this, then return to #1.a.
            (b) If they can, then develop a working hypothesis and test it.
                -1- If they cannot agree on the working hypothesis, then return to #1.a.
                -2- If they can, then obtain a mutual and desirable behavioral contract.
                    -a- If they cannot obtain agreement on a contract, return to #1.a.
                    -b- If they can, progress to Stage 2.

Diagnosis and treatment planning intertwine continually throughout the therapy, as illustrated by the diagnostic-intervention-therapeutic feedback loop shown in Figure 6.2.

As indicated, the therapist diagnostically examines the couple's readiness to move to the next step. If they are not ready, then he offers the opportunity to examine what is holding them back, individually and collectively. At the same time, he presents therapy as an intervention to more appropriately redirect their efforts. The couple's response provides

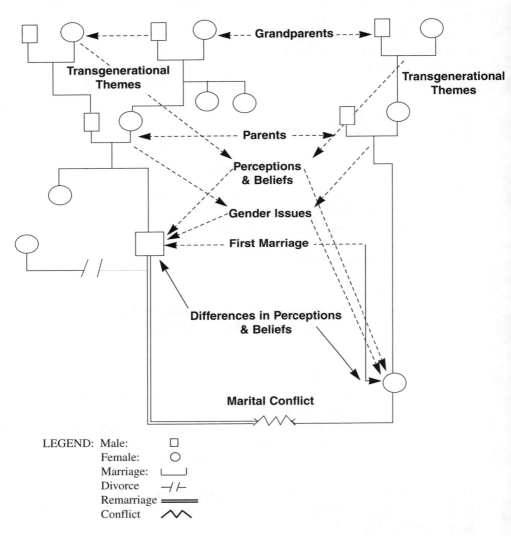

LEGEND: Male: ☐
Female: ○
Marriage: ⌐⌐
Divorce: ⊣⊢
Remarriage: ═══
Conflict: ⋀⋀

FIGURE 6.1 Multimodal diagnostic approach: tracing the families of origin (Genogram).

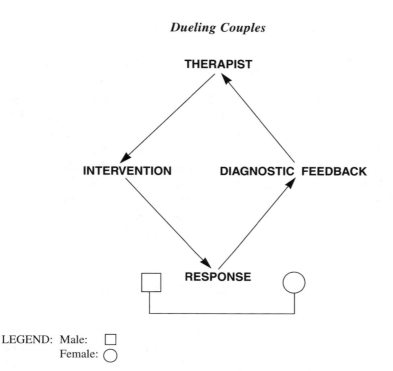

LEGEND: Male: ☐
           Female: ◯

FIGURE 6.2   Diagnostic-interventive-feedback loop.

the therapist with feedback as to how effective this intervention is and how well established their previous therapeutic work has been, individually and collectively.

Testing the Waters

The therapist's primary and most immediate task is to determine whether or not the couple can disrupt their own toxic interactional pattern. The opening move is to simultaneously test their ability to disrupt their negative interactional pattern and to assess their resistance, resolve, and resiliency. In essence, the therapist interrupts a heated conversation they are having with one another in order to ask them to interact with him. Are they actively pursuing the demise of their relationship, or do they hold any hope of staying together? If they are overwhelmed with failure, hopelessness, contempt, defensiveness, and alienation, then marital therapy will prove the "kiss of death." Therapy is an unhealthy venture in this case, since the proposition of staying together in a hostile relationship will only serve to further weaken shattered egos and immune systems. Helping the couple to separate becomes the only hope of ending the senseless brutalization, since this is the only *baseline* at which they can operate. If they have children, then divorce is probably better for the children if parents can be helped to maintain their coparenting responsibilities. If, however, the couple decide that they want to try to make their marriage work, then the possibility of divorce becomes the ultimate baseline, the bottom line, of which they may need to be reminded periodically. This is what Whitaker calls the "battle for structure" (Whitaker & Bumberry, 1988). The issue is whether this couple really wants therapy and whether they will be receptive to the therapist's recommendations.

ENTERING THE THERAPEUTIC PROCESS

The therapist has asked them if they wish to work with him and they have answered yes. Now they are ready to get up and take the hand of the therapist, who will lead them into the first sequence of steps of their new dance, a dance of renewed life. Now that the therapist has their attention, the "battle for initiative" begins (Whitaker & Bumberry, 1988). It becomes important to know whether the couple are willing to work on their respective problems within the marriage or whether they expect the therapist to do all of the work. The question is tested in the initial assessment process, as well as throughout the therapy. Assessment is a double-edged sword insofar as it not only obtains necessary information but also serves as an intervention and a feedback loop. Through the diagnosis-intervention feedback loop, the therapist examines the couple's readiness to move to the next step. Once again, if they are not ready, then he offers the opportunity to examine what is holding them back. At the same time, he presents an intervention, a way of more appropriately redirecting their efforts.

Individual or Couple Sessions

The next step in the dance of renewed life is to have each spouse describe his perception of the current marital situation. The "Battle of Initiative" (Whitaker and Bumberry, 1988) is confronted. The battle is concerned with whether the couple or the therapist is more anxious or motivated for change. Do they care enough about themselves or the marriage to take responsibility for describing their concerns and their pain? Many conflictual couples arrive in the office at the brink of divorce. They are already in a perpetual state of high physiological arousal, unable to tolerate one another's presence without falling into a defensive or antagonistic stance. Depending on the couple's volatility level, the therapist may see them conjointly or separately. In the interim, the couple is directed to avoid all unnecessary contact with one another during the assessment period. The therapist is now attempting to teach another therapeutic dance step: Each must refrain from interrupting the other's tale of woe. As in learning any new dance, the question arises whether they are born "klutzes" or are minimally able to follow directions. Referring also to the diagnosis-intervention feedback loop, if they cannot disengage from their toxic interactional pattern, then the therapist needs to meet with them individually. If they cannot effectively engage the therapist in individual sessions, while remaining disengaged from each other, then the therapist needs to help them become separated or divorced.

If the individual sessions prove unfruitful, in that at least one of the spouses cannot refrain from utilizing the session other than to chronically complain about the sins of the other or indulge in self-absorption, then one returns to the option of separation or divorce.

Minimal Marital Therapy

As highly volatile couples become more accepting of the conditions of therapy, or if the couple is somewhat less than highly volatile, then the therapist needs to provide them with what Gottman (1994) calls "minimal marital therapy." The couple are as yet unable to intellectually or emotionally benefit from anything that the therapist has to offer them, but they need to be prepared to perform the initial steps of their new dance. Like a dance instructor outlining what the steps look like for his students, the therapist in minimal marital therapy provides pretreatment that helps the spouses reduce their levels of high emotional reactivity and physiological arousal. Gottman's version of pretreatment (1994) trains them to monitor their heart rates when dealing with each other, and attempts to keep them within the normal range, 100 beats or less per minute. When the heart rate exceeds 100 beats per minute, they are to disengage from each other and individually involve themselves in a soothing ritual. In essence, this requires the couple to take a break from each other for approximately 20 minutes, and avoid thinking about what the other has done or said that upsets them. My version of the soothing ritual uses active mental or bodily manipulations. For example, when a spouse is confronted with the other's toxic behavior, the first spouse is asked to respond in *any other* manner than she usually does. This intellectual "change-up pitch" often serves to help them avoid having their emotional reactivity triggered or their automatic thought processes engaged.

Time-Out Management

The other techniques are concerned with having one partner physically and totally disengage from the other partner as soon as his physiological or automatic thought triggers are pressed. In addition, they are instructed to take a break from each other and avoid further contact until the disengaging one has cooled off. They are being sent off (by the therapist as choreographer) to practice their routines alone, without an audience. Once the fuse got lit, it cannot be put out. The exploding spouse, however, can prevent the explosion from going off in front of the other so as to avoid further escalation, which in many situations may lead to physical abuse. The instructions also direct constructive venting of the explosion. This works well when the therapist has been able to identify some activity, particularly a sport or physical activity like running, that the person finds enjoyable and stress reducing. Sometimes a client will spontaneously come up with such an activity. By venting his emotional reactivity in a constructive manner, he is achieving some sense of control in an uncontrollable situation. In less volatile situations, the disengaging exploding spouse is directed to return to the discussion when he is calmer. The abandoned spouse is usually agreeable to this approach, since he realizes that the intent is to avoid escalation and prevent him from having his emotionally reactive triggers pulled, while the other spouse still has the responsibility of responding meaningfully to him. The discussion has been temporarily put "on hold." Less volatile couples can remember to use a commonly agreed-upon term or phrase, which when uttered by one of them will signal that he is calling for a "time out" and will be respected and honored by the abandoned partner for already stated reasons. If the exploding spouse fails to return to the unfinished discussion, then the abandoned spouse is instructed to say nothing, bide his time, and bring up the matter at the next therapy session. In all cases, this procedure reassures them that issues are not to be forgotten or overlooked, but that the steps they are taking in dealing with one another are more important than any issue. Any of the variant forms of this procedure serve to slow down the interaction pattern, reduce the physiological arousal level, and prepare each spouse to be able to hear what the other or the therapist has to say. The therapist, like the dance instructor, is helping the spouse/student to walk slowly through the next step. In this way, any missteps can be readily averted; the student is guided into the correct way of performing the step. All of these initial procedural steps help to achieve three early therapeutic goals: to further define the therapeutic structure, disengage the spouses from their dance of death, and encourage them to accept responsibility for their behavior. Once these hurdles have been crossed, the battle for initiative and the therapy process can begin in earnest.

Beginning a Renewed Life

Beginning the dance of renewed life involves those who are motivated enough to proceed forward. This segment of therapy has several tasks: battling for initiative (Whitaker & Bumberry, 1988), deactivating spousal emotional reactivity (Kerr & Bowen, 1988), establishing a "holding environment" (Winnicott, 1969), seeking out object-relations projections (Scharff & Scharff, 1987), challenging irrational belief systems (Ellis, Sichel, Yeager, DiMattia, DiGiuseppe, 1989), and enlarging the spouses' positive behavioral repertoires. During this period, "care days" (Stuart, 1980) need to be introduced in order to reinforce the initial moves from a dance of death to one of renewed life and to relax the spouses in order that they may learn a more appropriate stance and manner of holding one another.

Care-days provides for a diagnosis-intervention feedback loop. The diagnostic question here is whether or not this couple can resume the activities they enjoyed together during happier times. Do they still or did they ever possess the ability to engage in such activities? As an intervention, it is moving them onto the next dance step of properly addressing and holding one another in order to begin the new dance. As a feedback loop, it helps the therapist determine an appropriate baseline of compatibility, the level at which they were first drawn to each other and that supported their desire to be together.

Emotional Deactivation

If the couple are able to sustain themselves in returning to premorbid conditions, then the therapist can move onto the task of deactivating their emotional reactivity; otherwise he reminds them of the option to divorce. The element of emotional deactivation is a component of most of the tasks in the early stage of therapy. The therapist begins the differentiation process by asking the more anxious spouse to review his role in the toxic interactional pattern, in order to understand its destructive behavioral cycle, as well as to suggest the reasons for each spouse's willing participation in it. During the one spouse's commentary, it is critical that the other spouses listen and remain silent. As from the beginning, the therapist controls the other. Each spouse learns to listen without reacting emotionally to the other. Here, the therapist acts as what Winnicott calls the holding environment (Winnicott, 1969) as the active spouse stretches the ability to remain unreactive during the telling of a toxic tale. This tolerance is also developed in the listening spouse, even if the therapist must insert periodic reminders to remain silent during the discourse.

The net effect of this procedure upon the telling spouse is twofold. First, it builds a greater sense of rapport and trust with the therapist, since the therapist is using the "language of caring" (Whitaker & Bumberry, 1988). The therapist is listening keenly, asking for more information about this or that, responding with reflection and empathy to the narrative, while at the same time, validating the speaker's ability to become less emotionally reactive to cited situations. She is better able to experience negative feelings and thoughts without becoming frightened or threatened or seeking to avoid the thoughts. This procedure is helping to create a safe place for exploring his behavior (thoughts and feelings), needs and issues. Once the tale has finished, the therapist provides the telling spouse with a transitional space for moving beyond present behavior. The destructive cycle has been temporarily broken.

The therapist now asks the spouse who was listening to be objective, observe herself or himself, and mentally run through the steps leading to the present. Antecedent issues from other relationships that might be evolving the current emotionally reactive steps also need to be explored. This is an attempt to induce a regressive experience in the service of the client's ego. As this spouse is encouraged to relate other similar experiences in his relational history, a metaphor or a resonating note may be struck within the therapist. Assuming countertransference is in check, the therapist shares these internal responses with the client. For example, the therapist might say, "Why don't you stop pretending that it doesn't hurt to feel ignored and just fly into your unhappiness?" This procedure offers another level at which to come to terms with the current marital experiences in light of previous relational experiences, issues, ungratified needs, and irrational beliefs. Repeatedly exploring emotionally reactive behavior in greater detail, as well as tracing its origins, has the effect of counterconditioning his classically conditioned response pattern, through the mechanisms of habituation or systematic desensitization. The spouse become less reactive about current events and more aware of their origins in previous relationships, transgenerational themes, personal misperception, or irrational beliefs.

The second step in the deactivation process is to have the listening spouse share the thoughts that occurred while the other was talking. This procedure invites the listening spouse to process the information intellectually instead of emotionally. In this way, the listening spouse is learning that there may be a difference between what is said and what is intended. Or, an awareness may dawn that what one does or says can mean two entirely different things to each partner in a marriage. The intellectual processing may reveal that what one says and does is really directed at someone other than oneself. In short, the listener is learning to understand intentions rather than simply react to words. The third step requires the listener and speaker to reverse roles, once the therapist feels that the first, most anxious speaker has a handle on the origins of his or her despair.

Dysfunctional Spouse Debunked

If one spouse was considered by the other to be dysfunctional or symptomatic, the deactivating emotional reactivity process begins with the "identified patient" as the speaker. The process serves to debunk the myth of the symptomatic spouse, since it becomes apparent to the listening spouse that he or she has underestimated the telling spouse's ability to cope with difficult situations. Proof of competence evident in the speaker's ability to give the therapist a description of personal behavior, to respond to the therapist's probing questions, and to explore these issues independently. The therapist must have established a strong relationship with the overfunctioning spouse before having the listening and telling spouses switch roles. The therapist may have to be quite forceful in helping the overfunctioning spouse overcome self-denial. For example, if the overfunctioning spouse's responses are minimal, the therapist will need to ask for greater elaboration. It is also not unusual to have both spouses resist the unmasking of the overfunctioning spouse. In cases when both spouses fear the loss of the protector's role, feelings may be stirred up to an unacceptable level. At these times, the therapist needs to enforce talk about the feelings rather than expression of them. If a partner is unable to do that, then the therapist needs to switch the topic to a more neutral one. When calm returns, the therapist may ask if it is possible to return to the original topic. The overall therapeutic goal, at this stage, is to enable both spouses to touch on areas known to be emotionally important to them and to discuss them calmly.

CONTRACT NEGOTIATION AND BEYOND

Once a couple have been able to describe their individual stories to the therapist, with minimal interruption, the therapist can move on to developing and testing a tentative hypothesis, based on the data received from them separately and/or jointly. The hypotheses, stated in their words, is presented to them for acceptance, rejection, or modification. This is another pivotal point in the therapy, since the therapist has put a therapeutic spin on his tentative hypothesis. The hypothesis is a reframed version of the relationship which reflects both their intentions toward and perceptions of, one another. Spouses are usually more accepting of their own maneuvers and intentions than they are of their partner's. However, the therapist's explanation usually allows each spouse to reserve judgment on the other's true intent. Either spouse's misgivings about the other's behavior are usually assuaged by the therapist's willingness to investigate. If the couple are unable to help the therapist formulate an acceptable hypothesis, then the therapist returns to Step 1.a of the decision tree. The joint agreement to the hypothesis constitutes the foundation of the therapeutic contract. It also forms the couple's new operative baseline to which the therapist can return instead of the divorce option. Once the therapist and the couple have agreed to and feel reasonably comfortable with the hypothesis in its finalized version, the therapist contracts with them their initial, short-term goal in therapy.

In developing a contract, the therapist asks the spouses to identify what changes they want in the relationship and what they are offering to do to improve it. This procedure directs each one toward awareness of his own and his partner's need system. In essence, the therapist is saying to them, "Here is where you stand. What do you want to do about it?" A "top ten" behavioral wish list and offer list are provided by each spouse. The therapist aids them in deciding for which of the wishes and offers listed each of the spouses mutually desire to reciprocity. This material is then finalized in a detailed manner, describing the nature and frequency of the behaviors. In this way, it lends itself to being easily monitored by all parties. When one spouse has failed to live up to his contracted behavior, the other spouse is directed not to engage him about it, but to bring it up in the next session. This procedure again ensures continued growth in tolerance, differentiation, and better management skills. The creation of the contract again serves to elevate the couple's operative baseline.

If either fails to live up to his part of the bargain, then the therapist can challenge his desire to either: (a) do what he willingly offered to do, (b) work on the marriage, or (c) return to step 1.a. of the decision tree. The bargaining procedure takes them beyond differentiation into relational consideration of the other's need system. They are becoming increasingly aware of the differences between themselves, while becoming emotionally indifferent to some of their spouse's toxic messages.

As the therapist continues to explore each spouse's emotional reactivity and its sources, focus shifts to families of origin, extended families and other interlocking emotional systems. These issues are generally more toxic but less difficult to manage than are spousal conflicts. In fact, spousal difficulties seem to disappear or take a back burner during this revolving, reverberating process. There are several reasons for this. For one, the marriage ceases to be the main focus of discontent. For another, they have learned through listening to one another's plight that their spouse's unhappiness, pain, and toxic behavior has much less to do with them than it does with preexisting relationships. In addition, they feel freed from the entire responsibility for the partner's unhappiness or pain. This new awareness also permits each spouse to become somewhat empathetic and understanding of the other's situation. They may even unite in an attempt to help each other solve their individual problems. The "option of choice" (Whitaker and Bumberry, 1984) is being employed by both spouses. Instead of automatically reacting to each other, each spouse is choosing to view the other's and his or her own reactions from a different perspective. In this way, both of the spouses are being helped to distance themselves from their dance of death and move forward toward a dance of renewed life. This principle is now replaced by the principal of mutuality as initially spelled out in a mutually developed behavioral contract.

Self-Redefinition

The redefinition of self in the presence of the other can now begin because the prerequisites have been met. The dueling parties (a) experience increased tolerance to their spouse's otherwise toxic responses, since they now understand, from a broader perspective, that the spouse's behavior does not have the same meaning for them as it does for the spouse; (b) realize that the spouse's responses are intended for someone else and therefore no longer personalize them; and (c) realize and accept that the spouse does not want to act out his or her partner's wishes; or (d) develop emotional indifference to the other's formerly toxic responses.

Changing the Interactional Pattern

The next step is to help clients identify the triggers of their respective emotional reactivity and the automatic thoughts that give rise to emotional reactivity. Becoming aware of these allows each spouse to catch them before they go off as well as to be able to sidestep the minefields laid by the other spouse. Each is then encouraged not to respond when the other touches a trigger. Cognitive restructuring aids in the achievement of this therapeutic goal. As the spouses learn how their response fits into their partner's emotional reactivity sequence, they are less likely to play into it. In other words, the therapist has helped them realize that they are actually colluding or cooperating with their spouse by providing them with the subconsciously desired response that will serve to further justify the spouse's negative behavior. The realization is a powerful inhibitor. Or, the offended spouse has learned that the offending response is not meant for them; and therefore, they are more readily able to sluff it off. With some practice, they can even help their spouse prevent triggers from being tripped by either identifying the toxic interactional pattern that is about to begin or by prefacing potentially triggering interactions with disarming statements, such as "I am not saying this to get your goat, but to. . . ."

In this respect, the therapist, using Whitaker's language of options in a different way, addresses the spouses' typical negative thinking, feeling and behavior. The therapist will ask them why they need to feel or perceive things in that manner. The couple's communication has improved since they have acquired new knowledge about family-of-origin issues that may be intruding into their relationship and are now under some degree of control.

The therapist continues building on their care day activity, looking for the origins of their emotional reactivity, and praising their ability to live up to their contractual agreements. The therapist also attempts to get them to generalize their newly learned behavior. The importance of generalizing positive behavior toward each other is addressed by Gottman's (1994) research finding. He indicated that those couples that maintained a 5 to 1 ratio of positive moments (e.g., mutual pleasure, passion, humor, support, kindness, and generosity) to negative moments (e.g., complaint, criticism, anger, disgust, contempt, defensiveness, and coldness) experienced marital satisfaction. This funding appeared to hold true across his three categories of couples: the validating, volatile, and conflict-avoiding couples. As he states in his article, it appears that this ratio determines the well-being of a marriage.

He also reports that in such marriages, no gender differences exist in emotional expression. Men are as likely to share their most intimate feelings as women are. In fact, it appears that men, under these conditions, not only improve their own mental health but indirectly improve their wives through their newly found ability to self-disclose. Gottman (1994) states that men are able to reveal more personal information or self-dissatisfactions (e.g., hurts, dreams, aspirations, reminiscences) than are their wives. Men also appear to let their wives know what they are feeling when they are angry rather than stonewall their wives. As a result, women are under less stress from their relationships to their husbands. Gottman also states that mutual and supportive involvement of the spouses in common tasks, such as doing housework, has physiological benefits and contributes to a sense for well-being for both.

Beyond the Presenting Problem

At this point, therapy is at a crossroads. Several things may happen regarding the couple's desire to continue or discontinue therapy. One possible outcome is that, having obtained symptom relief, they wish to stop therapy. Their original reason for seeking therapy has been satisfied. Another is that they may want to continue in order to obtain a deeper and more satisfying resolution. A third outcome may be the desire of only one to continue therapy. One factor influencing the decision whether or not to continue therapy is the willingness to be emotionally vulnerable, since physiological arousal levels are operating once again in the normal range. In marital therapy this vulnerability is double-headed, exposing both partners while bringing a deepening of their relationship. However, not all couples can afford this. Some are more comfortable with lesser degrees of commitment and sharing of experiences. Those who have or can develop a greater tolerance for vulnerability will be more willing to work on redefining their coupleship as a safe environment in which to develop and be themselves. These couples will be seeking to develop increased hopefulness, awareness, and intimacy, through risk taking and self-disclosure. They will be learning how to better manage their individual and collective experiences.

If the couple decide to continue, then core issues for each partner will be dealt with by the therapist. Family-of-origin or extended family becomes the focus. The work will require the inclusion of family-of-origin members in sessions from time to time. As issues are managed more and more effectively, the therapist's role is reduced to that of a consultant. Termination is close at hand.

APPENDIX A

Relational and Intergenerational Problem Areas?

Relational problems may arise for any of the following reasons:

1. There is a power struggle over self-esteem.
2. Frustration tolerance has peaked, due to daily pressures, and they view each other as additional sources of frustration instead of allies.
3. Codependency: One spouse needs to maintain the other as inadequate in order to maintain a satisfactory self-image.
4. One spouse struggles to resolve a previously unresolved relational conflict by attempting to have the other adopt the required complementary role.

5. One spouse is preoccupied with a third party, interest, or activity that provides tension release from marital involvement, but causes the other to feel abandoned (triangulation; loyalty issues).
6. Partners' initial perceptions of one another were faulty. They now have difficulty relating to one another because they are truly from different worlds with different languages.
7. The marriage cannot be sustained in the absence of an outside problem to unite them.
8. There is a conflict of coping or managerial styles.

Intergenerational patterns leading to marital problems may arise from:

1. The clashing of the managerial patterns or values of two individual's families or cultures
2. The constructing of the marital relationship to be similar to or different from the parents' marital relationship
3. The use of the spouse for upward mobility or as a noxious "hit man" to the family of origin. In the latter case, the maneuver leads either to marital conflict when the hit man's actions turn out to displease the spouse, or to marital dissolution when the services of the spouse are no longer desired.

APPENDIX B

Assessment Techniques

A. Family of Origin, Life Cycle and Contextual History
   1. *Genogram.* Identifying Bowenian emotionally reactive syndromes (e.g., cutoffs, triangulation, transgenerational themes, nuclear family dysfunction, and family projections) and prevalent themes and issues.
   2. *Behavioral Tracking.* Identifying the sequence of negative spousal interactions: who says what to whom.
   3. *Circular Questioning.* Deriving one spouse's perception of the other's behavior and intent.
   4. *Sculpting.* Obtaining a nonverbal presentation of the couple relationship from each spouse's perception, bypassing overintellectualized defenses.

5. *Structural and Functional Analysis.*
   a. Dating history
   b. Marital relationship, in terms of its:
      (1) structural hierarchy
      (2) organization of power
      (3) roles and expectations
      (4) interactional patterns
      (5) belief and value systems
      (6) boundaries
      (7) marital life cycle state
      (8) areas of conflict

B. Individual Strengths and Deficits
   1. General behaviors
   2. Conflict resolution strategies
   3. Communicative abilities
   4. Self-esteem
   5. Sex history
   6. Levels of differentiation

C. Therapeutic Readiness
   1. Why did they decide to enter therapy at this time?
   2. What are their individual goals for entering therapy?
   3. DeShazer's "miracle question" and other such questions, for example:
      a. "How would you know that any change has taken place?"
      b. "What would constitute the smallest amount of desirable change in the other's behavior that you would like to see?"
   4. Receptivity of each to a therapeutic intervention

Inventories

A. Individual
   1. Beck's Depression Scale (Beck, 1967)
   2. Rorschach (Psychodiagnostic, 1948, Grunet Stratton)
   3. Minnesota Multiphasic Inventory (MMPI) (University of Minn., 1982)
   4. Area of Change Questionnaire (Weiss & Birchler, 1975)

B. Relational
   1. Dyadic Adjustment Scale (Spanier, 1976)
   2. Marital Adjustment Scale (Locke & Wallace, 1959)
   3. Marital Conflict and Accord (Weiss & Margolin, 1977)
   4. Marital Satisfaction Inventory (Synder, 1981)

C. Sex
   1. Sexuality Satisfaction Inventory (LoPiccolo & Steger, 1974)

D. Marital Check-Up
   1. Is rejoining your spouse at the close of the day a pleasant event? If not, discuss the most important reason for regarding your mate's return home as unpleasant. Be specific: for example, "Very often I return home to screaming children and immediate pressure from my wife to step in and settle disputes"; "As soon as my husband walks in he gives me the third degree: 'Did you pick up the clothes, make those calls, walk the dog' and so on."
   2. Which aspect of your life gives you the most pleasure: your marriage, your work, your children, your hobbies, or some other area? Why?
   3. Describe five satisfactory aspects of your marriage.
   4. Is your sex life satisfactory to you? If not, what suggestions would you offer for improvement?
   5. Name five instances in the past month when you have expressed appreciation of your mate.
   6. Name five things your mate has done for you in the past month for which you felt appreciative.
   7. Recall three negative things that you have done—intentionally or unintentionally—to your mate in the last month. How could these occurrences have been prevented?
   8. Recall three negative things your spouse has done to you during the past month. How could these occurrences have been prevented?
   9. Recall a marital quarrel that took place in the recent past. Did it end with bottled up rage or resentment? Did it involve denigration of either participant? Review the quarrel in retrospect and discuss how it could have been handled more constructively so that it ended with an improved relationship instead of a bruised one.

10. Have there been occasions when you wanted to show affection to your mate and did not? What was the basis of your restraint? Give full details.

11. Name five pleasurable activities you've done together and five activities you've done alone in the past month. Which did you enjoy more? Explain.

12. Would you prefer more time alone? More time alone with your mate? More time in company? Explain.

13. What positive factors do you feel are missing from your marriage? Who do you think is more responsible for these voids, you or your spouse? Give reasons for this conclusion. In addition, discuss each of the factors you feel are missing. For example, if you feel trust is lacking and you are most responsible, discuss the difficulty in this area.

14. Briefly describe three things which you have requested your spouses to do, but which you have neglected to do either because you could not or did not want to.

15. Was there a period during your marital or premarital relationship when you would have been more accommodating to the requests described in question #14? If so, specify in detail the factors that account for your current unwillingness.

16. For each of the unfulfilled requests described in question #14 discuss the factors which, from your view, account for your mate's unwillingness or inability to please you.

17. Name five ways in which you'd like to change. Would these changes please your mate? Why haven't you implemented them?

18. Name five ways in which you'd like your mate to change.

19. If you have children, do they help or hinder your marriage? How so?

20. Do you know of a couple whose marriage appears more fulfilling than yours? If so, what factors account for their marriage being superior?

21. What are your aspirations and expectations for your marriage in the future? Be specific: for example, "I would like household tasks to be shared equally"; "I would like my wife to become more affectionate," and so on. Name at least five aspirations. Describe what you are doing to ensure that these hopes will be realized (Stuart & Stuart, 1973).

APPENDIX C

Styles of Conflict

Many conceptual schemes of negative interactional patterns have diagnostic value in classifying a couple's style of conflict. Some of these schemes offer a topological diagnosis, describing:

A. Discrete Categories of Disorders, such as:
1. Lederer and Jackson's (1968) marital types, based upon power relationships:
    a. Complementary—spouses behave in opposite ways
    b. Symmetrical—spouses behave in the same ways
    c. Parallel—partners ignore or retreat from addressing a problem.
2. Cuber and Harroff (1965) state that most successful middle-class marriages are constricted, conflict-ridden or zestless marriages.
    a. Conflict-habituated types actively entertain conflict but keep it within the marriage.
    b. Devitalized couples are preoccupied with interests outside of their families. They are restless but devoid of open conflict.
    c. Passive-congealed marriages are apathetic and restless but never desire closeness.
    d. Vital marriages are psychologically close and relate well to each other. Disagreements are settled quickly and without open conflict.
    e. In the total marriage, all aspects of life are shared.
3. Gottman's (1994) Three Affective Styles:
    a. *Validating couples* are defined as those who listen respectfully and empathize with each other's point of view. When they discuss a problem, they rarely interrupt each other. If they cannot persuade one another to either side of an issue, they negotiate a workable compromise.
    b. *Volatile couples* like to fight. They have intensely emotional marriages, characterized by brawls, high levels of jealousy, petty bickering, sarcastic remarks, "zingering" interactions, and triggered tempers. They rarely listen to what the other one is saying and fight dirty. They try to forcefully coerce the other over to their point of view. They feel free to say anything they want to each other without concern how harmful or damaging it might be.

    c. *Conflict-avoidant couples* seek to smooth over or ignore differences or incompatibilities. Stalemates are not uncommon. They have agreed to disagree, not to attempt to persuade the other to a point of view, nor hammer out a compromise. They don't consider unresolved conflicts as important and simply drop them. They do have many areas of common agreement that they do share.

4. Howell's Theoretical Family Types (1975):

    a. *Constricted* families exhibit excessive restriction over the family's emotional life and tend to suffer from somatic complaints. These families view outside intervention with antagonism and resistance, so that individual or marital approaches may appear more appropriate in handling newly reframed problems of repression, passivity, juvenile delinquency, maladjustment reaction, and perfectionism.

    b. *Internalized* families are inwardly focused and view the world with fear, pessimism, hostility and dread. They are hypervigilant. They have a well-defined role structure and exert powerful sanctions for misbehavior. Loyalty runs high. Their prognosis varies with the thickness of their walls. They are typically externally isolated, self-defined, enmeshed, somewhat suicidal, and display a family character neurosis.

    c. *Object-focused* families overemphasize reliance on children, the outside community or the self. Family cohesiveness and emotional closeness are low. Members use each other for personal reasons. Prognosis is however, generally good. They appear to be child-focused or externally focused, integrated, and adaptive but really are devitalized, egocentric and self-focused, with the rule of "every man for himself."

    d. *Impulsive* families contain troublesome adolescents or young adults. Their prognoses depend upon family characteristics rather than the presence of acting-out behavior exhibited through delinquency, aggressive or antisocial behavior, or childish maladjustment reaction.

    e. *Childlike* families never thoroughly separate from their families of origin. They need continued parentlike assistance. They display a great deal of immaturity, detachment behavior, demanding, and oral dependent behavior.

f. *Chaotic* families are poorly structured. They are decompensating families, where chronic psychosis and delinquency are rampant. Treatment outcomes tend to be unfavorable due to the lack of integration and instability.

B. Dimensional models, containing no such categories but attempting to locate clients along one or more dimensions, such as:
   1. Hill and Hanson's (1960) description of healthy, neurotic, behaviorally disordered, and psychotic families:
      a. *Healthy* families have the following attributes:
         (1) Separation and individuation is successful.
         (2) Ambivalence, anger, and sexuality are managed well.
         (3) An abstract code of morality is adhered to.
      b. Neurotic and behavior-disordered families tend to adhere to rigid and authoritarian rules. However, *neurotic family* parents:
         (1) Form coalitions to maintain enforcement of family roles, where one is dominant and the other subservient
         (2) Use repression to rid themselves of unacceptable feelings and thoughts
         (3) See impulses as unconscious or as not part of the self
         (4) Are successful in maintaining the status quo and entertaining few crises
      c. In comparison, *behavior-disorder families:*
         (1) Form no parental coalition
         (2) Use denial and projection as a means for dealing with rule-breaking incidents
         (3) See impulses as part of self and effort is expended to control them internally as well as externally
         (4) Frequently entertain crises which serve to maintain equilibrium by pointing to an increased need to control and restrict impulses.
   2. Mittleman's (1956) marital types are based upon an individual dynamic model, where the spouse is judged to be:
      a. Aggressive and dominating
      b. Emotionally detached
      c. Intensely competitive for domination despite fear of losing the other
      d. Helpless, out of consideration for the other
      e. Alternating between helplessness and assertiveness

   3. Gehrke and Moxon's (1962) marital types model is defined by the degree of conflict and power within the relationship:
     a. Masculine-feminine role reversal
     b. Sadomasochism
     c. Detachment or demandingness
     d. Oral dependency
     e. Use of neurotic illness

   4. Madanes' (1987) marital types are described along a continuum of:
     a. Hostility versus love
     b. Separation versus continuity
     c. Helplessness versus power
     d. Hierarchy versus equality
     e. Dignity versus future (present sense of being versus what you hope it will be)
     f. Past versus future
     g. Voluntary versus involuntary behavior
     h. Freedom versus dependence
     i. Loyalty versus betrayal
     j. Metaphorical versus literal communication
     k. Personal gain versus altruism
     l. Resistance versus commitment to change

C. Some schemes, called mixed models, contain both discrete categories and dimensional models:
   1. Ackerman's *theme dimension* (1958), primarily combine of external and internal, isolated and integrated family types:
     a. Externally isolated families fail to achieve emotional integration within the community and redirect their energies internally.
     b. Externally integrated families are overly active in community affairs due to their failure to become internally unified and self-gratifying.
     c. Internally unintegrated families are characterized by a split between parents and an alliance between at least one parent and one child, where hostility maintains the split and the resulting isolation keeps the inappropriate pairing in operation.
     d. Internally integrated families are characterized by a mutually protective alliance between the parents, in order to safeguard the satisfaction of their needs at the expense of the children.

Each spouse parentifies the other while both remain dependent on their own parents.

e. Deviant families express marked rebellion against community standards and they adopt deviant goals and values.

f. Disintegrated or regressed families are marked by open conflict, hostility, lack of integration. The potential dissolution of the family is great.

REFERENCES

Ackerman, M. W. (1958). *The psychodynamics of family life.* New York: Basic Books.

Cuber, J. F., & Harroff, P. B. (1965). *The significant Americans: A study of sexual behavior among the affluent.* New York: Appleton-Century.

Dattilio, F. M., & Padesky, C. A. (1990). *Cognitive therapy with couples.* Sarasota, FL: Professional Resource Exchange.

DeShazer, S. (1982). *Patterns of brief family therapy: An econsystemic approach.* New York: Guilford.

Ellis, A., Sichel, J. L., Yeager, R. J., DiMattia, D. J., & DiGiuseppe, R. (1989). *Rational-emotive couples therapy.* New York: Pergamon.

Fogarty, T. (1976). Marital crisis. In P. Guerin (Ed.), *Family theory, therapy and practice.* New York: Gardner.

Gehrke, S., & Moxon, J. (1962). Diagnostic classification and strategic techniques in marriage counseling. *Family Process, 1,* 253–264.

Gottman, J. (1994, May/June). Why marriages fail. *The Family Therapy Networker,* pp. 41–48.

Haley, J. (1976). *Problem-solving therapy.* San Francisco: Jossey-Bass.

Hill, R., & Hanson, D. A. (1960). The identification of conceptual frameworks utilization family study. *Marriage and Family Living, 22,* 299.

Howell, J. G. (1975). *Principles of family psychiatry.* New York: Bruner/Mazel.

Jacobson, N. S., & Margolin, G. (1979). *Marital therapy: Strategies based on social learning and behavior exchange principles.* New York: Bruner/Mazel.

Kerr, M. E., & Bowen, M. (1988). *Family evaluation.* New York: Norton.

Lederer, W., & Jackson, D. D. (1968). *The mirages of marriage.* New York: Norton.

Locke, H., & Wallace, L. (1959). Short marital adjustment and predicting tests: Their reliability and validity. *Marriage and Family Living, 54*(2), 251–255.

LoPiccolo, J., & Steger, J. C. (1974). The sexual inventory: A new instrument for assessment of sexual dysfunction. *Archives of Sexual Relations, 3,* 585–595.

Madanes, C. (1987). *Behind the one-way mirror: Advances in the practice of strategic therapy.* San Francisco: Jossey-Bass.

Minuchin, S. (1974). *Families and family therapy.* Cambridge, MA: Harvard University Press.

Mittleman, B. (1956). Analysis of reciprocal neurotic patterns in family relationships. In V. W. Eisenstein (Ed.), *Neurotic interactions in marriage* (pp. 88–100). New York: BasicBooks.

Nichols, M. P. (1984). *Family therapy: Concepts and methods.* New York: Gardner Press.

O'Hanlon, W. H., & Weiner-Davis, M. (1989). *In search of solutions: A new direction in psychotherapy.* New York: Norton.

Robinson, K. (1994, May/June). Which side are you on? *The Family Therapy Networker,* pp. 19–30.

Scharff, D., & Scharff, J. S. (1987). *Object relations and marital therapy.* New York: Jason Aronson.

Selye, H. (1956). *The stress of life.* New York: McGraw-Hill.

Snyder, D. K. (1981). *Marital satisfaction inventory.* Los Angeles: Western Psychological Services.

Spanier, G. (1976). Measuring dyadic adjustment: New scale for assessing the quality of marriage and similar dyads. *Journal of Marriage and Family Therapy, 38,* 15–28.

Stuart, R. B. (1980). *Helping couples change: A social learning approach to marital therapy.* New York: Guilford.

Stuart, R. B., & Stuart, F. (1973). *Marital pre-counseling inventory.* Champaign, IL: Research Press.

Weiss, R. L., & Birchler, G. R. (1975). *Areas of change* (unpublished manuscript). University of Oregon.

Weiss, R. L., & Margolin, G. (1977). Marital conflict and accord. In A. R. Cinimero, K. S. Calhoun, & A. E. Adams (Eds.), *Handbook for behavioral assessment* (pp. 346–377). New York: Wiley.

Whitaker, C., & Bumberry, W. M. (1988). *Dancing with the family: A symbolic-experiential approach.* New York: Bruner/Mazel.

Winnicott, D. W. (1969). *Child, the family and the outside world.* Baltimore: Pelican-Penguin.

CHAPTER 7

Physical Violence in the Family

Joan D. Atwood

SPOUSAL ABUSE

Case 1

Lisa and her three sisters were sexually and physically abused by their father as children. The abuse lasted until she was 12, when she told her mother. Dad overheard the confession that Mom chose not to believe, and severely beat Lisa. In need of medical attention and safety, she literally dragged herself to a police station where she recounted her story, but she was called a liar by the policeperson for not telling the police who the real perpetrator was. Lisa was then placed into a psychiatric group home for girls. Lisa married Thomas who also physically abused her. Many of the worst beatings occurred when Thomas was intoxicated or when Lisa was pregnant. In one incident, Lisa was raped by Thomas in front of their two young children. Lisa was nine months pregnant at the time of the assault, and the attack brought on the birth of their third child. Since she was 12, Lisa has been in some form of therapy. To date, even though Thomas continues to beat Lisa, he has never been in therapy.

Case 2

Karen was speaking with her counselor for the first time, when she sneezed and her front seven teeth came flying out of her mouth. When asked how this happened, she made a fist, and said her husband, Jason, had punched her in the mouth, knocking out her front row of teeth. Jason had a long history of violent drinking so his family walked on eggshells to avoid drawing his attention. They would tiptoe around the house, were acutely aware of where they sat, or stood, and would speak to each other in whispers. Although Jason had been arrested on several occasions for violent behaviors, he never once was seen by a counselor.

Case 3

Danny and Nicole grew up in Queens together. In search of a better way of life, they relocated to Long Island. Nicole described her father as physical and an alcohol abuser and recounted the days and nights when she and her siblings were "beaten up in the morning and beaten down at night." Danny continued where her father left off. Nicole reported almost miscarrying their youngest child, Stacy, because of a beating he gave her. Danny, heavily involved with drinking and drugs, fluctuated between leaving Nicole and the kids for months at a time and returning "down and out," only to abuse Nicole once more. Nicole, addicted to tranquilizers eventually went to a detoxification center. Danny, too, hit rock bottom and also went into treatment. After months in the center they came together again as a family, but many of the old stressors were still present. Eventually, the old ways of dealing with stress returned and the couple was separated. Nicole is currently in a shelter with two of her three children. Danny and their son are located somewhere in upstate New York.

Case 4

Carol is at an alcohol detoxification center because her husband told her she is an alcoholic and needs help. Carol, who has been isolated from family and friends throughout the years, feels she has no other choice but to believe him. Carol and her husband, Joe, live in an affluent area in the northeast. The police have visited them regularly. Although Joe has been arrested on several occasions for beating Carol to the point of hospitalization, he has had no encounters with the therapeutic community. On March 15, 1990, Joe called Carol's counselor at 1:00 AM to announce that there will be violence at his house. The counselor suggested separation and a call to the police if things got out of control. Joe refused to let Carol out of the house, but left for a hotel himself. Carol cannot financially provide for herself so she voluntarily checked into a detoxification center after learning that there were no beds available at a nearby shelter. Joe remains untreated.

Between 26 and 30 million spouses are abused annually (Wetzel & Ross, 1983). Up to 50% of all American wives have been hit or beaten

by their husbands, and it is estimated that one third of all married couples will experience violence at some time in their marital relationship.
A statistic even more surprising is that one quarter of abuse is husband
to wife, one quarter is wife to husband, and one half is mutual. Given
these statistics, why is it that more attention and sympathy is given to
wives of spouse abuse? In fact, in 50% of the cases, it is the wife that
initiates the first blow (Wetzel & Ross, 1983).

Domestic violence is an issue shrouded in myth, misconception and
misunderstanding. It has remained hidden for centuries in the sanctuary
of the home. This chapter seeks to dissect domestic violence into its
chameleon-like elements, to give the therapist an in-depth look at one
of the most complex and frustrating dilemmas a clinician will ever face.
Examples and explanations from current literary works and personal
communications are used to give the fullest account of domestic violence
in as many realms possible. Existing theoretical orientations and treatments are discussed as well as the problems associated with them, and
implications for the future treatment of domestic violence are offered.

Domestic violence today is something that thrives in secrecy, but it
was not long ago when it was part and parcel of marriage. The "laws of
chastisement" can be traced back as early as 750 B.C. and it was common that "before the nineteenth century, when a woman married she
lost property and personal rights. This had implications for wife-beating" (Stets, 1988, p. 2). The "rule of thumb," which meant that a husband could beat his wife with a stick no bigger than the size of his
thumb, was considered a normality until the late 1800s. As Stets noted,
"Women had no legal recourse when their husbands beat them. This
supported the patriarchal ideology and the accompanying hierarchical
social order that characterized most societies where men were in power
economically, legally, and religiously. It was not until the 1870s that
wife-beating became illegal in most states" (1988, p. 2). Even then, the
practice was to look the other way and minimize the discussion of violence, since it was something that occurred between husband and wife
in the privacy of the home. What we call marital rape in the 1990s was
previously called conjugal privilege.

"By the 1970s, domestic violence reached public awareness as a serious social problem that needed to be stopped. There were two major reasons for the sudden concern of domestic violence: society's intrusion into
the family and the feminist movement" (Stets, 1988, p. 2). In recent
years domestic violence has received more and more attention as violent

incidents have become increasingly public (Sullivan, 1991). However, exposure and awareness is not enough to stop the violence from occurring and continuing. As therapists who encounter and work with the effects of domestic violence on individuals and families, it is crucial to understand the psychodynamics of this problem.

Domestic violence is not a simple problem with quick, readily attainable solutions. It does not disappear. In addition to the hidden aspect of domestic violence, another obstacle in the path to effective intervention and resolution is its history. Okun (1986) points out that "against the backdrop of over 2,600 years of the laws of chastisement, it is modern feminist values absolutely opposed to conjugal violence that must be viewed as the historical aberration" (p. 10). In the war against domestic violence, we have only just begun.

With the acknowledgement of domestic violence as a serious familial and social predicament, professional and nonprofessional people alike have sought to address and explain its occurrence. While important insights into domestic violence have been made, perhaps an equal amount of myths and misconceptions have also developed. Cantrell (1986) cites the following myths in her book entitled *Into the Light:*

- Women who stay in abusive relationships are "asking" to be beaten and therefore must like it.
- Only low income, minority women are abused.
- Alcohol/drug abuse causes wife battering.
- Individuals who abuse their intimate partners are mentally ill.
- Wife abuse does not affect the children in the family. Often, they do not know it's happening. (pp. 6–8)

Other myths which have attempted in the past to account for domestic violence include the "the battered-husband syndrome," and a "mutual combat" theory which claims that "women usually employ violence in self-defense." (Pagelow, 1992, pp. 108–110). In regard to domestic disturbance calls, Pagelow (1992) noted that among law enforcement officers there was a "commonly accepted belief that these calls resulted in the highest rate of injury and death for officers" (p. 108).

Impressions such as these can actually prevent assistance for the family experiencing domestic violence. Incorrect assumptions also lend themselves towards a view of domestic violence situations as hopeless and, consequently, helpless. Some form of giving up then becomes the only real option for all involved.

Possibly worse are myths that assign or project blame onto women as illustrated the observation that "women (traditionally) have been considered at fault for the violence and, therefore, the symptoms they suffer as a result of their victimization have been minimized (Houskamp & Foy, 1991, p. 373). Gilbert and Webster (1982) reported the same misconception that "a battered women must have provoked abuse, otherwise it wouldn't be happening" (p. 138). Myths revealed by Okun (1986) included a "popular belief that women-battering developed recently as a symptom of a modern breakdown in the family" followed by "another popular myth that the epidemic of woman-battering has broken out only recently, as a backlash against feminism" (p. 10).

Besides the most familiar of conjectures are the ones that are not so apparent, as Okun discovered while seeking reasons why abused women stay in such destructive relationships. "In this fallacy, which was first described by Karen Horney, the actual experience of suffering is equated with a lust for suffering" (1986, p. 80). Believing any aspect of these inaccuracies hinders all attempts at alleviating the problem of domestic violence.

The myths and misconceptions that surround and protect domestic violence can be quite deceiving, although many of them cannot be substantiated with examples and explanations. As clinicians it is essential for us to distinguish fact from fancy if we intend to address this problem in any crucial way.

"Conjugal relationships and the family are supposed to be havens of love and warmth and tranquility. Violence is supposed to take place in the streets" (Okun, 1986, p. 91). Ideas such as these have been a part of the American culture for some time. Traditionally, television shows have reflected these beliefs. Strife was largely an out-of-the-house experience which became rectified through the love, support, and strength of the family members. More recently, however, movies and television shows have exposed the darker side of American life, portraying familial interactions where dysfunction and conflict comes from within. As Okun (1986) noted, "the foremost social factor influencing conjugal violence is the existence of cultural norms that permit conjugal violence" (p. 90). Unfortunately, our culture exposes us to and permits more than we may be willing to look at.

Regardless of the advances of the women's movement, our society is still primarily patriarchal. "It is the man who can give lawfully married status and who, therefore, has the power to dictate the terms; and it is the woman who is more interested in the connection and therefore willing to accept the terms at any cost" (Avni, 1991, p. 238).

For young women in particular, in American culture, early socialization creates pressures toward the quest for love and romance. To the majority, the ideal of being swept off their feet to marry Mr. Right and live happily ever after is at least a subconscious hope. When domestic violence enters this picture, the romance may still be maintained by inferring, "to love is to forgive; to batter is to love . . . beating stems from jealousy and therefore proves love" (Avni, 1991, p. 236). In many instances, the victims of domestic violence still love their mates—it is the violence that short circuits the love that they hate.

The notion of patriarchy does not exclusively manifest in the larger American sociocultural context but as Avni (1991) explains, "Its main concepts are power and authority and its chief setting is the home. Socialization, according to patriarchal attitude, stresses the hierarchial nature of the family, particularly male dominance and control over the female" (p. 233). "The patriarchal mentality operates before marriage so that it leaves its mark on the marriage itself" (Avni, 1991, p. 232). "Young ladies who are raised in patriarchal homes identify with the traditional sex roles, according to which a women should respect male authority, and her greatest aspiration is to be a good wife and mother" (Avni, 1991, p. 234).

It is the author's belief that patriarchy in and of itself is not problematic as long as boundaries and limits are clearly established, respected, and agreed upon. Domestic violence can occur in a patriarchal structure by breaching boundaries to brutal extremes and then by becoming the advocate for the violence.

It appears to be a rare occurrence that violence in a relationship is a one-time event. The cycle of violence theory originated by Gelles states that "children learn from violent families of origin that violence between intimates is acceptable and expected, physically stronger family members can perpetrate violence with minimal consequence to themselves, and violence is associated with controlling the behavior of physically weaker family members" (Downs, Miller, Testa, & Panek, 1992, p. 377). Walker (cited in Cantrell, 1986, p. 10) further elaborates by identifying three distinct phases in the cycle of violence: the tension building phase, the acute battering incident, and the honeymoon stage. At bare minimum, the honeymoon stage is sweet enough to keep a battered victim around for more.

THE PHYSICAL EFFECTS OF DOMESTIC VIOLENCE

The physical effects on female victims need not be embellished upon so much as an understanding of the effects and an analysis as to why women stay in such painful relationships. Much of the literature, as Houskamp and Foy (1991) report in their study, "suggest that a primary etiological variable for the development of post-traumatic stress disorder (PTSD) in battered women may be the intensity of their exposure to violence" (1991, p. 373). Downs, Miller, Testa and Panek (1992) concur and state: "Women who grow up in violent families may include violent behavior as part of their role expectations within families. These role expectations may then lead to normative approval of violence in their spousal relationship, and subsequently to the acceptance of violent behavior by their male partner" (p. 377). "When the girl is physically abused by her suitor during the courtship, one would expect that she would realize what would be in store for her if she were to marry him. However, there are several sociopsychological structures that inhibit this reaction. To start with, most of these women were physically punished in childhood" (Avni, 1991, p. 235), so the physical assault is not an unfamiliar event.

Aside from family-of-origin issues, other bearings common to domestic violence victims Avni (1991) saw were "the relatively young age at marriage" and "the relatively short courtship" (p. 234). Okun, on the other hand, found similarities in the characteristics between concentration camp prisoners and battered women. He lists the following as being common traits:

- guilt feelings, with an attendant sense of deserving the victimization
- significant loss of self-esteem
- detachment of emotion from incidents of severe violence, and extreme reactions to trivial incidents
- failure to observe the controller's rules because of the arbitrariness of punishment
- extreme emotional reactions
- difficulty planning for the future and delaying gratification
- fear of escaping the coercive control situation
- child-like dependency on the controllers, and identification with them
- limitation of controllers' aggressiveness, and adoption of their values
- maintenance of the hope that the controller is kind and just (1986, p. 87)

Gilbert and Webster (1982) feel that femininity can also play a part in the predisposition of women as victims of domestic violence. "Abuse, both in childhood and in adult life, makes it more difficult to change that program for victimization to something safer and more functional, because violation refeminizes us" (1982, p. 138). Gender specific roles even dictate that "it is unfeminine to be in touch with negative feelings. Women are not supposed to be aware of their aggression, rage, negativity, or nastiness" (Gilbert & Webster, 1982, p. 131).

The magical touch of love that sees the beauty in the beast must also be accounted for. Avni (1991) writes that "when the relationship is based on feelings of love and attraction, the girl may interprets the battering as a symbol of the strong bond between herself and her suitor" (pp. 235–236). Walker (1978) explains domestic violence from a codependency framework noting that "the woman becomes the victim because of her extreme dependence upon the batterer. . . . Interestingly enough, neither does the batterer believe he can stand alone. Both typically are traditionalists, who fear the religious, social, emotional, and economic ramifications of divorce. Death is a more acceptable alternative" (1978, p. 155).

In comparison to what is known about the victims of domestic violence, the data concerning the perpetrators is considerably less. Reasons for this lack of information pertain to self-protective measures, both conscious and unconscious. Denial of the battering is one reason. Davidson (1978) believed that "many middle-class men who are violent at home simply do not see themselves as wifebeaters at all" (1978, p. 25). Elusiveness, avoidance, and the refusal of assistance and treatments are other contributing factors.

WHY DO MEN HIT?

Why do men hit? Gilbert and Webster (1982) reply that "men do it because nobody stops them" (1982, p. 131). Stets' research, however, revealed that "control emerges as a central theme organizing their thoughts about the batterer's behavior and emotions: emotions and behavior are in or out of control" (1988, p. 1). In agreement, the coercive control theory of Singer and Serwin compares the actions utilized by a perpetrator to those of a brainwasher. "Batterers employ many techniques documented in the literature on brainwashing. These include imprisonment or confinement; social isolation; beatings; torture; starvation or malnourishment; sleep deprivation; threats of murder or of torture; random and unpredictable leniency, coupled with equally unpredictable punishment; humiliation and revilement; complete prescription of the use of time and space; manacling or other forms of bondage; coerced false confessions; and other methods of directly inducing guilt such as denunciations of the victim to authorities or significant others" (Okun, 1986, p. 87).

The perpetrator's family of origin may impact on the son's behaviors, as Downs et al. (1992) discovered that "violence from both parents was found related to each adulthood problem. There were also some gender-based findings. Mother violence was found slightly more important for adulthood experiences of severe partner-to-woman violence than father violence" (1992, pp. 376–377).

The Role of Alcohol

More significant, is the correlational relationship of battering behaviors and alcohol usage. Gottheil, Druley, Skoloda and Waxman (1983) concluded that "enforced repression of aggression in childhood might well inhibit the individual from displaying any form of aggressive behavior. If such an individual begins to use alcohol and finds relief of inner tensions, stresses, and strain, his or her inhibitions may be lessened and violent behavior might then be displayed. Individuals not socialized to conventional norms do not necessarily show restraint and thus engage in violence without the use of alcohol; however, one cannot dismiss the connection of alcohol abuse and violence, and domestic violence in particular. They tend to coexist" (p. 133). Pernanen (1991) hypothesizes that available data "has probably underestimated the involvement of alcohol in serious violent behavior" (p. 107), yet the existing literature is abundant with evidence of this most precarious association. Gottheil et al. (1983) noted that "in general, alcohol abuse . . . is more clearly associated with violence in the husband-wife relationship" (p. 121), while Pernanen draws the "descriptive conclusion that occasions on which people drink more than average are more likely to be related to physical violence" (1991, p. 113). Pernanen's investigation goes on to point out that "police-recorded violence in which women had been victimized had a higher degree of total alcohol involvement than crimes with male victims" (1991, p .102) and summarizes that "marital violence and domestic violence generally showed the well-documented pattern of a drinking assailant (with few exceptions, the husband) and a sober victim" (Pernanen, 1991, p. 127).

Batterers are not the only drinkers in a domestically violent lifestyle. Victims, although not as frequently, are also found to have a relationship with alcohol. Downs et al. (1992) believe that "daughters may perceive minimal ability to avoid further violence, due to the greater power of fathers, and turn to alcohol abuse in order to escape feelings associated with this violence" (p. 379). Bringing to mind the numbing effects of alcohol, it is of interest to note that studies showed "almost no violence among the most alcoholic group . . . the most severe alcoholics. These authors conclude that rather than being disinhibited by alcohol, they are in effect anesthetized" (Gottheil et al., 1983, p. 121). Aside from the multiple intricacies alcohol can induce in an already volatile circumstance, the chief purpose alcohol serves (if any) is as an overt excuse for the violence. "Attacking a family member while intoxicated provides the grounds for refusing to accept responsibility for one's own violent behavior" (Gottheil et al., 1983, p. 133).

Regardless of who the drinker is, Downs et al. (1992) distinguished a transgenerational transmission of alcohol abuse via domestic violence in that "father violence was found more important for development of alcohol problems in adulthood" (p. 377). In trying to understand the linkage between alcohol and family violence, Gottheil et al. (1983) submitted that the " 'social learning' and 'deviance disavowal' theory were explanations of the relationship between alcohol abuse and violence. By observing parents who behave violently or otherwise while drunk, people learn what is accepted, or at least 'excused' " (1983, p. 121). In searching for a solution, Minuchin acknowledged the correlational aspect of alcohol and domestic violence by reflecting that "continuing in the same way is not the answer; nor are the denial and concealment so often characteristic of both alcoholism and family violence" (1984, p. 174).

DOMESTIC VIOLENCE LAW

Domestic violence is a crime in every sense of the word but like its nature, this crime does not exhibit clear boundaries and, hence, legal recourse can be just as ambiguous. Part of the confusion lies in the history of domestic violence in which the abuse of women was viewed "as a legal and formally accepted institution in Western society" (Okun, 1986, p. 1). However, perhaps more pertinent, "family disputes are viewed as nobody else's business. The Fourth Amendment to the Constitution is the legal representation of this attitude, and it has often been interpreted as an obstacle to police intervention in domestic assaults" (Okun, 1986, p. 91). In addition, "abuse is an underreported crime. It is underreported for two reasons: (a) it occurs in the privacy of one's home where there are typically no witnesses aside from family members and (b) though violence is by no means restricted to the lower classes, middle- and upper-class violence is likely to go unreported to the police" (Stets, 1988, p. 3).

Each state within the United States handles domestic violence issues in their own way. For the purposes of this chapter, the following section is specific to a program operating in a New York State metropolitan area suburb. In an interview with the police officers of the Domestic Violence Unit at police headquarters, a 24-year veteran spoke of his belief that there was an increase in domestic violence reports since a pro-arrest policy was instituted in 1988 by the county executive. Under this policy, a perpetrator is immediately arrested if there has been a violation of an order of protection or a felony #2 (major assault). Arrest becomes the victim's choice if the incident is deemed to be a misdemeanor, which covers minor assaults and threats of violence (personal communication, November 10, 1992).

All officers agreed that holidays or any other occasion when families get together and alcohol is available contribute to a rise in the report rate. The officer cited above pointed toward the paradox of the laws' saying "don't" while the movies and TV condone violence (personal communication, November 10, 1992). Another female officer felt that ultimately it's "still a man's world" (personal communication, November 10, 1992). First-order changes may be made, she believes, but second-order changes concerning domestic violence may be unattainable in our society. Another officer voiced puzzlement over why driving-while-intoxicated (DWI) arrests are mandated for counseling, but domestic violence arrests are not (personal communication, November 10, 1992).

Pursuing this dichotomy of post-arrest treatment for abusers of drinking and driving versus abusers of family members led to a conversation with the county's Department of Probation, who along with the county's Victims Information Bureau, lead a treatment program for the perpetrators of domestic violence, as detailed in Table 7.1.

TREATING THE PERPETRATOR

The program director explained that the Domestic Violence Program was initiated in the family court system 4 years ago, but that it is currently utilized primarily in the district and criminal courts system at this time. It has been his experience through the Domestic Violence Program that alcohol is not causal to domestic violence, but influential. He firmly believes that no one can change while abusing a substance. He also noted that there is a high recidivism rate among perpetrators, as for alcoholics. He has faith that batterers can stop the abuse since most can and do control themselves in other arenas such as work, school, in public, etc. He feels that batterers "choose to lose it at home." In response to a question regarding the perpetrators not remembering the abuse they inflicted on their victims, he said that the men in his program realize that that program staff do not believe them when the batterers claim not to remember engaging in the abuse. Group leaders believe that the batterer consciously decided to use physical violence (personal communication, November 17, 1992).

Treatment Techniques

The theories that imply treatment techniques for domestic violence are largely individual oriented, but in no way are they exclusive of marriage and family counseling. The problem and the people are most adequately served when individual work precedes couple or familial work. Pressing for marriage and/or family counseling too soon may jeopardize the therapy at best and be a potentially dangerous situation at worst. Once individual work has been satisfactorily accomplished, a systemic framework may be employed. Stith, Williams, and Rosen (1990) suggest that "systemic-oriented couples therapy and family-of-origin work are recommended after partners are sufficiently differentiated so that relationship issues can be worked on in tandem without escalating possibilities of violence" (p. 48). "Approaching treatment from a systems

TABLE 7.1   Domestic Violence Program

- The Domestic Violence Program in County, Suffolk, New York, is a 16-week educational/treatment program designed for men who are batterers. It is partially modeled after the county Probation Alcohol Treatment (PAT) Program.
- The Domestic Violence Program is available to voluntary clients and for clients mandated by the courts.
- The program, which is both educational and therapeutic, is administered by the County Probation Department and the Victims Information Bureau.
- The workshops are led by a highly trained team of coleaders. Educational material is presented in each workshop through discussion and the use of visual aids.

The goal of the program is to stop domestic violence by reaching those who have been accused of battering with the message that:

- Domestic violence is illegal and there are consequences for those who batter.
- Violence is always damaging.
- Violence is learned and can be unlearned.
- Alternatives to violence exist and can be learned.
- Each individual is responsible for his own actions and his own violence.
- The batterer deserves help and support in changing his behavior and help is available.

The Target Population

- Those who have violated an Order of Protection
- Those who have a history of multiple family offenses (specific criteria applied here would be the commission of more than one family offense in a 12-month period)
- Those who have inflicted severe injuries on the victim

Maintenance Program

After successful completion of the 16-week program, the clients are invited to participate in a Maintenance Program. The purpose of the Maintenance Program is to help sustain and solidify the changes made during the previous 16 weeks. In addition, this maintenance program gives the participants an opportunity to continue to build their interpersonal skills and improve their competence in responding to stress. The program's content continues to focus on the basic premises elaborated during the 16-week Psycho-educational Program.

Fee

A nominal fee of $50.00 is charged. Sliding scale is available. The reason for a fee is based on the findings of other treatment programs. Participants tend to view the program with higher regard when they have to pay money for what they are receiving. Probationers are made aware that a report of payment of fee will be made to the Court as evidence of each participant's cooperation. Options of lowering the usual fee and alternative payment schedules are considered on an individual basis.

theoretical framework tak[es] the responsibility for the abusive behavior from the abuser. This framework, however, does allow for consideration of the role that society plays in contributing to the abuse" (Stith et al., 1990, p. 87). Extending therapy past the individual realm into the marital and familial domains can provide a stronger, more supportive foundation for the end goal of a violence-free environment.

No matter what theoretical orientation the therapist chooses, the treatment of a domestically violent family should be broken down into treatment phases—individual to couple to family—which must be handled slowly throughout, and delicately at the outset of each. Generally speaking, it is the author's belief that strategic, short-term and crisis-intervention modalities should be avoided in handling domestic violence cases since any of these could serve as a superficial bandaid and may discourage or sabotage the idea of the long-term therapy needed. If children are directly involved with the violence, it is important for the therapist to remember that they are mandated reporters under New York State law and that failing to report an incidence of suspected child abuse or maltreatment is a Class A misdemeanor.

The many issues that surround a domestically violent relationship ought to be probed in assessment, as they may serve as entrance points to treatment. Houskamp and Foy (1991) suggested "that a large percentage of women who have suffered domestic violence may experience PTSD as diagnosed by the *DSM-III-R* criteria" (p. 372). This diagnosis provides one approach to therapeutic intervention. Smith (1991) believes that "therapeutic intervention involves challenging the patriarchal expectations and attitudes (including excuses based on loss of self-control) that lie at the core of the abusive behavior" (p. 518), while Stith et al. feel that the concept of death should be examined: "Because of the insidiousness of abuse, the fact that it is a killing act is diminished in the minds of the participants. The death might not actually be a physical one, but small deaths occur with each abusive episode. There is the death of pride, of feeling valued, of trust, of respect, and of loyalty" (1990, p. 61).

One of the foremost issues regarding treatment is the safety of the family members. "The issue of self-protection is one that needs to be dealt with directly in therapy" (Stith et al., 1990, p. 61). "In dealing with the issue of protection, the female has a minimum of two tasks. First, she must become convinced of the seriousness of the abusive acts. Second, she must come to grips with the consequences of ending or attempting to end the relationship" (p. 63). These authors also recommend that systemic treatment be done in stages, from contracting for nonviolence, to teaching anger management skills, to enhancing the marital relationship.

Chapman and Gates (1978) propose that "the long-term expected outcome is economic and psychological interdependence. To be interdependent means to be capable of either independent or dependent behavior within a relationship as appropriate" (p. 154). Similarly, Minuchin (1984) agrees that "the goal should be to explore and improve people's interdependence" (p. 175).

In researching the literature, there is an abundance of material which emphasizes that "the most effective alternative for the battered woman is to end her relationship with the batterer" (Chapman & Gates, 1978, p. 155). Concurrent with the concrete and clinical goals of resources available to women in their communities, the majority of literary work advises that women leave their marriages relationships, if not permanently then temporarily, or to give their partners effectual threats of leaving. Loseke (1992) is of the opinion that "in the final analysis, a battered woman type of person requires help if she is to be able to remove herself from her plight" (p. 28). These conclusions trouble me because the impetus for change is placed on an already distraught, exhausted, and emotionally overburdened victim. As Cantrell (1986) stated: "The ultimate choice that you face is whether to stay with your abusive partner or to leave" (1986, p. 17).

The Therapist's Part

Domestic violence is one of the trickiest problems a therapist will ever face, because domestic violence is riddled with paradoxes and self-contradictions. For example: as prescribed above, some form of leaving the abuser is encouraged. Okun (1986) warns that "leaving the batterer sets up only a potential for cessation of the violence since the batterer's violence can continue after the legal termination of the relationship. In fact, leaving the batterer often increases the woman's risk of being murdered" (p. 81). Other complications in the victim's leaving is the "high incidence of battered women repeatedly leaving and returning to their assailants. . . . Many batterers may act on their best behavior when women first return to them and . . . battering sometimes escalates when women try to escape" (Sullivan, 1991, p. 52). As frustrating as it may be to hear, "estimates suggest that 50 to 75% of the women who separate from their abusers, return to live with them" (Stith et al., 1990, p. 49).

Minuchin (1984) says, "I cannot support family maintenance when the family organization is destructive to its members. The goal then is to help the family separate" (1984, p. 177).

The inherently problematic nature of domestic violence is not only limited to the client's domain but to the therapist's as well. In many domestically violent families the mother can be found somewhere in the sibling subsystem, and a crystal-clear picture of how to treat this family from a structural framework emerges. But therapist, beware: Mom is in a one-down position for a reason and if the abuser is not in treatment, structural intervention can be life threatening for the victim. Raising her up into the marital or parental subsystem too soon may leave her open to attack. If the spouse cannot emotionally beat her down from this new position, then a physical beating may be the answer to return her to a comfortable place for the abuser. One can never predict the amount or harshness of abuse that the perpetrator will inflict. It is the perpetrator who will decide when enough is enough, not the victim.

A primary reason for the long-term ineffectiveness of treatment in domestic violence cases is the inaccessibility of the perpetrator. There is only so much a therapist can do with the individual who wants to maintain the relationship. As Chappel pointed out, even though the Domestic Violence Program is on a voluntary or court-mandated basis (1992), no one comes into the group voluntarily (Personal communication, November 17, 1992). The lack of physical attendance in therapy by batterers is only one obstacle in resolving domestic violence. Another is described by Stith et al.: "With limited self-awareness, abusive men tend to suppress and mask what they feel" (1990, pp. 69–70). Besides intrapsychic reason for refraining from therapy, Minuchin believes, a general bias exists which reinforces men to keep from becoming involved. As he explains, "Many . . . refuges maintain a policy that keeps their doors closed to men, not only the abusing relative but any other variety" (1984, p. 174).

Internal defense mechanisms can also inhibit therapeutic gains, as described by Stith et al. (1990): "Victims of abuse often deny the reality of their situation. They deny the seriousness of the abuse, the dangerousness of their partners, their fears, insecurities, and often the actual source of the injuries. They rationalize behaviors in such fashions as to make the batterer incapable of being responsible for his abusing behaviors" (p. 51).

Houskamp and Foy (1991) caution that bringing these issues to awareness may be especially precarious. "For women still in an abusive situation, acknowledging the extent of psychological distress they are experiencing from the violence may create additional unwanted internal and psychosocial conflict" (1991, p. 373).

Inciting thought processes must be handled delicately or they can also prove detrimental to symptom relief in the victim. Most often, the victim has already been thinking for quite some time. "The painful paradox contained in dedicated thinking about a problem that almost certainly will not be solved in this manner is a part of the victim's psychological character and burden" (Blackman, 1989, p. 73). Blackman (1989) also notes that "battered women 'think hard' about how to prevent and avoid future violence and that the activity of 'thinking hard' stymies them" (p. 75). She also states most intelligibly that "high levels of fear do not promote complex cognitive activity" (1989, p. 75) and may severely limit how much the victim may be able to absorb, process, and act on while undergoing therapy.

Another factor which may hinder intervention is the concept of isolation for the victim in dealing with self-protective measures such as time-outs, respite or a short separation from the abuser. Blackman (1989) generalizes that "in the domain of 'seeing alternatives', isolation is a potent deterrent. Isolation diminishes the perception of alternatives" (p. 72). Due to this fear of being left all alone, the victim may not be willing to trade her sense of security with the abuser for her own personal safety. Okun (1986) points out that, "People often place higher priority on potential losses than on potential gains in weighing the merits of risky options" (p. 81). This ideology can even be reflected in the mate selection process, where Avni (1991) observed the rationale that "to marry this man, with all his shortcomings, is preferable to maintaining the status quo" (p. 237). Blackman's (1989) research found that "other women may make similar choices between what is known and a seemingly worse unknown" (p. 74).

Domestically violent relationships are by no means exclusively the result of a lesser of two evils choice made by the victim. "A more complicated dynamic is that which involves love. This emotional factor has a significant effect independent of whether it is her love for him or his love for her" (Avni, 1991, p. 235). Coupled with this matter is the fact that "victims of abuse often live in a fantasy land of illusions of how they want their lives to be" (Stith et al., 1990, p. 51). A fine line exists between actuality and illusion in this context for both client and therapist. Avni notes that "patriarchy does not necessarily spell violence. On the contrary, it can be dangerously disguised as chivalry and care" (1991, p. 235). The therapist should remain at optimum alertness while working in this realm. The empathetic pull towards the victim is very strong and, if the perpetrator is also in therapy, his seductiveness can be as equally powerful. "It is common for a battered woman to believe that her man is himself only at those times of remorse and reconciliation" (Gilbert & Webster, 1982, p. 145) and for the therapist attempting to find the middle ground between destructive monster and repentant sinner, the presentation can be quite challenging. In this situation the therapist can draw upon constructivist techniques by scripting a more functional narrative of the victim's perceptions and by assisting the perpetrator and victim in redefining their ideas of love, romance, patriarchy, and the like.

More therapeutic impediments derive from aspects connected with the "big picture" ranging from the familial to cultural arenas. "One of the critical areas that sets domestic violence apart from other traumatic events is its tendency to involve multiple occurrences of violence, over an extended length of time, within a setting that is familiar and assumed to be a place of safety" (Houskamp & Foy, 1991, p. 374). While I wouldn't claim that we have a negligent society, we seem to live in one that stands in horror at the revelations of abuse, but permits the abuse to continue through active avoidance. Okun feels that "the tolerance of conjugal violence is related to our society's priority on the privacy of the home and of the nuclear family" (1986, p. 91). Blackman draws attention to a stagnating attribute: "Cultural norms and values may profoundly limit individuals' perceptions of alternatives" (1989, p. 70). These norms and values change with time as do their impacts; "contemporary society now expects women actively and hedonistically to enjoy sexual activities, rather than to submit to coitus in the passive and self-sacrificing fashion which Freud seems to have equated with female sexuality" (Okun, 1986, p. 81). The one thing that has not appeared to change in our society is the use and acceptance of violence as the quick way to get what one wants, while being feared and therefore respected at the same time.

Specific concerns regarding the treatment of domestic violence were voiced by Stith et al. (1990), who suggested that "treatment tends to lag behind theory" and that "some professionals have suggested that systems theory implies the blurring of boundaries between batterer and battered spouse" (p. 86). In an interview with the county Victims

Information Bureau, a bureau representative estimated that victims make eight to ten attempts at intervention before they are willing to leave an abusive relationship, and that a majority of the women want to stay with their abusive partners. The representative stressed that it is very difficult to get victims into counseling, that there's a 50% no-show rate and that there's a high dropout rate. She also cited that through a course of years a pattern has emerged with the end goal being a state of readiness to leave the relationship. The victims will seek: (a) an Order of Protection, (b) legal aid, (c) counseling, and last, (d) assistance to leave (Suffolk County Victims Information Bureau, personal communication, November 9, 1992).

Each literary quote used for this paper was specifically chosen not only for its content, but for its thought-provoking quality as well. It is the authors' belief that each issue of domestic violence requires a thorough examination if we as therapists are at all serious about guiding our clients to a place where the love does not have to physically hurt.

Future treatment considerations include:

1. teaching our female clients how to "be free to choose to enter a relationship, rather than believing it is her only alternative" (Chapman & Gates, 1978, p. 155);
2. being aware of and "conceptualizing domestic violence in a way that does not contribute to blaming the victim" (Houskamp & Foy, 1991, p. 373);
3. "incorporating the batterer's perspective and identifying the processes that are characteristic of violent relationships overtime" (Stets, 1988, p. 1) and, perhaps the most significant but most overlooked key to treatment;
4. reviewing "the commonalities in the characteristics and theoretical explanations of alcohol abuse and domestic violence [that provide] the framework for common treatment programs. The abusers and victims, as well as other family dependents, would be served effectively and efficiently under one umbrella program" (Gottheil et al., 1983, p. 135).

Finally, an historical perspective urges us to consider that "the demand for domestic non-violence does represent a breakdown in traditional family life, a breakdown that is better termed a breakthrough" (Okun, 1986, p. 10).

SUMMARY

The purpose of this chapter was to present the reader with information on the widespread problem of domestic violence and its effect on individuals and families. Some of the effects of domestic violence were discussed, along with a domestic violence program that has been implemented in a court system in a New York State metropolitan area suburb. The view of the chapter is that domestic violence is a social, interpersonal, and intrapersonal problem and must be treated from a multisystemic perspective if this problem is to be eradicated.

REFERENCES

Avni, N. (1991). Battered wives: characteristics of their courtship days. *Journal of Interpersonal Violence, 6*(2), 232–239.

Blackman, J. (1989). *Intimate violence: A study of injustice.* New York: Columbia University Press.

Cantfell, L. A. (1986). *Into the light: A guide for battered women.* Washington, DC: Franklin.

Chapman, J. R., & Gates, M. (1978). *The victimization of women.* Thousand Oaks, CA: Sage.

Chappel, J. N. (1992). Effective use of Alcoholics Anonymous and Narcotics Anonymous in treating patients. *Psychiatric Annals, 22,* 409–418.

Davidson, T. (1978). *Conjugal crime: Understanding and changing the wife-beating pattern.* New York: Hawthorn.

Downs, W. R., Miller, B. A., Testa, M., & Panek, D. (1992). Long-term effects of parent-to-child violence for women. *Journal of Interpersonal Violence, 7,* 76–94.

Gilbert, L., & Webster, P. (1982). *Bound by love: The sweet trap of daughterhood.* Boston, MA: Beacon.

Gottheil, E., Druley, K. A., Skoloda, T. E. J., Waxman, H. M. (Eds.). (1983). *Alcohol, drug abuse and aggressions.* Springfield, IL: Thomas.

Houskamp, B. M., & Foy, D. W. (1991). The assessment of post-traumatic stress disorder in battered women. *Journal of Interpersonal Violence, 6,* 367–375.

Loseke, D. R. (1992). *The battered woman and shelters: The social construction of wife abuse.* New York: State University of New York Press.

Minuchin, S. (1984). *Family kaleidoscope.* Cambridge, MA: Harvard University Press.

Norton, A., & Glick, P. (1986). One-parent family; a social and economic profile. Special issue: The single-parent family. *Family Relations, Journal of
Applied Family and Child Studies, 35,* 9–17.

Okun, L. (1986). *Woman abuse: Facts replacing myths.* New York: State University of New York Press.

Pagelow, M. D. (1992). Adult victims of domestic violence: Battered women.
Journal of Interpersonal Violence. 7, 87–120.

Pernanen, K. (1991). *Alcohol in human violence.* New York: Guilford.

Smith, M. D. (1991). Male peer support of wife abuse: An exploratory study.
Journal of Interpersonal Violence, 6, 512–519.

Stets, J. E. (1988). *Domestic violence and control.* New York: Springer-Verlag.

Stith, S. M., Williams, M., & Rosen, K. (1990). *Violence hits home: Comprehensive treatment approaches to domestic violence.* New York: Springer.

Sullivan, C. M. (1991). The provision of advocacy services to women leaving
abusive partners: An exploratory study. *Journal of Interpersonal Violence,
6,* 41–54.

Walker, L. E. (1978). Battered women and learned helplessness. *Victimology,
2,* 525–534.

Wetzel, L., & Ross, M. A. (1983). Psychological and social ramifications of battering: Observations leading to a counseling methodology for victims of
domestic violence. *Personnel and Guidance Journal, 61,* 423–428.

CHAPTER 8

Intimacy Dissolution: Divorce

Joan D. Atwood

DIVORCE RATES

The divorce rate (number of divorces per 1,000 marriages) began to increase in the United States early in this century, seemed to peak after World War II and then drop back a bit. It has been rising again in recent years (Ditzions, 1978), resulting in approximately 2.2 million marriages and 1.1 million divorces each year, creating a pattern which results in almost 2.5 million persons entering this single status each year. Current figures indicate that over 11 million people in the population are divorced (Arditti, 1992), with divorce affecting one million children every year. The divorce rate is higher for nonwhites than whites and generally higher among lower-class than middle- and upper-class whites (Glick, 1988). The average age at divorce from first marriage in the United States today is 27 for females and 29 for males. Divorce appears to have become so common that 60% of Americans who get married today report that they do not expect the marriage to last the rest of their lives (Yankelovich, 1981). In addition to the already divorced, a sizable number of people are between marriage and divorce. At any given time, individuals who are separated from their spouses constitute a very large population. In March, 1984, the census reported 1.5 million men and 2.4 million women who were separated (Norton & Glick, 1986).

However, it should be noted that these figures probably represent underestimates, inasmuch as an unknown number of persons report that an absent spouse is "visiting relatives." It is basically impossible, then, to measure separation in this group, either through agreement to separate or desertion, since there are basically no formal reporting techniques; only a few couples go through the formalities of legal separation. These statistics mean that American society has the highest divorce and/or separation rate in the western world. It is clear that there is a large segment of the population confronted with the task of readjusting to postmarital life.

Explanations of Divorce Rates

There are many ways to interpret the fact that a growing number of marriages end in divorce. Rising divorce rates are a common topic in the popular media, and they often are interpreted as a sign of societal rejection of the institution of marriage or the demise of the family. This explanation is questionable because available divorce statistics are not necessarily an entirely reliable indicator of the current state of marriage. While it may be true that fewer people value the commitment of marriage, it is also possible that expectations of marriage are higher than they were historically and that people are more easily disappointed.

In the days of arranged marriages, many people tolerated unhappy or unsatisfying situations and adjusted to them. Now, fewer people are kept from divorce by religious prohibitions, legal barriers, and social disapproval and sanctions. With the increased life span, others are unwilling to adjust to an unhappy marriage for 50 or so years, resulting in more dissatisfied couples terminating the marriage. Divorce is probably also more common now because women (about one family in seven now has a woman as the head of the household) have more opportunities economically and emotionally, to support themselves and their children and to receive financial aid from governmental agencies. Finally, changes in gender roles and gender role expectations may have led to increased dissatisfaction with the institution of marriage in general. However, it is important to keep in mind that the number of divorces may reflect dissatisfaction with a particular marriage more than with the institution of marriage itself and the great majority of people who divorce eventually do remarry (75% of women and 80% of men), thus indicating that the dissatisfaction may reflect the person rather than the institution of marriage.

There are several other factors that could have bearing on the way divorce statistics are interpreted. Not all the states in this country have developed uniform standards for divorce recordkeeping. What this probably means is that the records reflect variable data collection procedures. Also, recently there have been many legal changes regarding divorce and the recent rise in divorce rates could reflect the increased ease of the legality of obtaining a divorce rather than a rise in dissatisfaction with marriage itself. In many cases, obtaining a legal divorce has become a relatively simple and less expensive legal process. Added to this is the fact that a significant percentage of the divorce rate is composed of individuals who have had more than one marriage and divorce.

Using most measures, though, the research does appear to indicate that the proportion of marriages ending in divorce has almost doubled since the 1950s, lending credence to the fact that there is a large and still growing divorced population who are confronted with the emotional task of adjusting to new social, psychological, and sexual roles.

Because of these high percentages, one is likely to believe that "divorced" is as acceptable a status as "married" and there is some indication that there has been an increase in the tolerance of divorce (see Gerstel, 1987; Spanier & Thompson, 1983; Thorton, 1985). So why is it then that persons going through the divorce process feel as though they are social deviants? Unfortunately that which is frequent is not necessarily considered "normal" so that even though it appears that reported disapproval of divorce has declined, the absence of the socially negative meaning does not necessarily indicate that it is acceptable to be divorced (Atwood & Genovese, 1993). In the United States persons practicing alternative lifestyles are still frequently frowned upon and are subject to stigmatization so that divorced persons are still often defined (and see themselves) as participating in a lifestyle that is less than ideal (Atwood, 1992, p. 206). If we continue to accept the concept that those who do not achieve the ideal are failures, then we are a society of failures. It is these very same social definitions that create the legacies of "broken homes" and "broken dreams"—responding to social definitions that no longer (probably never did) reflect the world.

RESEARCH ON DIVORCE

With the above statistics in mind indicating the prevalence of divorced families in United States society, it would seem that there would exist a wealth of research in the area of divorced families. Unfortunately this is not the case. The quality of research on the divorced family is poor in that most studies looked at minor aspects of divorce; researchers failed to examine interpersonal relationships or the range of emotional experiences of family members; there have been few longitudinal studies of single parent families in formation; the normal processes of families in transition have not really been defined; the longitudinal studies that do exist did not measure large representative samples before and after changes in family configuration; several statistical studies based conclusions on unrepresentative or small sample sizes (for example, see Lee & Hett, 1990) or arguable quantitative methods; there has been inadequate attention given to the process variables that may mediate the effects of family configuration, leading Emery (1988) and Marsh (1990) to conclude that there are serious methodological problems in the study of family configuration effects that have not been adequately addressed. Baydar (1988) furthered this notion by suggesting that researchers have failed to confirm large negative effects of divorce on children.

Perhaps, though, the most blatant problem is that most divorced family research is based on comparisons with intact first families. Family researchers have generally been consistent with society's negative views, using a problem- or deficit-oriented approach to studying the single parent family (Coleman, Ganong, & Gingrich, 1985; Duncan & Brown, 1992; Hoffman, 1991). Inherent in this type of research approach is the assumption that the intact nuclear family is the normal family and anything outside this range is less than or negative. This creates the construction for researchers to perceive single parent families within a problem-oriented framework or within a deficit model, thereby focusing on documenting the difficulties of the divorced family. As Gilligan (1984) states, "There is a tendency to construct a single scale of measurement . . ." (p. 4). According to Fassel (1991) the tendency to compare these two groups results in dualistic thinking. She suggests that there are both functional and dysfunctional families in both divorced and intact families and indicates that comparing children from intact and broken homes results in an oversimplification of a complex reality.

As for the children living in divorced families, otherwise known as "the children of divorce," perhaps the most frequent and unfortunate problem is that many of the studies on the effects of divorce on children relied upon the ratings of teachers. Guttman (1988) reported that bias by teachers and school psychologists, participants in many studies, reflects a low reliability. Since these school personnel not only participate in evaluations of children but also read and utilize the studies for educational purposes, their observations are seriously questionable (see also Blechman, 1982). To further test their hypothesis, Guttman (1988) studied moral behaviors in children of single parent and two-parent households and concluded that differences could be found only on teacher ratings. A very important question arises in light of this discussion. Does teacher bias, in fact, cause the finding of lower student functioning for children of divorce?

In 1978, Santrock and Tracy showed a 20-minute video to 30 teachers. The subject was an 8-year-old boy. When teachers were told that the child was from a divorced family background, they rated him lower on happiness, emotional adjustment, and the ability to cope with stress. This led Guttman to conduct a further study. Teachers were asked to view a film of a 9-year-old child from Tel Aviv. The results concluded that children were judged less favorably if the rater was told that the child was from a divorced family. In a later study, Guttmann and Broudo (1989) showed that teachers rated the identical behaviors of fictitious "cases" negatively when they were told the children were from single parent or remarried families. Similarly, Atwood and Genovese (1993) found that when school counseling, teachers, and marriage and family counseling graduate students were asked to rate identical behaviors of fictitious children from two-parent and one-parent households, they consistently rated identified behaviors lower in children from one-parent households. This small study and the research cited above indicate that mental health professionals need to examine their own assumptions about this type of family system. As Fassel (1991) suggests, we need to question the manner in which research in the area of divorce reflects the bias of society in favor of the intact family. She feels that this research carries the implication that children of divorce are flawed, but this is not necessarily true.

Ignoring the strengths of the single-parent family and focusing on the problems that these families experience may create a negative self-fulfilling prophesy. Since there is such an emphasis on, resulting in the documentation of, the problems, divorced families themselves may come to accept that problems are normal and to be expected. In fact family researchers may be partly responsible for behavioral confirmation—the phenomenon in which beliefs about a group of people (in this case, constructions about divorced families) may influence their behaviors (Snyder & Swan, 1978). "Seek and ye shall find." W. I. Thomas believed that if men define situations as real, real consequences are incurred (Thomas & Thomas, 1928). When a person believes something is true, she or he is likely to act as though it is true, and the action then further confirms the belief. Beliefs can facilitate solutions to problems or impede them. They can create problems where none exist or create solutions that create more problems (Watzlawick, Weakland, & Fisch, 1974). The identification of strengths in the divorced family does not exist in the literature. We do not know what makes divorced families work when they do.

The Newer Research on Divorce Outcomes

Deficit models of divorce present a pathological picture citing prominent studies proclaiming that where divorce is deviant and its effects deleterious. For examples of the deficit model, please see Dublin (1992) and Sable (1992). Additional research indicates that there can be healthy reactions to and because of divorce, indicating that parental separation, in and of itself, need not be a factor in emotional disorder (Kelly, 1988; Watts & Watts, 1991), leading researchers to increasingly conclude that many other variables may be factors in creating functional and well-adjusted children, despite or because of the divorce process (Baydar, 1988).

The following studies are representative of the more recent research on children of divorce. They are in no way meant to discount the uncomfortable feelings that some children experience as a result of divorce; they are presented to inform the reader that there is a "flip side to the coin" crucial to examine. For example, Weiss (1979) has studied the experience of growing up in single parent households and found that one-parent families are able to forgo traditional hierarchical power structures within the home, with children taking on greater responsibility for the household, possibly promoting maturity and responsibility. He believes that single-parent households are characterized by greater closeness between the parent and the child. Emery and O'Leary (1984) noted that divorced families can tap into the experiences of the transitional situation and strengthen a child's ability to cope and be independent. In a review of studies between 1970 and 1980, Cashion (1982) concluded that children in single-parent households are likely to have good emotional adjustment, good self-esteem and school success, and as much school success as children from two-parent families, when socioeconomic factors are controlled. This concurs with Hutchinson and Hirsch's suggestion, as cited in Everett (1989), that children of divorce can be good decision makers, and that they are stronger and more mature as an outgrowth of divorce. This positive research promotes a "reframing approach" which focuses on seeing children of divorce as healthy and successful. These researchers believe that it is significant that mental health professionals and educators hold misleading and at times careless assumptions that children of divorce often display behavioral changes and perform lower academically. They prefer to see divorce-resultant symptomology as a potentiality rather than an inevitability (see also Hutchinson, Valutis, Brown, & White [1988] and Warren, Illgen, Grew, Konac, & Amara [1985] who found no statistical differences in children from intact and single parent homes). They also cite that adolescents living in single-parent families are characterized by greater maturity, feelings of efficacy, and an internal locus of control (see also Guidubaldi & Perry, 1985; Kalter, Alpern, Spence, & Plunkett, 1984; Wallerstein & Kelly, 1974; Weiss, 1979).

In a landmark study examining the impact of marital status of parents on the academic performance of children on the Iowa Test of Basic Skills, Beer (1989) found no significant impact. In a study of the academic achievement of over 4,000 Canadian high school students from two parent and one parent households, Watts and Watts (1991) found that, of 11 variables most affecting student achievement, ability and educational aspirations of the student have the largest direct effect on student academic achievement, whereas the effect of family configurations was negligible. McCombs and Forehand (1989) studied low, medium and high-achieving adolescents in an attempt to identify family factors that could mediate the "negative" influence of divorce on school achievement noted in earlier studies and found that school performance after the divorce is far from uniform, and is possibly caused by other more complex factors than the divorce itself. Garber (1991) examined the long-term effects of family structure and conflict at home on the self-esteem of students and found that inter-parental conflict may have long-term effects on general and social self-esteem of young adults, while family structure does not. See also Albert, 1971; Besidine, 1968; Cornelius and Yawkey, 1986; Guidubaldi and Perry, 1985; and Wallerstein and Kelly, 1980. Wood and Lewis (1990) caution teachers to beware of basing their judgment of student's behavior or school performance on their assumptions about the home life of the child, in particular, status as a member of a single-parent family.

Mulholland, Watt, Philpatt, and Sarlin (1991) examined psychologi-cal resilience and vulnerability in 96 middle school students from a suburban school district. Their research indicated that nationally formed tests of scholastic aptitudes and other factors such as absence from school showed no significant difference when regressed from family configuration. Despite a similar background (i.e., marital dissolution), a minority of children of divorce showed vulnerability in the pattern of academic achievement over time, while the majority demonstrated academic careers similar to the controls. The authors state further that research suggests that divorce by itself is not detrimental to children's academic performance. The term *resiliency* is also discussed in an arti-cle by Hetherington, Stanley-Hagan, and Anderson, (1989) who believe that some children exhibit remarkable resiliency that in the long term may actually be enhanced by coping with these transitions; others suf-fer sustained developmental delays or disruptions.

The literature also points to longitudinal studies dealing with perfor-mance and children of divorce. A 5-year study (Kaye, 1989) involving 457 children (50% from two-parent homes) revealed that although achievement scores dropped in the months after divorce, the overall grades did not seem to be adversely affected. Using data from the National Centre for Educational Statistics, Marsh (1990) tracked a large repre-sentative sample of high-school-aged students. Marsh's article states that family configuration had remarkably little effect on student growth. Even Wallerstein (1984), known for reporting on the deleterious effects of divorce on children, reported that after 5 years of a longitudinal study of children of divorce who were brought for therapy, about 34% of the children studied were happy and thriving. Schwebel, Moreland, Steinkohl, Lentz, and Stewart (1982) believe that parental divorce forces children to engage in personal adjustment. According to a study by Kurdek and Siesky (1980), children of divorced families are signifi-cantly more androgynous than children of intact families, who tend to be traditionally sex typed (Demo & Acock, 1988; see also MacKinnon, Stoneman & Brody, 1984). The shedding of restrictive sex role orien-tation could be a positive growth factor, opening new doors for the newly single and their children.

In a recent review of the literature, Veevers (1991) has identified 17 factors that may contribute to growth, rather than trauma, as an out-come of divorce. Her review of other studies shows that divorced per-sons may experience divorce on a continuum from relatively painless to causing relief. She believes that given the current statistics on divorce in our society, the social stigma and psychological stain associated with divorce as a deviant activity should no longer apply. Antithetical to the pathogenic model is the contention that divorce per se need not be a trauma, but may be a "stren," a strengthening experience. She points out that the extreme trauma felt by some divorcing persons does not belie the fact that for others the experience is merely a short-lived unpleasantness, and for some, it is actually defined in positive terms.

The research summarized above represent but a few of the studies indicating that divorce per se may not have negative effects on children and that marriage and family therapists, educators, psychologists, social workers, and other mental health professionals must not carelessly assume that it does. There is positive evidence cited in clinical, empirical, and theoretical studies which suggest that children of divorce often experience outcomes less or no more difficult than do children from two-parent structures. As Heatherington et al. (1989) point out, "When I first began to study children in divorced families, I had a pathogenic model of divorce. However, after more than two decades of research on marital transitions, depending on the characteristics of the child, available resources, subsequent life experiences, and especially interpersonal relationships, children in the long run may be survivors, losers, or winners of the parents' divorce or remarriage" (p. 12).

These studies are in contrast to the monolithic view that people who experience parental divorce are universally maladjusted. It is becoming increasingly clear that we must stop making these sweeping generalizations. A rethinking of the social value system that fuels the thought that divorce is bad and shameful should begin. For example, Thiriot and Buckner (1991) found that the custodial parent's own subjective sense of well being was the strongest single predictor of divorce adjustment. They point out that parents who feel good about themselves also feel good about their parenting, and conveyed their feelings to the child. Certain types of parental behavior foster favorable outcomes in children following divorce. Kaslow and Hyatt (1981) state that parents who cope well model for their children how to deal with strained interpersonal relationships and major life crises and provide vicarious experience that may increase children's feelings of self-efficacy. Research findings imply that the better adjusted the parents are to the divorce, the better adjusted the children. It is important to take these newer findings into account when we see individuals who are getting a divorce.

PSYCHOLOGICAL ASPECTS OF DIVORCE

Although the chain of events leading to marriage and/or an intimate relationship is varied, most people do marry with the hope and expectation that the marriage will last. The emotional reactions to divorce are equally varied. As stated earlier, ideas about divorce are socially constructed, with marriage and the two-parent family socially sanctioned as the ideal family form. For some, divorce can represent the loss of a "forever" dream and may represent other losses as well: one's spouse, the extended family of the spouse, sometimes one's children, possibly a lifestyle, often the security of familiarity, and perhaps most importantly, part of one's identity. Changing status from being married to being single can present varied difficulties in emotional adjustments for the person whose self-definition was primarily in terms of coupled status.

Psychological Stages

It usually takes 2 to 3 years to form a strong attachment to a person and for some persons, if separation occurs after this time, it involves separation shock for the individual. It is a myth for people to assume that couples who are married 30 years suffer more than couples who are married for 7 years. In each case, if the individuals are going to suffer separation shock they will do so regardless of the time spent in the couple relationship. The major difference, perhaps, is couples who are married longer may be more entwined in relationships with external systems. More of their couple life has extended outside the immediate marriage, leading to possibly more difficulty in extricating themselves from the network after divorce. Although stages of divorce resolution are presented, it is important to keep in mind that not everyone passes through these stages and not everyone passes through them in this order. They are presented simply to describe the processes that some divorcing persons experience in American society.

In other societies, depending on the social definitions of divorce, reactions may be different. For example, Benedict (1934) found that among the Zuni people of the northwest have a casual view of marriage and divorce. If the couple are not happy together and thinking of separating, the wife will serve at a ceremonial feast. This symbolizes that she is looking for a new mate. After the woman finds a new husband, she gathers together her old husband's possessions and places them outside the door. When the husband comes home in the evening, he sees the little bundle, picks it up and cries, and returns to his mother's house. It is more dignified for a man to live with a wife than in his mother's house and so the statuses are redefined. The ex-husband's family weep together and are regarded by the tribe as unfortunate, but this living arrangement is considered ordinary and there is little display of emotion. Rarely is there any display of anger and/or jealousy. In the Doboans, a tribe off the southern shore of eastern New Guinea, the reason for divorce is the failure of the yam garden. The husband and the wife each have their own yam garden; It is their ultimate pride and possession. Each plants his or her own yam garden with seeds from their respective families of origin. There is no sharing of seeds. These seeds are made to grow by magical incantations and rites that are inherited from each of the couple's blood line. Thus a failed garden is seen as a worthless heritage.

As is evident by examining the cross-cultural reactions to divorce, social definitions and the resultant psychological reactions are socially created and defined. What marriage and divorce means in any given society is created by that society. In the United States, divorce is viewed as failure by many individuals and as a result divorced people and children often feel less valued than their married counterparts. Many divorced persons experience some of the following emotions.

Stage I: Denial

Although the reactions of the divorce process are varied, for some individuals going through it, there is a typical and predictable series of psychological stages to pass through. It is helpful to be aware of these stages in order to understand persons in this sociopsychological process. For purposes of clarity, the four stages are labeled denial, conflict, ambivalence and acceptance.

SEPARATION SHOCK. Stage I of the emotional divorcing process, denial, is mainly manifested in some individuals by separation shock. During separation shock, the individual may experience relief, numbness, or panic. Relief is often felt when the divorce has been a extended process. The most typical reaction to separation is fear of abandonment. The emotional response to this fear is often apprehensiveness and anxiety.

> Linda, a 32-year-old housewife, separated from her husband of 8 years because of constant arguing. For the most part, she was comfortable with

her decision. However, she said that she felt shaky, not on solid ground almost once a week. During these times, she would doubt her decision to divorce, feeling that she had made a mistake. Often, she would go to bed, feeling anxious and upset, stay there for days, and leave the care of her children to her mother. Eventually, she would feel a little better and, after a few days, would get up and function as usual. She would be fine for a while; however, after a few weeks, the pattern would repeat.

These anxious feelings may be accompanied by disturbances of sleep or appetite patterns. If there are increases in food intake and decreases in number of hours spent sleeping, the person usually experiences anxiety. Decreases in food intake and increases in time spent sleeping may be related to depression. In any case, both symptoms are indications of separation shock. Often, during this time, individuals will report that they are unable to concentrate on work or carry on conversations with people. They may experience sudden outbursts of tears or anger.

Other people report that they often lose control of their anger and for what later seems to them to be an insignificant reason, explode into sudden flashes of rage. For many individuals, though, feelings of numbness or the absence of feelings are experienced. Numbness can be a way of muting or denying feelings which, if experienced, might be too overwhelming for the individual to handle.

When Linda felt shaky and went to bed, if asked how she felt, she would reply, "I feel nothing. The world feels numb. I don't love anyone or hate anyone. I just don't feel anything." In this case, Linda is overwhelmed by the reality of the situation and responds with denial, temporarily turning off her psychological system.

Often during this stage, the person vacillates between emotions— feeling first anxious, then angry, and then numb. For many persons, these emotions are often combined with feelings of optimism about their new life. This stage of separation shock can last anywhere between a few days to several months.

THE LEAVER AND THE LEFT. Often one partner desires the divorce more so than the other. There are typical reactions to the impending divorce depending upon whether or not one initiates the divorce. For example, the person who leaves is often burdened with enormous amounts of guilt and self-blame; whereas, the remaining person potentially feels more anger, hurt, self-pity and condemnation of other. The person who requests the divorce may fear being labeled a deserter, whereas the person who is left may feel embarrassment and a fear of being labeled a loser. Both individuals suffer. The partner left by the other may feel anger or pity or may feel blamed by the other. The process of divorce can have effects far greater than simply the dissolution of an unworkable marriage or relationship. Even when the marriage ends because one of the partners has fallen in love with someone else, there can be profound pain in the partner who asks for the divorce.

In sum, for some persons, Stage I emotionality involves coming to grips with the fact that the marriage is ending. The emotional task of the person at this stage of the divorcing process is to accept the reality of the separation.

> Linda requested the divorce. The arguing in the marriage had nearly escalated to physical violence. Steve, her husband, often came home at 2 or 3 AM in the morning. This would enrage Linda. On these nights, she would wait up for him and question him extensively as to his whereabouts because she had correctly inferred that he was having an affair. Then, she would feel guilty about arguing and accusing him. During and after the divorce she felt tremendous guilt over depriving him of his family and hurting him.

Stage II: Anger and Conflict

ANGER.   Once Stage I is resolved, the divorcing person may enter into Stage II, anger and conflict. Shortly after separation shock, the individual may begin to experience a multitude of emotions, one occurring right after the other. One minute the person may feel perfectly comfortable with the new lifestyle and a minute later they may find themselves in tears, reminiscing about the former spouse. Then, remembering a negative event or an argument, rage may surface.

> After being in therapy for about 6 months, Linda started to feel good about herself. She had taken up racketball, she had lost 10 pounds, and she had started a part-time job. She reported to the therapist that for the first time since she got married, she was focusing on herself—her own needs, her own wants and desires. She was learning who she was as a person. Before she had always focused on Steven's needs, trying to anticipate them to avoid conflict. These feelings of well-being lasted about 2 weeks; then Linda came to therapy reporting that she didn't know what

she was doing; she had made a mistake; "being married and miserable was better than not being married at all." Her feelings had "fooled" her again: Just when she thought she was doing better, she came crashing down.

FEELINGS OF UNPREDICTABILITY AND DISORGANIZATION.   For many people who experience these reactions, the only predictable thing in this stage is the unpredictability of feelings. Feelings of disorganization may also occur. One day there may be a sense that the entire world has turned upside down; the next day persons may feel perfectly comfortable with their new-found freedom. Volatile, explosive emotions may unexpectedly surface during this time. Individuals in this stage typically feel that they may fall apart at any time. Feelings of guilt and anger become strong. Persons may feel enraged at their spouse and then, a few hours later, feel ashamed and guilty about their angry feelings. They may experience periods of anger at themselves and their spouses for having failed at their marriage or for their current lonely situation. This stage is typified by conflicting emotions: At any given time the individual cannot predict which feeling he or she will be experiencing.

GUILT.   While swayed by these feelings, a divorced person may also ponder the wisdom of the divorce; they may feel as though they made a mistake. At times, there may be feelings of regret. These feelings usually come in waves and they may catch the person off guard.

SCANNING.   Also during this second stage of the divorcing period, the individual may do what is called "scanning" (Krantzler, 1975). Scanning persons will reminisce about what went wrong with their marriage, who was to blame, what their own role was in the failure. They also relive the best times in the marriage and mourn the loss of the more intimate aspects. Scanning, in many ways, may be a way of preserving the attachment bonds; it may also provide much constructive insight to individuals about their own constructive and destructive patterns in relationships. In this sense it could be a valuable learning experience.

REGRET AND LOSS.   The review process may go on for months and may contribute to the mood swings the divorcing person experiences. Each memory and each new awareness causes the person to feel different emotions. During this stage of emotional upheaval, for some persons, a sense of loss and loneliness may develop. This process, although emotionally uncomfortable, enables individuals to release pent-up feelings which might otherwise cause them much distress at later points in their lives.

LONELINESS. Loneliness in this phase manifests itself in many ways. Some individuals may sit in front of the TV set for hours. Gradually, they may withdraw from social contacts. Others may experience a more active type of loneliness. Instead of sitting at home, they frequent old restaurants, pass by their spouse's homes or go from one singles bar to another, desperately looking for solace from their loneliness. During this time also, any negative feelings and emotions the person experienced as a child, such as separation anxiety, low self-esteem or feelings of worthlessness, may resurface, causing the individual much distress.

EUPHORIA. Although individuals may typically experience strong emotional swings, at times they may experience periods of euphoria. Hunt and Hunt (1977) found that there was a small percentage of individuals in their sample who, after separation, felt a sense of relief, increased personal freedom, and newly gained competence. There was also a reinvestment of emotional energy into themselves which had been previously directed toward the marriage. These euphoric feelings tend to appear suddenly and for no apparent reason, causing the person to feel "on top of the world." These happy feelings may last for days or weeks or forever.

THE EMOTIONAL SEESAW OR THE ROLLER COASTER. The danger during this phase is that the person may think that the worst is over only to suddenly plunge into the depths of depression. Unfortunately, it is usually during this time when the emotions are changing so rapidly that the person is required to deal with lawyers and make major decisions. In sum, for people going through Stage II ride an emotional see-saw, characterized mainly by psychological conflict. The emotional task of individuals at this stage is to achieve a realistic definition of what their marriage represented, what their role was in its maintenance, and what their responsibility was for its failure.

Stage III: Identity Work

Stage III, ambivalence, involves changes in the person's identity. In many ways, this is the most psychologically stressful aspect of the divorce process. Being married is a primary source of self-identity. The two individuals enter the relationship with two separate identities and then co-construct a coupled identity defining who they are and where and how they fit into the world. They create social definitions which are consonant with the social definition of marriage. When their relationship ends, they may feel confused and fearful, as though they no longer have a script telling them how to behave. Often during this time period, they may try on different identities, attempting to find one that is comfortable for them. At this time, the divorcing person faces a major change in self-perception. Instead of a husband and father, a man may find himself living in a small apartment seeing his children every other weekend. Instead of a wife and homemaker, a woman may find herself labeled as a "divorcee," a term that sometimes means promiscuous to the uninformed person.

Sociologist W. I. Thomas believed that if men define situations as real, they are real in their consequences. When a person believes something is true, she or he is likely to act as though it is true, and the action then further confirms the belief. Beliefs can facilitate solutions to problems or impede them. They can create problems where none exist and where the solutions then create more problems. Often divorcing persons begin to believe the stereotypes, which could result in behaviors or affective states which might otherwise might not have been present. This is especially relevant with regard to children when they believe that they cannot get good grades because they are children of divorce or that they are from a dysfunctional family because they live in a one-parent household.

Sometimes, during this period, people go through a second adolescence. As in the first adolescence, persons may become very concerned about how they look, how they sound. They may buy new clothes or a new car. Many of the struggles of the teen years may reappear and persons may find themselves trying to decide how to handle sexual advances or when to kiss a date good night. Sexual experimentation may occur as the individual makes attempts to explore their new sexuality outside of the marital situation.

The emotional task for someone at this stage is to make the psychological transition from being married to being single again. This constitutes an identity transformation which for many is psychologically the most difficult and stressful undertaking of the divorcing process.

Stage IV: Acceptance

PEACE AND CONTENTMENT.   Finally (the time varies for individuals from months to over a year), the person enters Stage IV. In this stage individuals typically feel a sense of relief and acceptance about their situation (Krantzler, 1975). After a while individuals start to experience a new sense of strength and accomplishment. For the most part, in this stage, they feel quite content with their lifestyle and no longer dwell on the past. They now have a new sense of awareness and knowledge of their own needs.

If, after months of separation, a sense of acceptance of the past is not developing, the person may seek professional help. Hunt and Hunt (1977) and Weiss (1975) feel that the most painful aspects of divorce mourning peak within the first several months of a divorce and then tend to level off by the end of the first year. They believe that the complete emotional resolution of a divorce occurs when the spouses are no longer significantly influenced by the previously described reactions. This, they believe, usually takes about 2 years.

MOVING ON.   Although many of the feelings triggered by divorce are painful and uncomfortable, they ultimately lead toward resolving the loss so that, if the individual desires, he or she will be emotionally able to reestablish an intimate relationship.

> Linda typifies feelings experienced while going through these emotional stages. As stated earlier, originally, she wanted the divorce. She was tired of fighting and felt that she wanted to find a loving relationship. Most days she felt this way. Occasionally, however, she would remember the good times, a party they went to together, a funny episode which occurred with one of the children.

> Sometimes when her husband came to pick up the children, she would feel a resurgence of tenderness. A moment later, she would experience the rage she felt when he would stay late at work after promising he would be home early. Then she would feel certain of her decision once again. The emotions experienced during a few seconds, however, can be extreme. When she felt tender toward him, she also felt guilty about having deserted him. The emotional swings would leave her exhausted, so she would spend the next few days in bed.

In therapy, Linda's feelings eventually began to stabilize. Her feelings of well-being began to take precedence over her feelings of anxiety and anger. She was able to pursue her own interests and put her former spouse and former marriage in a comfortable perspective. She started to date someone she liked and, although she felt he was not the "right" one, she was content in her situation.

Socially Single Again

While the language used in this and other chapters refer to the divorcing couple, the social and psychological reactions reported refer to any couple who had an intimate relationship—whether married or not. There are many social stereotypes of the divorced or separated person. Traditionally, the divorced male or female was seen as a social loser, sitting alone in his or her apartment with four or five cats and newspapers piled to the ceiling. This stereotype invokes the image of the sad, depressed, psychologically devastated victim of divorce, struggling over the trauma of this life change, who experiences devastating problems in his or her interpersonal and sexual relationships.

Social Stereotypes

Today, the image of the single person has changed. Along with the lonely loser image, the contemporary divorced single is now typically viewed as a young, swinging, upwardly mobile career person without a worry in the world and with the sexual fantasies of many as his or her reality. There is the "gay divorcee" image, the person, who, feeling released from the bonds and burdens of marriage, then supposedly lives amidst constant parties and entertainment, plentiful sex (before AIDS), and general abandonment in sexual and other areas of life. Of course, none of these stereotypes is completely accurate, but they probably contain elements of truth applicable to many people's adjustment to divorce or separation. Becoming single again for most people generally falls somewhere between these extreme stereotypes.

> Lois, a 39-year-old social worker, was married for 15 years. She separated from her husband when she learned that he was involved in a long-term extramarital relationship. Now, 5 years later, she lives in a condominium on the beach, realizing a long-time dream. For the most part, she is happy with her life. She is currently dating someone she likes but reports that there are many times when she feels lonely and misses the sharing and intimacy of married life.

Advantages and Disadvantages
of Being Single

As with almost everything else, individuals report both desirable and undesirable aspects of singlehood. On the one hand, for some, it may offer independence which they feel is rarely achieved in marital relationships. Singlehood also offers time alone when one wants it. It provides the opportunity to examine individual needs and desires, a concern of many young people today. For individuals who value privacy and time alone, singlehood can be defined as a very positive lifestyle. It may be easier to gain self-knowledge in the absence of a partner who may become the primary focus of self-definition. It also offers variety in terms of both interpersonal and sexual relationships. Some people believe that only singles can truly experience the human diversity in interpersonal sexual relationships, an opportunity that many people find rewarding in terms of the uniqueness of each person and each relationship. As Hayes (1993) learned in his national study of divorced women over the age of 40, the majority were quite content in their divorced lifestyle and reported that they rejected proposals of marriage.

Time Alone versus Loneliness

On the other hand, many people report disadvantages to being single. Some people define being single as lonely rather than as being alone. Perhaps more important for the average single person, there are many times when the price paid for independence and time spent alone is having no one who is intimate or close with whom to share day-to-day living. Individuals report that little things may also be problematic. Such necessary life events as errands during the day, doing laundry, washing the car, and the like must be accomplished alone.

Social and Emotional Adjustments
to Being Single

Changing status from married to single may involve varied difficulties in emotional adjustment. For many, there are also social adjustments that must be made. Many individuals have established friendships and social relationships as couples rather than as individuals. The divorcing individual may feel awkward being alone or with others who are in couples. At the same time, other couples may not be comfortable including single persons in their activities. Often, then, a sense of security or belonging that accompanies being part of a couple is replaced with sudden autonomy that may be uncomfortable for many individuals.

> Mel, a 54-year-old business executive, divorced his wife, Ellen, of 25 years, because he wanted to experience other women. Initially feeling secure with his support network of friends whom they both had known for many years, he didn't feel lonely. Over time, however, his friends tended to side with Ellen, and Mel became increasingly uncomfortable in their presence. So he stopped seeing them. Eventually, he began to experience depression—feeling alone and abandoned by his friends. After 2 years of therapy, Mel began to establish a support network of his own, consisting mainly of persons who were single again like himself.

New Social Contacts

Divorcing individuals often want to establish new social contacts which include new groups of single people. Many cities have organizations where single people can meet and form new friendships. However, for many individuals, giving up old relationships and seeking out new friendships can be a frightening experience.

Changes in Social Roles

Divorced men and women also undergo changes in social role, from wife or husband (and thus part of a couple) to an unattached person for whom society has established no definite role or expectations. For this reason, recently divorced people may often feel anxious and rootless. They may watch helplessly as the friends who saw them as half of a couple drift away. These social definitions, expectations and assumptions about marriage and divorce which delineate the appropriate contexts for sociosexual behavior create the setting within which individuals experience the many psychological reactions to the divorcing process.

While many individuals feel relief during and after the divorce, many others experience a wide range of discomfort at the ending of their marriage. Sometimes those who experience extreme amounts of discomfort do not go through the stages and simply experience resolution. Some individuals get stuck. Although most people would benefit from therapy while going through this major change, those who get stuck would especially find therapy most useful.

Terry, an attractive 57-year-old bookkeeper, couldn't accept the idea that her husband had left her to move in with his young, pretty secretary. After her husband had moved out, Terry withdrew from all her friends and eventually they stopped calling her. She spent all her evenings at home, alone and preoccupied with thoughts of her ex-husband and his girlfriend. All she could think about was the two of them together.

Becoming obsessed with these thoughts, she was determined to discover what they were doing in their daily lives. She decided to set her alarm clock for 2 AM, at which time she awakened, dressed, and drove to their home. She snuck out of her car, stole their garbage, took it home, and examined it on her kitchen table. In therapy, she exclaimed to her therapist, "You'd be surprised how much you could learn from people's garbage. I know when they're sick, what they eat for dinner, when she has her period!" After 2 years of therapy, Terry was able to develop her own support structure, become involved in meaningful activities, and begin dating. Eventually, she gave up the possibility of a reunion with her ex-husband.

Under most circumstances, separation and divorce represent a life-cycle transition. Even in mutually agreed upon, friendly terminations of a marital situation, many significant lifestyle changes occur. The newly single person often faces adjustments in social and sexual relationships, financial arrangements, living arrangements and, if applicable, in parenting roles. Many divorces, however, do not occur under the best of circumstances; typically, divorces are not logical or rational agreements. Rather, they tend to be emotional or irrational conflicts full of bitter contention. During this time, an individual's self-confidence may be shattered because the individual believes he or she has failed at the relationship or marriage. Extensive changes such as these, even if accompanied by the relief of ending an undesirable situation, can cause stress. But ultimately the person emerges from the stress challenged by the experience and ready to go forth in their new life.

Sexually Single Again

While divorced women sometimes have been falsely depicted as lonely and sexually deprived, divorced men have been incorrectly portrayed as having full sex lives with scores of partners.

Linda's postseparation experience portrayed the ambivalent feelings women often have at this time. Initially, when she first began dating, she was unsure of herself. She didn't know if men would find her attractive; she thought she was too fat; and she felt she didn't know how to behave. She had never had sex with anyone but her husband and felt strange about the prospect of "being with" another man. She felt so unsure that after her first date, she asked her therapist if perhaps she "should" have slept with him because he had bought her dinner. She was insecure in her role as newly single person. She had entered marriage at a young age and now many years later she felt cast out into the "singles scene" unprepared.

Generally, it appears that immediately following a divorce some divorced men and women engage in a short period of increased sexual experimentation but, in most cases, they soon settle down to a more stable sexual style within the context of a longer term relationship. While the onset of AIDS has eliminated some of the carefree sexual behavior of the seventies and early eighties and more and more single-again persons are hesitant about entering into sexual relationships, there still are indications that following a dissolved relationship, some persons enter into a short period of sexual experimentation.

In some situations, increased sexual activity is indicative of less emotional attachment and commitment to sexual relationships. Some divorced persons report confusion about and difficulty with suddenly finding themselves required to date and engage in various types of courtship behavior after years of being in a monogamous situation. They say that they often did not know the current appropriate behavior in dating situations, frequently felt insecure with members of the opposite sex, and were often unsure of themselves, feeling value conflicts about their actions. It was not unusual for men to have erectile dysfunction while attempting intercourse with new partners whom they perceived as being sexually more demanding and aggressive than their former wives.

After divorce it appears that most individuals are too weary for another involvement. They may feel lonely, rejected and sexually unsatisfied. A typical initial reaction, although occurring less frequently since the AIDS epidemic, is to have casual and friendly sexual relationships with little commitment. These new relationships can serve the important psychological function of healing a wounded ego and thereby may encourage people to involve themselves in an intimate relationship again. And, for some, they can even result in more satisfying sexual expression.

Sex and Single Parents

Many divorced individuals are single parents. If there are children involved, even if an individual is not awarded custody there are still times when he or she is primary caretaker. Census experts estimate that about 50% of children born in 1985 will live with one parent for at least a while before they are eighteen. In 1980, 20% of children under the age of 18 lived with only one parent. About 25.7% of all living arrangements including a child under 18 are with the mother only, with about 1.6% of living arrangements are living with a custodial father (in Hanson & Sporkowski, 1986).

The Single Mother

Since mothers are more likely to be given custody of their children in cases of separation and divorce, and since mothers are more likely to be widowed, it is not surprising that most children in single parent homes live with their mothers. Over eight million children in this country live with their mothers alone, while 800,000 live with their fathers.

FINANCES. Money is an especially critical problem for single parents. One-parent families in general have considerably lower income than two-parent families and a great many of their problems are often tied to economics. Not surprisingly, single working mothers make less than half of what single fathers make and since childcare must often be arranged and paid for, single motherhood is constantly fraught with financial worries. It is no wonder that some writers speak of the "feminization of poverty." Because of these very real economic pressures, the single mother may find it difficult to attend social events without her children. She may be unable to buy new clothing or she may not have extra money for a babysitter. In some cases she might not even have money for food. These factors may restrict the likelihood of single parent mothers' entering dating situations. She may not only not have funds for babysitters or appropriate clothing, she may also feel uncomfortable about bringing new men to her home to meet her children.

The Single Father

Relatively few (about 10%) one-parent families are headed by men. Usually though, male-headed households arise because the mother has died. In these cases, the widower experiences many of the same psychological and emotional problems faced by widowed mothers such as loneliness, sorrow, bitterness, and a sense of being overwhelmed by the full responsibility of childcare. Motherless families tend to have fewer economic problems than fatherless families. Using traditional definitions, if many single mothers are at least initially unprepared for the work role, many single fathers are unprepared for childcare responsibilities and home management tasks such as shopping, cooking, doing laundry and cleaning house—tasks formerly done by their wives. Some men do these chores themselves, while others rely on relatives or friends for help or hire outside workers.

The Parental Child

Where there are teenage daughters, they are sometimes put in the role of "little mothers" or the "parental child" and given considerable responsibility for the house and the younger siblings (George and Wilding, 1972). In the case of the male parental child, he may become the "little man of the house." There is often resentment on the part of this child. He or she is unable to enjoy childhood activities and often feels overburdened by responsibility for the emotional well-being of the parent. Other children in the family system may feel resentment toward the parental child, believing that he or she holds a special favored position in the parent's eyes. The father or mother may come to rely on the company of this child and in some cases, their relationship may prevent the parent from seeking out appropriate social partners of the opposite sex.

> Ron is a 47-year-old construction worker. Ron's wife left him with two children, a boy and a girl, ages 13 and 10. Initially, he was lost, unfamiliar with their physical and emotional needs. He was unfamiliar with housekeeping and gradually his 10-year-old daughter began to take on more and more responsibility. As a result, her grades began to drop at school and she hardly ever went out with her friends. She didn't have time. Her teacher called Ron one day to tell him his daughter was sad and depressed.
>
> As for Ron, all his extra time was spent with the children. He planned weekend activities with them, took them on vacations, and tried to monitor their lives. When he visited relatives, all he spoke about was his involvement with them. Gradually, his friends dwindled, and his adult activities virtually ceased. Two years later, both he and his daughter went to therapy for depression.

With the aid of a therapist, Ron eventually hired a cleaning person to manage the children and the household tasks. He also began joining several singles clubs. By hiring a housekeeper, his daughter was released from her parental-child role and she too began playing with her friends. Her grades began to increase

Meeting sexual and intimacy needs while taking care of children without a partner is sometimes fraught with problems of privacy, energy, and time. In an interview study with 38 single parents, Greenberg (1979) reported that most of her sample believed that their sexual activity should not be known to their children. The double standard was evident, since more men than women accepted sex among single parents even if it were apparent to their children. In a study of 127 separated or divorced fathers with full or joint custody of their children, Rosenthal and Kesshet (1979a) found that most of their serious dating relationships were with younger, childless women. When the father dated a new woman and stayed overnight, it was more typically at her home rather than his. The women involved in the sample reported that they felt more comfortable and more romantic in their own homes or apartments. They reported that they did not have to worry about their date's children in their own homes. If after a while a serious relationship developed, then a sense of a new couple emerged.

Eventually, 75% of the single fathers asked their new partners to sleep over, (Rosenthal and Keshet, 1979b) although they reported that it was initially very difficult for them to do. Single fathers also reported that they were generally uncomfortable about having a girlfriend spend the night when the children were present. They reported that they worried that their children might feel that sex should be totally uncommitted and free. This idea was uncomfortable for them (Rosenthal and Keshet, 1979b).

It may be especially important for the single father that whomever he becomes involved with get along with his children. If the relationship leads to marriage, the woman might be expected to assume much of the responsibility for managing the household and caring for the children. Single mothers, on the other hand, may consider financial security more important in their mate selection. They might consider the possibility that the children's biological father would renege on support payments thereby making the step parent more responsible for the child's welfare. In this sense, then, for single mothers financial security of the future mate is an important variable while for single fathers the person's

ability to assume responsibility for childcare and household maintenance might be more important considerations.

Other Single-Parent Concerns

Time Considerations

The decision to begin dating may lead to guilt feelings concerning the
children. If the single parent works and his or her children are in childcare all day, he or she is faced with the choice of either going out or
spending time with the children.

Potential Parent Considerations

The single parent generally also looks at dates not only as potential
marital partners but also as potential parents as well. A new criterion then
enters the process by which the single parent evaluates the person. The
individual who is fun to be with, may not be interested in assuming
parental responsibilities. This relationship is probably time limited. In
another situation an individual may be willing to assume parental responsibilities but the children may be so threatened by his or her presence
that they may sabotage the relationship between him or her and their parent, attempting to maintain the status quo.

Financial Considerations

Finances and fatigue may collude to restrict social life. Aside from all
of the above dilemmas, there are all the practicalities of dating to worry
about, the costs in time and energy, and money. If the children are small,
dating requires finding and paying a babysitter. Both men and women will
need to have up-to-date clothes in good order. If finances are limited, there
may be competition between these needs and the needs of the children.
Going out also imposes a cost in fatigue. It means less time to get other
things done and less time to sleep and rest. It also means less time for
the children. Single parents who work may also feel that they spend too
little time as it is with their children. Dating means that the children will
be left once again with a babysitter. A great deal of guilt is sometimes
generated in the parent who opts to leave the children with a babysitter
for a purely social occasion. Potential guilt also creates much conflict in
the single parent deciding whether or not to date in the first place.

Reputational Considerations

Some individuals, especially those from very traditional families who live in traditional neighborhoods, may worry about their reputations. In family neighborhoods, there are the neighbors to worry about and what they might think, and the repercussions of their judgments on the children. It is also possible that the single parent fears that the former spouse would use the parent's dating to malign the parent to the children or to argue in court for renegotiation of support or custody. Most single parents also worry about their children's reactions. They are likely to be aware that their children will now see them as having sexual needs. They may be concerned about their children's reactions to the people they date. The children may actively discourage parents who are already uncertain about entering into dating. And although parents may feel it a relinquishing of their rights as independent adults to permit their children to control their personal lives, their children's objections may in fact affect their dating behavior.

Personal Considerations

Single parents recognize that not only has society changed while they were married, but so have they. They are older. They may feel less attractive. They may worry about the condition of their bodies. Women may be concerned about sagging breasts and stretch marks. Men may worry about pot bellies, thinning hair, and impotence. And now they are parents. They come as a package deal: adult with children. The person with children is likely to feel himself or herself less marriageable, for many prospective partners are hesitant to take on the added responsibility of parenthood with someone else's children.

Sociosexual Considerations

Meeting eligible mates can be difficult and when they are met, children may cause immediate problems, either by being negative to anyone they see as possibly taking their mother's or father's place or by being excessively positive and frightening others off immediately by asking, "Are you going to be my new Daddy?" Furthermore, a single parent must decide whether to permit a date or a lover to spend the night when the children are present. To allow someone to spend the night who is not the children's mother or father is often an important symbolic act for the parent. For one thing, it generally involves the children in the relationship with the person. If there is no commitment to the person, the parent may fear that the children will become emotionally involved with the person. If the relationship ends, then the parent will have to deal not only with his or her own feelings about the break up but also with the children's feelings as well. Allowing a date or a lover to sleep over also reveals to the children that their parent is a sexual person. This, in many cases, may make the parent feel somewhat uncomfortable. He or she may feel that the children are passing moral judgment. And they very well might be.

Right Person Considerations

Single parents, both men and women, can easily despair of finding the right person. Single fathers may have an easier time meeting contestants. But they may complain that those they meet are too young or, if older and never married, then are too involved with their careers or are too prudish. Divorced women may feel bitter toward all men. If the woman is a widow, she may idealize her former husband, creating an unrealistic ideal person to whom she compares the single father. Single mothers who are themselves in their thirties or forties have similar complaints. There may be men around, they report, but not the right type. If the men have never been married, then it is probably because something is wrong with them and no one else wants them: they are unwilling to settle down or perhaps they are still tied to their mothers, or else they may be homosexual. If the men have been married, then they are likely still to have responsibilities to their former families, still have wives to whom they must furnish child support and children whom they must see. Many single parents, male or female, feel themselves drawn to the conclusion, "Why bother?"

All single parents at times experience the difficulties of providing for the physical, social, and emotional needs of themselves and their children. There are problems of fatigue and role overload irrespective of the family's financial situation, though surely those with financial difficulties are more likely to experience such problems. The pressure of family responsibilities can prevent the single parent from arranging long periods of time with members of the opposite sex in order to get to know them better. Many single parents will not have a date or lover sleep over because they believe that their children should not be exposed to their sexual lives in this way. They may not be able to spend the night at another's home because they do not have a babysitter. Similar child-care problems make the chance of going away for an evening, weekend, or vacation with someone of the opposite sex very slim. There is less movement into marriage from the world of single parents than from some of the other unmarried populations. Some of these structural impediments certainly add to and account for the general lack of desire for remarriage of many of these single parents. Thus, on the one hand, there are emotional, physical, and social needs pressing the single parent toward finding a new partner. On the other hand, there are very real reasons for hesitancy, including the costs of dating, and concerns for dignity and self respect.

THERAPEUTIC APPROACHES

As stated throughout this book, traditional models of therapy, based on modernist assumptions, embrace a position of certainty in that there is a model of normalcy, to which the therapist then compares the person or family in therapy. In so doing, a focus on how different the family is from the norm (i.e., deficit focus) dictates which interventions are needed to bring the family closer to the norm. Solution-focused therapy, although accepting of postmodernist assumptions, in many ways is a therapy of certainty because of its focus on competencies, resources, and strengths—to the exclusion, in some cases, of the reason why the person/family came to therapy in the first place. Both models represent a one-sided view of the phenomena they study. Although there is much overlap, traditional psychotherapies and the solution-focused therapies could be seen as operating from a position of certainty, and thus are representative of an either/or perspective that tends to leave out half of the picture.

Applied to single-parent households, these models either focus on the deficits, often presenting pathological pictures supported by prominent studies where divorce is considered deviant and its effects deleterious, or by comparing boundaries, rules, and roles (or the lack thereof) against a norm for healthy family functioning, or by emphasizing the healthiness, resources, competencies, and strengths of single parent households in an attempt to replace the problem definition with one of competency.

The problem here is that clinicians, theorists, and researchers compare these families to theoretical models of normative family functioning in an attempt to understand all families. This approach assumes that there is such a thing as a normal family and that anything outside its range is less normal or negative. The resulting constructions lead clinicians to perceive families within a problem-oriented or competency-based framework, both within a deficit model. Therapy then involves bringing the family closer to the normative. The therapist, entrenched in theoretical groundings, defines the situation, discovers the truth.

Certainty-Based Assumptions

Following are some common general assumptions about divorce and the single parent household from a position of certainty.

On Single-Parent Households:

- The high divorce rate represents a breakdown of the institutions of marriage and the family unit and is the reason for most social problems.
- Whether due to death or divorce, single parent families are borne of loss. Those borne out of a death are more stable, in more need of support than those of divorce and are usually less damaged.
- Single-parent families are characterized by overburdened adults who balance care for children and careers outside the home and cannot possibly provide the amount of supervision, nurturance, time, discipline and love that their children need.
- Single-parent homes are predictably unstable, overemotional or underemotional, unreliable, and parents are usually too busy to partake in community activities.
- Single parents are usually guilty for leaving the family or angry and resentful for having the burden of caring for the children alone.
- When adults in single-parent homes socialize, it is at the expense of the children. Further, they are indiscriminate in their intimate life, negatively affecting impressionable children.
- Single-parent families rely on the older children to carry the extra burden in the family, fail to adequately provide children role modeling of both sexes, and have adversarial relationships with their ex-partners.

On Single Mothers and Fathers:

- Mothers are more competent than fathers as custodial parents and therefore should receive custody in the great majority of cases.
- It is worse for children if the missing noncustodial parent is the mother.
- Mothers, because of their socialization, should always be custodial parents of infants and toddlers.
- Mothers in single parent households are generally enmeshed with their children and lack adult companionship.
- Men usually do not take custody of their children following divorce because children prefer to stay with their mothers.
- Fathers are better able to raise teenage boys.
- Men do not bond as much with their children as women do and are therefore not likely to pay child support, visit their children as often as they should, keep promises to their children, etc., and therefore are not fit to be custodial parents.

On the Children of Divorce:

- Children from single-parent homes are deficiently prepared in school, are overstressed, and are poorer students than children from two-parent households.
- An absence of role modeling by the noncustodial parent has long-term damaging effects.
- Divorce and its transitional aftermath always damage the children involved.
- Financial losses that occur during a divorce are massive and have detrimental effects on children and their development.
- The change from a two-parent family to a one-parent household causes irreparable damage for children, since change produces anxiety.
- Girls growing up in homes with a custodial father will be more masculine than if they had grown up in a home with a custodial mother. There is a higher chance of a boy becoming homosexual if he grows up in a home with a custodial mother.

Therapists holding these views also make assumptions:

From a Traditional Psychological View:

- Divorce is the result of some personal deficiency or personality flaw, and can be blamed on one of the partners.

- Problems that manifest themselves in divorcing situations are likely to manifest themselves in future relationships.
- The deficiency in the person who is divorced needs to be understood and worked through in order for the person to avoid further emotional problems or further difficulties in future relationships.
- Once the person understands the cause for the personality problem which led to the divorce in the first place, he or she will know how to fix it.
- Both the adult and the children experience loss of attachment which manifests itself in troublesome behaviors that are subtle or overt.
- The earlier the divorce, the more the child will be deprived and the greater likelihood that psychopathology will develop.
- All divorcing families need counseling to prevent and repair the psychological damages of the children and to facilitate normal growth.

From a Structural View:

- One of the parents is missing and therefore it is likely that one of the children will take over the missing parental role.
- If a single-parent mother returns to the home of her parents because of financial difficulties, there is a high likelihood that cross-generational coalitions will develop.
- If a mother is in charge, there will be less disciplining of the children. There will be more disciplining in a home with a custodial father.
- Single-parent families tend to be more chaotic than two parent families because of less role definition, less discipline, and less hierarchy.

From a Solution-Focused View:

- Single-parent households are more flexible, collaborative rather than hierarchical, and therefore are more successful in today's changing world.
- It is most helpful to look at developing a solution to the problem rather than understanding the cause.
- Seeing single-parent households as healthy and viable encourages and empowers families.
- Getting a divorce is better than living in a conflictual two-parent household.

A Therapy of Uncertainty

Implications of the Therapeutic Models

The field of family therapy has progressed from a traditional deficit model, as typified by the early psychodynamic therapies, to the problem-focused or problem-solving therapies, to the solution-focused model. The social constructionist model of therapy presented in this chapter explores the family meanings that incidents, behaviors, and encounters with single parent households have for individuals and how these are determined by the sociocultural environment. The sociocultural environment equips persons with methods and ways of understanding and making judgments about aspects of the single parent households, ranging from how they felt about their divorce to religious values. These ways of making sense of experiences are embedded in a meaning system which is accepted as reality by the social group and in the scripts (ways of behaving) that are a part of the individual's meaning system. The dialectical relationship between individual realities and the socially constructed meanings about the single parent household is one focus of this chapter.

Based on a postmodernist assumption that divorces occur due to a myriad of social, cultural, and psychological reasons, rather than something inherently defective in an individual or family structure, social constructionist therapy expands the vision for the therapist and the family. Instead of confirming diagnoses of depression following loss through a *DSM-IV* classification, escalating cycles which serve to reinforce a problem-focused view of the family's dilemma, or focusing on positiveness, *tentative talk* is used. The therapist avoids characterizing family configuration, predicting future concerns and constraining options; instead, the tentative talk opens ground for the family and the therapist to see the context of the family, not only the structure. Here the therapist gains information by learning about the gender roles, finances, and emotional network that support the family, thereby increasing the potential for the family to liberate themselves through dialogue. The client defines the situation through interacting with the therapist. The conversations that ensue between client and therapist are vehicles for helping the client develop an increased sense of awareness.

The underlying premise in social constructionist theory is that social problems and problem resolution occur in language. Therapy is the "management of the conversation" (Gergen, 1985). The co-creation of new meanings occurs in the dialogue while the therapist works with the family. Together the conversants construct and reconstruct a new reality for the family.

Assumptions About Divorce from a Position of Uncertainty:

- Divorce occurs because of a myriad of social, cultural, and psychological reasons. It is impossible to categorize these reasons into deficit- or solution-focused categories.
- Divorce or relationship problems in general are best viewed in terms of interactional patterns which are inadvertently maintained in the hope of resolving the original difficulty.
- Problems persist because individuals, couples, and families do not know how to respond to them in a way that would eliminate them.
- Divorce does not necessarily reflect any type of individual or family deficiency nor does it necessarily reflect strength in a person or a solution to a problem.
- Single-parent households are too diverse a group to categorize them in certainty terms. Contradictions between and within families abound. "Single-parent family" is descriptive rather than prescriptive.
- Any predictions about family configurations are shaky at best. Single parent families do not reflect any kind of deficiency nor do they necessarily reflect strength, competency, growth, or an improved family form.
- Context gives us more information about a family than does family structure or configuration. To understand or predict behavior, other qualities of a family are more informative than the number of parents in the home. For example, it is just as useful to look at gender roles, support networks, finances, problem-solving skills, and other attributes.
- Family configuration is characteristic of all families whether they be one- or two-parent households.
- As therapists, our choice of language and the questions we ask, however benign they may seem, have the potential to limit and/or liberate our conversations about and with single-parent households. Tentative talk with single-parent families makes room for unique information.

Therapy Flowing from a Position of Uncertainty

Therapy from a position of uncertainty assumes that the meaning of behavior and emotion is relative and proposes that psychological and emotional characteristics are as much a product of the observer's interpretation or assessment as they are of the characteristics of the person. Therapy, in this view, seeks to include the responses of the clients in the analysis, thereby establishing levels of normalcy that are client generated. Questions are used as interventions (Tomm, 1987). Questioning families from a position of uncertainty allows for the possibility of alternative, nonproblem definitions. For example:

- Can you tell me what it's like living in your family?
- In what ways do you arrange or organize your family? Your household?
- I am curious about what that means for you.
- What words do you use to describe your family?
- Do you think your experience of your family is typical, atypical, or both? In what ways? Why?
- What is your assessment of how things are going in your family?
- Do you see any similarities/differences between living in your household and living in a two-parent household? What is your experience of these similarities/differences?
- Is there anything else that I should have asked but didn't that would be relevant to your family situation?
- What would you hope to accomplish here with me?
- At any point in our conversation do you feel we neglected anything important in our conversation?

For a comprehensive review of the theory and social constructionist therapy the reader is referred to the first chapter of this book.

To adhere to the standard of uncertainty to the point of denying or ignoring one's own or the counseling field's professional values would be silly. While presenting information in a way that leaves room for additional possibilities, the therapist can remain uncertain and simultaneously offer the client the benefit of his/her experience and knowledge of research in the field. Atwood and Genovese (1993) have composed a comprehensive review of divorce and single-parent family literature and research that therapists may find useful.

SUMMARY AND DISCUSSION

This chapter has provided the reader with an overview of the social and psychological aspects of the divorce process. Stages of the divorce process, implications for sexuality, and issues for single-parent families have been discussed. Traditional, solution-focused, and social constructionist approaches to therapy with divorced families are compared. Through a look at societal assumptions about divorce, divorced parents, and children of divorce, notions of how therapeutic assumptions are embedded within societal ones were explored. Both society's and therapeutic approaches' assumptions dichotomize things into good or bad, right or wrong, true or false. These dichotomies presume that one can know for sure that these assumptions are correct. The social constructionist approach is reviewed with special attention to how therapy might be conducted from a position of uncertainty. Questions were provided as examples of how a therapist might evoke the client's experiences without imposing personal, societal, or theoretical assumptions.

Fifty-seven percent of all first marriages end in divorce. It is time for us to rethink the notion that marriage is a failure when it ends in divorce. There is a growing body of research that suggests that the consequences of divorce are far from uniform, and that many adults and children appear to be able to cope well with the stressful events that we generally associate with divorce. What we have learned is that while divorce may be painful, it is a fact of our society. It is important that we do not regard divorce as evidence that the family is falling apart but rather as evidence that the institution of the family is an incredibly adaptive one. Families continue even when marriages end. As professionals we must not carelessly assume that divorced families are one way or another. We must not make the careless assumption that all divorced families are pathological any more than we can make the assumption that all two-parent nuclear families are healthy. Bilge and Kaufman (1983) comment eloquently on the malleability of families:

> Whether or not the single parent household—or any other kind of domestic grouping, for that matter—becomes a personal or social disaster depends upon the availability of sufficient material resources, supportive social networks, and the tenor of culturally structured beliefs toward it. (p. 60)

> No single family form produces an optimal milieu for a growing child. No family type is more "natural" to the human species than any other.

Children should have their emotional and physical needs met, but this can be accomplished by a wide variety of social arrangements. It is not necessary that this be done exclusively by biological parents in a nuclear family structure. (p. 69)

The purpose of this chapter has been to point out that even though the divorced in U.S. society outnumber the first-time married, and even though reported tolerance for the divorced appears to have increased, the bias associated with the process is alive and well. The implications of this are enormous, because as social workers (one among many groups that make these assumptions), we unwittingly phrase our questions or notice behaviors that fit with our preconceived ideas, thus in many ways creating conditions for self-fulfilling prophesies. However, as social workers we are also in a unique and advantageous position to assist in the process of attitude change around this issue.

Marriage and family therapists can be important leaders in the process of reassessment of attitudes, policies, programs, and therapeutic interventions that affect families involved in divorce. Marriage and family therapists need to be aware of the new research so that they may begin to reevaluate policies designed to "repair" students from "broken" homes, to refocus efforts on creating positive therapy environments, and to provide support to mobilize family members' strengths.

In sum, marriage and family therapists should view the divorce process as a process effected by gender, cultural socialization for men and women, and the social, economic, and political realities of our society today (see Hartmann, 1993). We are accustomed to thinking of ourselves as an enlightened and modern society, and it is certainly true that divorce today is far more commonplace than was the case a hundred years ago—but have we ever truly left behind our early prejudices?

REFERENCES

Albert, R. (1971). Cognitive development and parental loss among the gifted, the exceptionally gifted, and the creative. *Psychological Reports, 29,* 19–26.

Arditti, J. A. (1992). Factors related to custody, visitation, and child support for divorced fathers: An exploratory analysis. *Journal of Divorce and Remarriage, 17*(3–4), 23–42.

Atwood, J. D. (1992). *Family therapy: A systemic-behavioral approach.* Chicago: Nelson Hall.

Atwood, J. D. (1993). Comprehensive couple's therapy. In B. J. Brother (Ed.), *Couples therapy, multiple perspectives: In search of universal trends* (pp. 41–66). New York: Haworth.

Atwood, J. D., & Maltin, L. (1993). Relationship traps. In B. J. Brother (Ed.), *Attraction and attachment: Understanding styles of relationships* (Vol. IV, pp. 1–2). New York: Haworth.

Atwood, J. D., & Genovese, F. (1993). *Counseling single parents.* Alexandria, VA: American Counseling Association.

Baydar, N. (1988). Effects of parental separation and reentry into union on the emotional well-being of children. *Journal of Marriage and The Family, 18,* 149–159.

Beer, J. (1989). Relationship of divorce to self-concepts and grade-point averages of fifth grade school children. *Psychological Reports, 65,* 104–106.

Benedict, R. (1932). Configurations of culture in North America. *American Anthropologist, 34,* 1–27.

Besidine, M. (1968). The jocasts complex, mothering, and genius: *Psychoanalytic Review, 55,* 259–277.

Bilge, B., & Kaufman, G. (1983). Children of divorce and one-parent families: Cross-cultural perspectives. *Family Relations Journal of Applied Family and Child Studies, 32,* 59–71.

Blechman, E. (1982). Are children with one parent at psychological risk? A methodological review. *Journal of Marriage and the Family, 44,* 179–195.

Cashion, B. (1982). Female-headed families; effects on children and clinical implications. *Journal of Marriage and Family Therapy, 8,* 77–85.

Coleman, M., Ganong, L. H., & Gingrich, R. (1985). Stepfamily strengths: A review of popular literature. *Family Relations Journal of Applied Family and Child Studies, 34,* 583–589.

Cornelius, G. M., & Yawkey, T. D. (1985). Imaginativeness in preschoolers and single-parent families. *Journal of Creative Behavior, 19*(1), 56–66.

Ditzions, S. (1978). *Marriage, morals, and sex in America, a history of ideas.* New York: Norton.

Dublin, P. (1992). Severe borderlines and self-psychology. *Clinical Social Work Journal, 20,* 285–294.

Duncan, S. F., & Brown, G. (1992). RENEW: A program for building remarried family strengths. *Families in Society, 73,* 149–158.

Emery, B. (1984). A new format for the community meeting. *Psychiatric Quarterly, 56,* 35–44.

Emery, R. E. (1988). *Marriage, divorce and children's adjustment.* Thousand Oaks, CA: Sage.

Emery, R. E., & O'Leary, K. D. (1984). Marital discord and child behavior problems in a nonclinic sample. *Journal of Abnormal Child Psychology, 12,* 411–420.

Everett, C. (1989). *Children of divorce: Developmental and clinical issues.* NY: Haworth.

Fassel, D. (1991). *Growing up divorced: A road to healing for adults and children of divorce.* New York: Pocket Books.

Forehand, R., & McCombs, A. (1989). The nature of interparental conflict of married and divorced parents: Implications for young adolescents. *Journal of Abnormal Child Psychology, 17,* 235–249.

Garber, R. J. (1991). Long-term effects of divorce on the self-esteem of young adults. *Journal of Divorce and Remarriage, 17*(1–2), 131–137.

Gately, D., & Schwebel, A. I. (1992). Favorable outcomes in children after parental divorce. Special issue: Divorce and the next generation: Effects on young adults' patterns of intimacy and expectations for marriage. *Journal of Divorce and Remarriage, 18*(3–4), 57–78.

George, V., & Wilding, P. (1972). *Motherless families.* London: Routeledge and Kegan Paul.

Gerstel, N. (1987). Divorce and stigma. *Social Problems, 34*(2), 172–186.

Gilligan, C. (1984). New maps of development: New visions of maturity, *Annual Progress in Child Psychiatry and Child Development, 52,* 98–115, 199–212.

Glick, P. C. (1988). The role of divorce in the changing family structure: Trends and variations. In Wolchik, S. A. & Karoly, P. (Eds.), *Children of divorce: Empirical perspectives on adjustment* (pp. 3–34). New York: Gardner.

Greenberg, J. (1979). Single-parenting and intimacy: A comparison of mothers and fathers. *Alternative Lifestyles, 2,* 308–331.

Gutman, N. (1988). *On Skinner and Hull: A reminiscence and projection.* New York: Mcgraw-Hill.

Guttmann, J. & Broudo, M. (1989). The effect of children's family type on teachers' stereotypes. (Special issue: Children of divorce: Developmental and clinical issues.) *Journal of Divorce, 12*(2–3), 315–328.

Guidubaldi, J., & Perry, J. D. (1985). Divorce and mental health sequelae for children: A two-year follow-up of a nationwide sample. *Journal of the American Academy of Child Psychiatry, 24,* 531–537.

Hanson, S. M. (1986). Healthy single-parent families. (Special issue: The single-parent family.) *Family Relations Journal of Applied Family and Child Studies, 35*(1), 125–132.

Hanson, S., & Sporakowski, M. (1986). Single parent families. *Family Relations, 35,* 3–8.

Hartman, A. (1993). *Challenges for family policy.* New York: Guilford Press.

Hayes, C. (1993). Creating a political climate that values and supports children. Albany, NY: State University of New York Press.

Heatherington, E. M., Stanley-Hagan, M. & Anderson, E. R. (1989). Marital transitions: A child's perspective. (Special issue: Children and their development: Knowledge base, research agenda, and social policy application.) *American Psychologist, 44,* 303–312.

Hoffman, L. (1991). A reflexive stance for family therapy. *Journal of Strategic and Systemic Therapies, 10*(3–4), 4–17.

Hunt, J. G., & Hunt, L. L. (1977). Race, daughters and father-loss: Does absence make the girl grow stronger? *Social Problems, 25*(1), 90–102.

Hutchinson, R. L., Balutis, W. E., & Brown, D. T. (1989). The effects of family structure on institutionalized children's self-concepts. *Adolescence, 24,* 303–310.

Kalter, N., Alpern, D., Spence, R., & Plunkett, J. W. (1984). Locus of control in children of divorce. *Journal of Personality Assessment, 48,* 410–414.

Kazlow, F., & Hyatt, R. (1981). Divorce: A potential growth experience for the extended family. *Journal of Divorce, 5*(1–2), 115–126.

Kaye, S. H. (1989). The impact of divorce on children's academic performance. (Special issue: Children of divorce: Developmental and clinical issues.) *Journal of Divorce, 129*(2–3), 283–298.

Kelly, J. B. (1988) Longer-term adjustment in children of divorce: Converging findings and implications for practice. *Journal of Family Psychology, 2*(2), 119–140.

Krantzler, M. (1975). *Creative divorce.* New York: New American Library.

Kurdek, L. A., & Siesky, A. E. (1980). Effects of divorce on children: The relationship between parent and child perspectives. *Journal of Divorce, 4*(2), 85–99.

Lee, J. M., & Hett, G. G. (1990). Post-divorce adjustment: An assessment of a group intervention. *Canadian Journal of Counseling, 24*(3), 199–209.

MacKinnon, C. E., Stoneman, Z., & Brody, G. H. (1984). The impact of maternal employment and family form on children's sex-role stereotypes and mother's traditional attitudes. *Journal of Divorce, 8*(1), 51–60.

Marsh, H. W. (1990). Two-parent, stepparent, and single-parent families: Changes in achievement, attitudes, and behaviors during the last two years of high school. *Journal of Educational Psychology, 82,* 327–340.

McCombs, A., & Forehand, R. (1989). Adolescent school performance following parental divorce; are there family factors that can enhance success? *Adolescence, 24,* 871–880.

Mulholland, D. J., Watt, N. F., Philpott, A., & Sarlin, N. (1991). Academic performance in children of divorce: Psychological resilience and vulnerability. *Psychiatry, 54,* 268–280.

Rosenthal, K., & Kesheet, H. (1978). The impact of childcare responsibilities on the part-time or single father. *Alternative Lifestyles, 1,* 165–492.

Sable, P. (1992). Attachment theory: Application to clinical practice with adults. *Clinical Social Work Journal, 20,* 271–283.

Santrock, J. W., & Tracy, R. L. (1978). Effects of children's family structure status on the development of stereotypes by teachers. *Journal of Educational Psychology, 70,* 754–757.

Scwebel, A., Moreland, J., Steinkohl, S., Lentz, S., & Stewart, J. (1982). Research based interventions with divorced families. *The Personnel and Guidance Journal, 60*(9), 523–528.

Snyder, M., & Swan, S. (1978). Hypothesis testing, processes in social interaction. *Journal of Personal and Social Psychology, 36,* 1202–1212.

Spanier, G., & Thompson, L. (1983). Relief and distress after marital separation. *Journal of Divorce, 7,* 31–49.

Thiriot, T. I., & Buckner, E. T. (1991). Multiple predictors of satisfactory post-divorce adjustment of single custodial parents. *Journal of Divorce and Remarriage, 17*(1–2), 27–48.

Thomas, W. I., & Thomas, O. S. (1928). *The child in America* (pp. 571–573, 575). New York: Alfred A. Knopf, Inc.

Thompson, L., & Spanier, G. B. (1983). The end of marriage and acceptance of marital termination. *Journal of Marriage and Divorce, 45*(1), 103–113.

Thornton, A. (1985). Changing attitudes toward separation and divorce: Causes and consequences. *American Journal of Sociology, 90,* 856–872.

Tomm, K. (1987). Interventive interviewing: Part 1. Strategizing as a fourth guideline for the therapist. *Family Process, 26,* 3–13.

Veevers, J. F. (1991). Traumas versus strens: A paradigm of positive versus negative divorce outcomes. Special issue: Marital instability and divorce outcomes: Issues for therapists and educators. *Journal of Divorce and Remarriage, 15*(1–2), 99–126.

Wallerstein, J. S. (1984). Children of divorce: Preliminary report of a ten-year follow-up of young children. *American Journal of Orthopsychiatry, 54,* 444–458.

Wallerstein, J., & Kelly, J. (1974). The effects of parental divorce: The adolescent experience. In G. Anthony & C. Koupernik (Eds.), *The child and his or her family—children at a psychiatric risk, III.* New York: John Wiley & Sons.

Wallerstein, J. S., & Kelly, J. B. (1976). The effects of parental divorce: Experiences of the child in later latency. *American Journal of Orthopsychiatry, 46,* 256–269.

Wallerstein, J. S., & Kelly, J. B. (1980). Effects of divorce on the visiting father-child relationship. *American Journal of Psychiatry, 137,* 1534–1539.

Warren, N., Illgen, E., Grew, R., Konac, J., & Amara, I. (1982). *Parenting after divorce. Evaluation of preventive programs for divorced families.* Paper presented at APA meeting, Washington, DC.

Watts, D. S., & Watts, K. M. (1991). The impact of female-headed single parent families on academic achievement. *Journal of Divorce and Remarriage, 17*(1–2), 97–114.

Watzlawick, P., Weakland, J. H., & Fisch, R. (1974). *Change: Principles of problem formulation and problem resolution.* New York: Norton.

Weiss, R. S. (1975). *Marital separation.* New York: Basic Books.

Weiss, R. S. (1979). Growing up a little faster: The experience of growing up in a single-parent household. *Journal of Social Issues, 335*(4), 97–111.

Wood, J. I., & Lewis, G. J. (1990). The coparental relationship of divorced spouses: Its effects on children's school adjustment. *Journal of Divorce and Remarriage, 14*(1), 81–95.

Yankelovich, D. (1981). *New rules.* New York: Random House.

CHAPTER 9

When a Loved One Has a Chronic Illness

Estelle Weinstein and Joan D. Atwood

UNANTICIPATED ILLNESS

Case 1

Matt and Diane expected, when they married, to spend most of their lives together in relatively good health. While serious illness had affected their elderly grandparents, it appeared a long way off for them. Then at 45, Matt suffered a serious heart attack and the future became unpredictable—their life's plans were in shambles.

Case 2

When Jim and Marie's two children Kelly and John were born 13 years ago, their lives were right on schedule. Their parenting plans had begun and each knew what part they would play in their children's development. As their daughter Kelly approached adolescence they expected her teenage years to be filled with usual adolescent crises, but they did not anticipate the crisis a diagnosis of juvenile diabetes would bring.

Case 3

Here it was, what they thought was "a time for them"! The children were grown, they had achieved success in their jobs; accumulated a fair amount of money and were ready for what they envisioned the next part of their lives to be—travel, skiing, golf, tennis, and retirement. Jack and Sharon were late middle-aged and in what appeared to be excellent physical condition, when she was diagnosed with breast cancer.

Case 4

Sara and Frank had retired from professional careers in teaching and dentistry several years ago and moved to a community that supported their interests in music and theater, several states away from their grown children. Both of them performed in the local semiprofessional theater group. Then, Frank noticed that Sara was confused at times, mixed things up quite a bit and sometimes she was not able to recall her lines. He attributed this to their "getting on in years" but, it continued to get worse. As the tempo of deterioration increased over the next year, they sought medical attention and eventually learned that Sara had Alzheimer's disease.

These unexpected, health-related life events raise many questions for therapists and other health service providers. What are the factors that determine the onset of serious, chronic, and degenerative diseases and how does the progression of an illness affect families? To what extent does gender, the life cycle stage of those affected at the onset of the illness (childhood/adulthood), roles, couple relationships, social support systems, and finances contribute to the way families cope? Can family systems be strengthened rather than weakened in the face of health problems? How do marital and family dynamics, belief systems, rules and boundaries determine the physical well-being of its members and their ability to adapt to physical health problems? This chapter will provide a foundation for understanding the role illness plays in family systems and the implications for effective intervention.

A BIOPSYCHOSOCIAL PERSPECTIVE

Until recently, disease was thought to be a function of the breakdown of biophysiological processes (Engel, 1980a; Sarafino, 1990). This biomedical model of disease assumed that there were distinct separations between the mind and the body. Within this framework, health was an exclusive function of a person's physical state. While there are some changes emerging, the medical system in this country is still primarily a product of this model (Sarafino, 1990), and within this belief system, interventions consist almost entirely of medical technologies. The medical system concerns itself with the treatment of the biology of an illness in an individual. Little attention is paid to the person's mental health or his or her family.

Only recently in our history have we begun to consider a newer, theoretical conceptualization of health and disease known as the biopsychosocial model (Engel, 1977). This multifactored perspective suggests that an interaction of the biological, social, and psychological aspects of a person's life are the determinants of his or her health, the onset of illness, and often the prognosis. Even the immune system, which was thought to be a strictly biological response, is now thought to be influenced by emotional factors and the course of chronic illness largely influenced by lifestyle behaviors (Sarafino, 1990). Now, it is believed that psychological factors such as cognition, emotion, and motivation in behavior and mental processes have been known to contribute to a person's proneness for illness and speed of recovery (i.e., positive attitudes decrease recovery time, negative attitudes extend recovery time (Sarafino, 1990). Thus, the social systems in which a person functions (family, work, and community) influence their belief systems, lifestyle, and experiences with health and how they use health providers. These social outcomes recursively interact with many other health-determining factors.

Biopsychosocial factors change systematically in response to developmental stages (Sarafino, 1990). For example, the biological functioning of older people is challenged by many more chronic diseases than middle-aged people or children suffer just by virtue of more years of normal wear and tear on their bodies.

The sociological impact of family or cultural membership affects belief systems, family rituals, and the way people use the health care system differently at different times during the life cycle. The response to a child's illness, the role sick family members play, the respect for or willingness to use health professionals, have roots in family-of-origin dynamics. Hence, interventions that increase people's ability to delay the onset of or cope with serious illness must include an understanding of disease entities, expected physical prognoses, and psychosocial implications for interpersonal relationships, coping styles, and family dynamics.

Out of this broader biopsychosocial model have come changes in the preparation of medical providers and changes in the thinking of mental health personnel. In the field of marriage and family therapy, the specialty of family systems medicine has emerged. New thinking offers an opportunity for medical practitioners and family therapists to collaborate in their efforts to help families with serious, chronic, and debilitating illnesses. Such collaboration means learning about the training, theoretical paradigms, languages, and working styles of each other's profession, which serves to decrease power issues and increase communication between fields (McDaniel, Hepworth, & Doherty, 1992). For family therapists it means understanding the biology of disease and the medical approaches to treatment. Conversely, the medical practitioner is learning about how family systems effect health and how health status effects families.

RESEARCH ABOUT ILLNESS

The research that is presently available addressing the interaction between family and health is mostly anecdotal and therefore difficult to generalize. The literature that does exist addresses medical conditions and the burdens associated with the provision of care (by spouse or other) to the exclusion of how the interrelationships in the family are affected or effect the physical health of its members (Creasey, 1990 #1). However, interrelationships between social and psychological factors including economic and demographic variables and their influence on the impact of illnesses and family dynamics can not be ignored. The discussion below defines terminology and provides a framework for understanding the important issues with regard to chronic, serious illness and the family.

Until recently, the medical and scientific community had virtually conquered or controlled most communicable diseases (e.g., smallpox, measles, diphtheria). Even in the era of the human immunodeficiency virus (HIV), the major causes of death in this country are chronic degenerative diseases, especially heart disease, cancer, and stroke. (Although HIV infection is communicable, it destroys the immune system and persons with acquired immune deficiency syndrome (AIDS) actually die of opportunistic chronic diseases.)

Chronic diseases develop over time, progress symptomatically, result in permanent, compromising changes in the person's health, are mediated by lifestyle, and often have a genetic component. The effects of a chronic disease are sometimes predictable, but more often vary over time and from patient to patient. Serious communicable or infectious diseases that also affect health status are transmissible from one person to another and have a limited range of recovery time or result in more chronic conditions, if they do not end in a relatively swift death.

While risk factors for chronic diseases have historically been identified as behavioral or genetic in the diagnosed person, recently health professionals are exploring interpersonal relationship factors as they relate to risk for illness. Some of the questions considered are: To what extent do personality, lifestyle, behaviors, and other factors in one spouse increase the likelihood of serious illness in the other? Can characteristics in a well spouse be the cause of an illness in the partner? How will individual characteristics or couple dynamics affect the way a couple lives with an illness when it occurs? How do parental characteristics affect children's experiences with illness and their belief systems?

Haynes (Haynes, Eaker, & Feinleib, 1983) was one of the first to demonstrate less conventional risks for coronary heart disease (CHD), including those associated with and heightened by certain characteristics in a spouse. Swan, Carmelli, and Rosenman (1986), studying this phenomenon, named it "'cross-spouse' risk factors" (p. 172). They found that such characteristics as higher social mobility, increased life pessimism, high school or above education, higher levels of activity and dominance, were characteristics of women married to Type A personality men with CHD. Although these characteristics have been identified, what has not yet been determined is if, and how, this notion of interactive causality may be functioning. Had the disease in husbands resulted in the wife's pessimism, which in turn affected his coping? Is her increased activity or dominance a response to his illness?

A serious illness often results in the disruption in the social and recreational activities for the diagnosed person as well as the other family members but it has specific implications for a marital couple. Research indicates that an ill person's contact with friends outside the family diminishes considerably because of such things as medical limitations, physical exhaustion, and embarrassment about physical appearance that has resulted from the illness. This in turn limits the spouse's social activities. For example, in the case where an insulin-dependent diabetic needs to adhere to a strict diet, attending dinners and parties might be too tempting. Or, in the case of a cancer patient undergoing chemotherapy or radiation treatment, the ill person may be just too exhausted to be sociable. If there is disfigurement resulting from an illness, the person may be afraid of rejection from close friends or of people staring in public places. And so the couple avoids these social functions. The spouse or other family members may begin to feel isolated, in need of social stimulation, guilty if they partake, and, often, angry at the ill spouse.

Swan et al. (1986) found that for up to a year or so after a diagnosis or onset of a serious illness, spouses of the ill partner reported increased depression, anxiety, and a major disruption in their routine. Yet, over time the couple's balance returned. Levenson and Gottman (cited in Swan et al.), studying marital interaction and satisfaction as it relates to serious illness, found greater physiological symptomatology among couples who reported dissatisfaction with and conflict in their marriages than with those who reported being satisfied.

In addition to the emotional distress that occurs in an ill spouse, the well spouse often experiences a revisit of—or a host of new—physical and psychological symptoms of his or her own. And, the data indicate, well-spouse difficulties significantly influence the coping and psychological well-being of the ill partner (Manne & Zautra, 1989).

The research suggests that when a relationship is stable and positive, couples are better able to withstand the struggle of serious illness and in some cases report their relationship is even strengthened by it, whereas if the relationship is troubled it may be destroyed (Shlain, 1979). Mullan (1983) looked at longer term effects (over 10 years after a coronary incident), and found that less than 20% reported less satisfaction with their marriage and 25% actually reported increased satisfaction after chronic illness entered the family. While the passage of time generally helps people adjust to new and possibly life-threatening life cycle situations, some couples report that their relationships and commitment deepened as they reevaluated what was important to them.

REACTIONS TO A DIAGNOSIS OF A SERIOUS ILLNESS

A diagnosis of a serious illness provides medical practitioners with a label and frame of reference with which to approach patients. While the diagnosis speaks to the biophysiological factor, it does not begin to suggest the psychosocial demands that the diagnosed individual, couple, and family will face (Rolland, 1993). The label of the disease itself often addresses the beliefs and past experiences of the people involved with the illness. When a person is diagnosed with cancer, for example, several expectations may be made. If there is the belief that cancer is not treatable or beatable and is physiologically devastating, then compensations often begin even before any severe symptoms manifest themselves. The person may develop a "sick" role by virtue of the diagnosis alone, and tend to surrender responsibilities to others. This attitude can result in a shift in the family power that further encourages the diagnosed person to define him or herself as "no longer capable." This sick role may have some advantages: for example, in a disease that runs a particular course, it may give the diagnosed person an opportunity to rest and recover with a respite from the usual responsibilities. On the other hand, it may discourage the person from maximizing remaining abilities. Even in the case of a disease requiring the ill person's constant self-monitoring, people who have taken on the sick role tend to relinquish their decision-making rights and caretaking to health providers or significant others. On the other hand, for some people cancer is not a death sentence but an opportunity to deepen their lives, to bring new meanings to their relationships, to increase their religious affiliations, or to take control and "be strong," perhaps for the first time in their lives. These responses can result in many positive changes in family systems.

Shontz (1975) outlines a common sequence of reactions persons tend to have when they are diagnosed with a serious illness. The first reaction, shock, is characterized by bewilderment. The person behaves in an automatic fashion, exhibiting feelings of detachment from the immediate situation. These avoidance reactions are a means of getting distance from the overwhelming feelings. In the second phase a person may exhibit disorganized thinking, and feelings of loss, grief, and despair. This second phase is more typical when a diagnosis comes without warning to a seemingly healthy person. The third phase is characterized by a denial of the circumstances, along with an acknowledgement of the existence of the health problem.

However, in most cases, the reality of the situation returns slowly as the person's ability to cope increases. If avoidance and denial are maintained over too long a period of time, a person may become immobilized, especially in the ability to gather information about the problem. Immobilization can prohibit one from making timely decisions about treatment or care needs and sometimes results in another family member's taking over the decision-making role, evaluating treatment options, and providing daily care. It is in this situation that power shifts, role reversals, and conflicting triangulations occur. Or, as the family surrounds the ill member, they may bond more closely, strengthening each member of the support system. Increases in family support increase healing and promote coping.

While shock is a fairly consistent initial response (Shontz, 1975), some persons who become ill do not become disorganized or evidence avoidance behaviors. They seem much more in control and accepting of the illness and begin to structure their lives around the necessary accommodations. Family-of-origin "tapes," sociocultural beliefs about illness, and economic and social circumstances affect immediate reactions to serious health problems. People's beliefs about the identity of an illness (Meyerowitz, 1983), about the cause and duration, and about the consequences of their conditions are important predictors of their ability to adjust.

Health Locus of Control

Reactions to health concerns have also been explained by theories of "locus of control" and self-efficacy (Phares, 1987) Rotter (1966) developed the original scales for measuring internal and external locus of control, and Wallston, Wallston, and DeVellis (1978) applied these concepts to a health-related measure called the Multidimensional Health Locus of Control Scales.

People with an internal locus of control believe that they are in control of their own successes and failures. Hence, people with a powerful internal locus of control believe that something they do or do not do determines their health status. These individuals are also more likely to believe that their ability to overcome a serious illness is determined by themselves and their behaviors. They verbalize things like, "If I give in to this, I will get sicker," or "I'll decide what is best for me!" These individuals tend to make their own informed decisions about their care and adhere to regimens that they believe will work.

People with an external, "powerful other" locus of control are likely to believe that professionals or others outside themselves determine their successes or failures. These individuals believe that the outcome of their illness is determined by their doctor, surgeon, or other professional, and generally leave their care in the hands of a medical professional, doing only what they are told.

Chance locus of control is exhibited by people who believe that luck, fate, or God determines their successes and failures. Persons with a chance locus of control will say things like, "If I'm lucky, I'll get over this" or "If my time is up it's up and nothing I can do can change that."

As people move from middle to older age their bias toward chance or powerful other locus of control increases (Lachman, 1986), and they are more likely to turn to medical professionals to make their health-related decisions. People who optimize their health by living healthy lifestyles believe that they can determine their own health status. People who exhibit less stress and those who have coped with serious illnesses tend to have stronger internal locus of controls.

Externality or internality of control also influences the way people use the health care system. Individuals whose belief systems incorporate notions like "the doctor knows best" and turn their care over to the practitioner are less likely to seek second medical opinions or try alternative medical procedures unless their primary physician suggests it. Few questions are asked about the treatment process, treatment expectations, or the protocol, and they tend to perform as the "good patient." On the other hand, believing in fate or God often causes people not to seek treatment or limits the treatment they seek, because they do not believe it will make any difference in the outcome.

As stated before, belief in one's ability to control health-related events and the degree to which a person falls on the locus of control continuum are largely determined by family-of-origin experiences, culture, and social groups. In the case of couples who hold diverse beliefs about their ability to control or determine outcomes, a more chaotic response is generally observed when a chronic illness diagnosis is made.

Poor physical health in general, and especially chronic disease, tends to erode individuals' sense of control over their life and destiny (Baltes, Hans-Werner, & Schmid-Furtoss, 1990). Emotional well-being is likely to decline as health status is compromised. Hence, the tasks for managing serious chronic illnesses include achieving some measure of control over the symptoms of the illness; adhering to complex treatment regimens; coping with the uncertainty of a prognosis; supporting and maintaining family, work, social relationships and responsibilities within the parameters of the illness, and continuing to set goals and plans for the future. Furthermore, a sense of self-efficacy or the belief that, "That can succeed at goals we want to accomplish" is another factor in maintaining a sense of control in the face of serious illness (Bandura, 1977).

Adherence/Compliance

When a crisis period of serious illness subsides, the medical treatment plan for controlling the disease and preventing additional problems is to a major extent reliant upon the ability of a person to select and adhere to medical protocols that have been found to be successful and for the family to support these protocols. This is presently referred to as *adherence* (DiMatteo & DiNicola, 1982; Turk & Meichanbaum, 1991). In the medical literature, adherence occurs at two levels: primary adherence that refers to a person's ability or willingness to carry out activities that prevent the initial onset of illness; and secondary/tertiary adherence that refers to following prescribed procedures that are aimed at controlling a specific health condition (Turk & Meichanbaum, 1991). The term *compliance,* rather than adherence was more commonly used in the past, suggesting that people with diseases follow the steps assigned to them by medical practitioners. The notion of adherence requires that people make informed decisions, select, and then adhere to a specific protocol. It is this commitment to the decision and the following of the particular protocol that is believed to determine the physical outcome of an illness rather than the medical effectiveness of a particular drug or procedure (Epstein, 1984). This taking of action on one's own behalf often results in feelings of self-confidence, an increased sense of well being and an increased likelihood of participating in ancillary healthful behaviors that ultimately limit or control the effects of serious illness. Movement from the language of compliance to adherence in the health field signals shared decision making about health behaviors between practitioners and patients.

Several factors have been identified as affecting people's ability to adhere to specific health behaviors. These include:

- a simplified understanding of the protocol or regimen
- an ability to implement a protocol with a minimum of life changes
- satisfaction with and a feeling of confidence in the source of the regimen
- the specificity of the regimen, including such factors as length of time needed, cost, etc.

- the social and psychological factors in the person's environment that influence the activities (Sarafino, 1990; Turk & Meichanbaum, 1991).

When individuals make a commitment to a protocol that is in concert with their belief systems and the roles and behaviors of their significant others, there is a greater likelihood that the process will be followed. Sometimes, individuals have persons in their family to whom they look for the family's health matters and decisions. Adherence successes can be closely associated with approval from these pseudo–family doctors.

Oftentimes, the family's support in adherence activities deepens the family's trust and intimacy, but families have also been known to sabotage the process. In the authors' clinical practice, it was suggested to a man who recently suffered a heart attack that diet and exercise would help him to control his disease and decrease his risk of sudden death.

He discussed what this would mean to each of them with his wife. The family ate together often and their dietary habits did not resemble the required diet. Moreover, the only social activities the couple participated in together were dining out. At first the adjustments seemed easy, as the risk of dying from heart disease was central to their fears. The family shopping and meal preparation was the wife's duty and she indicated her complete support of the new eating behavior and better eating habits by decreasing her own weight. The exercise protocol required of him included exercising regularly at a rehabilitation center after work which, while she completely supported it, would decrease their dinner time together. As distance from the acute heart attack and the possibility of death was achieved over time, the couple began to lose interest in maintaining the healthier behaviors. The restrictions it posed on their social structure became problematic for them. As his health became less central to their fears, she began to pay less attention to what they ate and he went back to his "couch potato" evenings. They argued frequently, she accusing him of not taking care of himself and leaving all of the burden to her and he accusing her of putting him at risk for another heart attack by planning social dinners with friends at places where he could not choose healthy meals. At a support group they met other couples with serious CHD illnesses who encouraged them to join a local health club and a bicycle traveling group. The definition of themselves as a diseased couple receded as these new social activities enabled them to participate in a new, healthier social life, and created renewed interest in each other.

IMPLICATIONS FOR THE FAMILY

Although a serious illness manifests itself in one member of the family, it is perceived as an intruder by other family members. Eventually the illness itself becomes an independent functioning member of the system, with its own separate identity. It is demanding in that it requires readjustment of schedules, roles, finances, and other aspects of life. It elicits anger in that it is often uncontrollable and causes pain and fear. It is selfish in that its demands for attention must be met despite other interests. It is isolating in that it often changes intimacy and friendship patterns. While the family's task is to meet the ill person's medical and other caregiving needs, the emotional well-being of the entire system is challenged.

This may lead to couple or family discord that aggravates health status, which in turn negatively affects family dynamics. Family scripts and experiences with illness have implications to the functioning of the system and its ability to adapt. If, for example, the family defines the illness as something that could have been prevented or something that was caused by themselves or another family member, then a place to lay blame is sought. The family diet was not healthy because it was not a priority of the meal preparer, or the ill person spent too many hours at work, or the children caused too much stress. This type of thought process attempts to explain or offer some level of control over what feels like an uncontrollable situation. Hostility, low self-esteem, and other negative patterns may develop as the family system is threatened. These patterns tend to create distance from the problem or create distance between family members, closing down communication and leaving little room for accommodation to the new situation.

In some cases, blame is placed outside the family system, usually with the medical profession. The doctor is accused of incorrectly diagnosing the ailment or taking too long to recognize it. In these cases there is a loss in faith in the medical system, which may result in the delay of necessary treatment.

The demands of an illness often deplete energy, dissolve optimism, and create depression. Chronically ill persons may experience depression, leading other family members to have increased risk for depression themselves (Coyne & Delongis, 1986). Also, those family systems with existing problems, tend to adjust less well to their new situation and exaggeration of the negative patterns may occur (Swan et al., 1986).

When an illness compromises the diagnosed member's physical capabilities and personality characteristics, there is a constant struggle on the part of the person to maintain equilibrium. In some cases, this struggle creates growth, development, new closeness, and trust in the primary or family relationships as needed adjustments in roles, power, and responsibilities emerge. In other cases, as the person's self-care capabilities decrease, resentment, jealousy, and a feeling of being overburdened occur as the family relationships deteriorate. The task of maintaining the family support and intimacy is ongoing for all members. In order to effectively accommodate and regain equilibrium, family members challenged by serious illness should receive information about the expected patterns of the particular disorder or illness and the resultant practical and emotional demands these patterns may create for them over time (Rolland, 1993). It would be helpful for them to address their mythical notions in light of the medical realities about the health problem and to find language to discuss their fears with each other.

The onset of an illness, whether an acute attack or a gradual development of symptoms, has implications for how families will function, as does the nature of the expected progression of a particular disease (progressive, constant, or relapsing) and the expected outcome for survival. Can a course of events be outlined for an individual upon diagnosis, including the degree of disability, pain, and other likely outcomes, or is the future entirely vague and uncertain (Rolland, 1993)? What medical interventions are available and how can people access them?

The family definition of health and illness contributes to their ability to set boundaries around a health problem. Finding the appropriate place for the illness so that it does not become the central focus of the family limits the boundaries of the disease. When boundaries are not established and maintained, the illness invades all aspects of the system and the family becomes narrowly focused on it. The individual's physical limitations become the family's limitations. Plans and activities for all members center around the activities associated with the illness (going to doctors, taking medication, etc.).

Power Shifts

Disengagement

Disengagement may occur among family members who cannot cope or are unable to give care in ways that are acceptable to themselves or the system. Others become so enmeshed in the symptoms and the disease entity that it becomes difficult to distinguish between the sick member and the well others. While the ill person is still able to maintain his or her past roles or tasks with some modifications, the enmeshed family might usurp that ability and elicit a lack of competence. When the sick role is assigned to an individual with a previously dependent spouse, the latter can become stronger and better functioning. But, as one spouse gains, there is an obvious shift in the power in the relationship away from the ill spouse.

Inverted Hierarchies

Timing is also an important component of the systems' well-being. In some cases, the type of serious illness determines the timing factor. In cases where the onset of an illness is acute, changes occur very quickly. Often the ill person is hospitalized during acute attacks. In an acute phase of illness, the family may become off balance; much of the decision making falls to the medical community and the family tasks become survival and treatment. Family members spend much of their time at the hospital. The outside world and day-to-day activities recede as the illness comes to the foreground. Social relationships may change as family members become unavailable to their friends, especially when they are involved in the immediacy of the illness.

When a person enters a hospital or other medical inpatient facility, the family's identity is lost, as is the ill person's. The rules and behaviors specific to that family are disregarded as the hospital rules become the governing forces. The concerns of the hospital staff center on the patient in need of services rather than on the individual with an independent identity. Care and day-to-day life become routinized according to hospital schedules. The ill person may take on the role of the good patient, handing destiny over to the medical staff. This type of medical environment is conducive to doctors or nurses and patients creating parent-child relationships or inverted hierarchies. The nonassertive family often is carried along with this redefinition, feeling safe that someone in authority has assumed the caretaking.

The Rigid Hierarchy

In other situations, patients and their families fight hard not to give up their rights and roles to the facility. The complication of maintaining one's independence and needing to be cared for is a difficult balance. Family members often rebel against the routine and the limited access they have not only to each other but to information about care. Anger is not an uncommon emotion.

Triangulations

In some cases, a more chronic debilitating illness results after the acute phase. In these situations, medical personnel will likely become a permanent, important influence on the family if not full-fledged members of the system. In some cases the medical practitioner will be triangulated into the family system. The triangular relationship may involve the caregiver or the patient and can contribute to conflict and confusion in the system.

When the acute phase ends and the person survives, a period of rehabilitation or healing may begin. The participants in the system work toward regaining their balance and helping the ill person maximize health functioning. At this time, assessment and understanding of the more chronic conditions and disabilities that will remain a part of the person's life forever occurs.

The threats of loss and disability have considerable implications to the family's ability to function. Changes in physical appearance and emotional state result in the sick person's revisiting most of the important components of their life, roles, and future plans. As a result of the illness, some of these plans vanish while others will become stronger as a new identity is sought. The family system reorganizes as the chronic illness is given its family position. Changes in the rules that govern the system are effectively made as the family becomes centrally or peripherally (depending upon the severity of the symptoms) organized around the illness.

When there is a particular health problem that has an expected progression, the changes tend to be more subtle and can be planned and managed as the family adapts to the definition of the disease. Time allows for adaptations to occur with less disruption as a full understanding of the impending physical changes emerge more slowly.

The Roller Coaster

Chronic illnesses such as cancer can have periods of remission between bouts of serious debilitation, which can create a roller-coaster-like effect. During remission, there is a slow "lulling" away from the immediacy of loss, fear, and suffering. During the recurrence periods, impending loss, helplessness, feelings of anger, confusion, and fear return. The individual's short-range goals and future plans are severely disrupted and life seems to take on an unpredictable dimension.

Finances

In situations where the ill spouse has held a primary role (e.g., breadwinner, caregiver) or which, because of the illness, has ended or will do so shortly, there is fear of the future. In addition, sometimes guilt arises. An ill spouse may have to make decisions that demand acknowledging the outcomes of his or her illness. It is a challenge for the family to verbalize emotions and assist the ill person to maintain as much independence as possible while letting go of responsibilities. This can sometimes be accomplished by shifting and changing roles rather than giving them up.

Life Cycle Issues

The life cycle of the sick person and the developmental stages of the other family members have implications for the family's ability to adapt. The impact of disabilities on the expectations and skill mastery may differ considerably from one stage to another, but no matter what the stage of life, illness and disability have a profound effect on family systems. For example, if chronic illness enters the family in a child who has not achieved independent living skills, it has a different impact than if it occurred later in the child's life. If a certain level of success is achieved at a career that requires skills that cannot be maintained, it may have a different effect on the individual and the family than if it occurred at the end of the career or before a career had been selected.

Rolland (1993) suggests that families need support in establishing "beliefs that sustain hope and empower, instead of those that foster blame, shame, or guilt" (p. 15). Independence and an ability to maintain optimal functioning within the parameters of the illness need to be fostered. Furthermore, to avoid hostile imbalances in power and control, Rolland (1993) identifies the need for families to see health problems as couple or family problems.

Serious chronic illness can lead families to create a reconstruction of the past in an effort to find meaning for the future. People who have remission from serious illness can achieve a much greater meaning for each life event. The powerful experience of vulnerability can be an opportunity for the strengthening of marital bonds, deepening emotional intimacy, expressing caring and commitment, opening communications, and increasing trust (Chekryn, 1984). The disruption in the family that occurs when illness enters the system may contribute to positive changes. Family members can develop new and better ways to interact with one another.

Chronic Illness and the Children

Bronchial asthma, juvenile diabetes, leukemia and other cancers are among the more serious chronic and debilitating diseases that affect children and young adults. Although these diseases were once fatal, as a result of medical technology and effective pharmacology, children now often live with them and their related problems for the whole of their lives.

A preconceived notion of a chronic illness has implications for a family's ability to cope and adjust. Marteau and Johnston (1986), in their study of parents with children who have chronic diseases, found that parents rated diseases that their own children had as less serious than others. Moreover, there were less negative feelings about a health problem that they were living with than one their child did not have.

In early childhood, long inpatient separations when the child's needs are met by doctors or nurses can interfere with the parent-child relationship. If the physical disabilities interfere with attempts at independence, children's self-confidence may be compromised. Overcompensating parents can inhibit a child's developmental task mastery or the child can become rebellious in an attempt to push out the boundaries.

The peer system in later childhood and early adolescence provides a yardstick by which children measure themselves and develop their self-image. If a child has a chronic illness at this life cycle stage, peer relationships may become problematic. Peers can be cruel and it may be difficult to develop a social network if the disabilities are severely restricting. The family may become strongly protective of the child and meet more of the child's needs than are necessary. This stage of childhood is a particularly crucial and difficult time for families, as children with disabilities attempt to negotiate close friendships and personal values that are different from the family's. Sometimes the withdrawal and loneliness experienced by an ill child result in anger and self-recrimination. If the family has been invested in maintaining the child's health without encouraging the child's maximum input, adolescent rebellion may be expressed in refusal of treatment or medication.

When the day-to-day activities of the family are adjusted to the child's needs, other family members, especially other siblings, may become angry. Wilson-Pessano and McNabb (1989) found that the diagnosed child's care often took away from the needs or restricted the other children in the family. Other children adapted best when family schedules, visits, and vacations, were adjusted to the total family's needs wherever possible, rather than entirely to the diagnosed child's. When siblings identities and importance in the family are supported and appreciated, less resentment and anger is felt. Moreover, a family's encouragement in maintaining a child's involvement in his or her own care and decision making (where developmentally appropriate) will maximize the child's confidence and coping ability.

Shapiro's (1986) research looked at maternal influences on families with chronically ill children and found that a mother's ability to adjust correlated strongly to overall family adaptation; where mothers were depressed, siblings and other family members had negative feelings toward the ill child. Moreover, when families are unable to express their frustrations, fears, and anger, the family's ability to accommodate to the changes is weakened. The interactional patterns, communication, and feelings of the entire family unit are important therapeutic material (Minuchin, Rosman, & Baker, 1978). The resources external to the family system (financial assistance, childcare, etc.), can support or weaken the stability of the family and its ability to accommodate to the illness. Helping families with the multitude of support services they might need to survive a serious childhood illness requires a multisystemic intervention.

Less explored in the literature are the problems young children face when a parent is seriously ill. The separation and the fragility of the diagnosed parent may result in feelings of insecurity in the child. The protective environment of the family may be compromised when attention is placed on the ill parent. Temporary caregivers may not set appropriate boundaries so that children may feel particularly vulnerable. Children may feel excluded from the family interactions, especially when they are given little or no explanation for the changes in the system or about their parent's health status. There is more than one case in which the parent of a young child died after being taken to the hospital and the child was given no more explanation than "Mommy /Daddy went to heaven." Later, in therapy sessions, the adult explores the anger experienced from the abandonment.

As children reach adolescence they may be expected to take care of their ill parents or be responsible for siblings during acute phases of the illness. Their caregiving may inhibit their opportunities for social development and peer relationships. Children, like adults, may feel angry with their ill parent, or ill sibling, sometimes secretly wishing them dead. These secret feelings need to be expressed and resolved to alleviate the guilt that often accompanies them or to make sense of the reactions to grief they experience if the loved one dies.

Chronic Illness in Adults

When serious chronic illness emerges in adulthood, it can occur in the primary family or in elderly parents. When it occurs in early adulthood it may interfere with people's ability to marry, have children, or become successful in their careers.

In middle adulthood, illness can be perceived as disrupting the family and work systems. Midlife is the time when major financial and other responsibilities for young children are completed. People are established in their roles and couples are often readying themselves for their retirement in good health. Plans that were long put off put the future close at hand, if not in place. Couples in midlife are always aware of the potential for illness but their scripts postpone it to older age.

With recent sophisticated medical technology, a first acute attack of an illness (cancer, heart attack) ends in death less frequently than ever before. A couple will often have an opportunity to live for several, if not many years with some quality of life. The quality of life is sometimes associated with their ability to change their definition of themselves to accommodate the changes in their physical ability. Their quality of life is to some extent also dependent upon how their finances cover their medical and caregiving needs.

Caregiving can compromise their definitions of each other. Changing from an intimate couple relationship to a caregiving and care-receiving one is a difficult task for couples. If the spousal relationship is compromised by some loss of ability to do basic hygiene tasks, it may upset sexual and social boundaries. For example, in the case of sexuality, spouse caregivers of partners with dementia or Alzheimer's disease have reported finding particular distress with partners who make sexual overtures to them yet do not remember who they are or that they have participated at all (Litz, Zeiss, & Davies, 1990). When the sexual intimacy of a relationship is changed by an illness, the couple or the caregiver may have to redefine their relationship from lovers to companions.

Caregiving may also change family's roles. For example, when there is a loss of control over body functions and the caregiving partner takes on diaper changing and dressing responsibilities, a marital relationship may be perceived as being replaced by a parent-child dynamic. The ill person may become ashamed of acquired inabilities, withdrawn, angry, or despondent.

Finding new meanings for accommodations to the relationship must be done in the context of communication between the partners. While dependency in physical needs may be real, the therapist can assist partners to elicit maximum participation from the sick partner in family decisions and in any other ways that are possible. Encouraging self-participation to the fullest extent throughout the course of the illness maximizes the quality of the relationship.

Gender factors have been known to play important parts in how care is given (Brok, 1992; Gwyther, 1990; Vinokur, 1990). Because of differing socialization, women tend to accept caregiving roles more readily than do men. Studies on postcardiac incidents indicate that women are better able to provide environments for their husbands to rest and recover because they have generally been responsible for the family chores (Badger, 1990). On the other hand, men tend to seek caregiving or housekeeping assistance from others when their wives are recuperating from acute illnesses. In less acute cases, (e.g., in Alzheimer's disease), the caregiving responsibilities tend to be transferred over time (Gwyther, 1990). The caregivers most frequently sought are adult daughters although the health care system does provide some nursing and home health aide assistance, most often by women. Caregiving tends to isolate people and increase the caregiver's own risk for illness.

The status of a midlife couple's social system in terms of other experiences with illness can affect their quality of life, if and when one member becomes chronically ill. If others in their peer group have had similar experiences, adjustment and support systems may be available. If there are adult children close by, they may provide a social support network. The less overall disruption in social activities or family gatherings, the easier the adaptation. Families can be encouraged to include the ill member in social situations wherever possible and discouraged from taking over all of the sick person's responsibilities. In the case where support networks are not available, medically based peer groups (Heart Clubs, Partners of People with Parkinson's Disease, etc.) offer a setting for families to reestablish themselves. These groups often provide a setting for new friendships to form. By providing psychoeducation about support groups, the therapist can assist the family to minimize their loneliness and isolation.

Chronic Illness in the Elderly

Chronic illness has often been defined as the illness of old age. It is also believed that if one lives long enough one is expected to encounter a chronic illness, thus, leading individuals to assume that they will someday be ill. It is estimated that 85% of the elderly population in this country have a chronic illness, about half of which result in serious physical limitations (Schienle & Eiler, 1984), and yet only about 5% of the population live in nursing homes (Stone, 1987). The life situation, experiences with loss, socioeconomics, and support systems of older people are often directly related to their stage of old age (65–75, 75–85, 85+) and their ability to cope with illness.

Belief systems about aging often affect the way families and the health care system respond to chronic illness in this stage of life. If illness is defined as an anticipated, expected component of advancing age and elderly people are not expected to be able to care for themselves, then their care may be taken over by family members or the health care system. If they themselves share this notion, they may relinquish themselves to the caregiving situation. Comments like "I'm old" are often synonymous with "I'm feeble" or "unable." These self-determinations may result in self-fulfilling prophecies that are often encouraged by well-meaning health providers or children who become parents to their elderly parents. Furthermore, if it is acceptable for an elderly person to be unable to perform self-care and regain health after a serious illness, then there may be no encouragement to do so. Yet many older people do not succumb to these definitions, and fight hard to maintain their independence and self-sufficiency. They recover and refuse care, sometimes to their family's distress.

The family's definition of themselves as caregivers of elderly members determine their willingness to give care, their style of caregiving and the effect it has. The caregiving needs of the elderly may be provided by a spouse, siblings, or children. In long-term relationships, spouses usually have a vision about caring for one another in old age and are most comfortable when they can carry these out. Their scripts incorporate "till death do us part." Oftentimes, children interfere with these efforts in fear that the well parent's health is being irrevocably compromised. Sometimes this interference disrupts the lifetime promise and the well spouse caregiver responds to family pressure either by giving up the role or by keeping the family at a distance. Older spouses who give up responsibilities often feel that they have deserted their ill spouse and become depressed and withdrawn. Other times, well spouses continue as caregivers, compromising their own health.

In cases of spousal relationships entered into during later life, the role of caregiver and the expectations of families can become imbalanced. Boundaries between the "new" well spouse and the birth children or other relatives of the ill spouse often need to be established when serious illness occurs. Who makes the decisions, who does the caregiving and where it will occur are problems that need to be resolved. Reconstituted families become engaged in inevitable power struggles as they react protectively. Environments that support older persons belief systems and independent decision making wherever possible should be encouraged.

Sometimes couples have never expressed their feelings or their fears about who will die first, or who will care for whom. These are difficult times for couples.

The Extended Family

In the case of children as caregivers, the extended family's proximity and responsibilities to their primary family may also influence how needs are met. Family-of-origin belief systems about what responsibilities adult children are "supposed" to have, how the different genders determine who does what, under what circumstances people should be institutionalized, and other value-laden issues have implications to the delivery of care. The effects of caregiving an elderly parent may be profound on the family of the caregiver (spouse and children), especially when the ill parent comes to live with their child's family. Many marital relationships have deteriorated in the process of caregiving a parent, especially when the caregiving couple does not agree on the extent of responsibility or involvement.

GENERAL CAREGIVING ISSUES

Fairly recently, changes in hospital payment systems based on diagnostic related groups (DRGs), have resulted in financial incentives for hospitals to get people out in the shortest possible time. This has dramatically changed the face of caregiving. Professional home health care has emerged, and there is increased time pressure on families to make provisions for its sick members. In these circumstances, people outside the family system invade the system constantly. Some actually become enmeshed with the family itself. Sociocultural factors, such as the distribution of families around the country, reconstituted family systems, women in the workforce, and other considerations, have complicated the system further. Yet, caregiving still remains a family issue.

Because of the changes in medical payment systems, changes in family proximity, and the aging of the population, recent research has been devoted to alternatives for the giving of care. Historically, care of infirm people was the responsibility of the family and where no family existed, the religious institution. In families, men were responsible for the money to pay for the health needs of their ill and women for the hands-on care.

Caregiving has several meanings: love and intimacy, forgiveness, proving one's maturity, obligation, and more. Caregivers experience enormous frustration and sometimes "irrational anger, ambivalence, death wishes or escape fantasies" (Rolland, 1993). Intense feelings can result in distancing and guilt on the part of the caregiver. Directing the caregiver's intense, explosive frustrations at the illness rather at the ill partner can diminish the guilt and bring families closer together.

SUMMARY AND CONCLUSIONS

There was a time when the primary care doctor in this country was a long-time friend of the family, lived in the neighborhood, and was an integral part of the social systems in which a family functioned. This trusted other person (usually male) had almost exclusive rights to the diagnosis and care of people in his practice who became ill. He engineered or directed care that went far beyond medical treatment approaches and involved many family considerations. When the illness was long or serious the family often deemed him the "father." This model of treatment for people with chronic illness rarely exists any longer. Medical personnel come in and out of family systems and play several different roles at different times. They rarely know much about the individual or the family system.

The acceptance and understanding of ethnic and culturally diverse ways of using or not using the health care system and the ways families care for their ill has also changed dramatically in this country. The health and delivery systems, however, have not yet accommodated to these changes.

Chronic illness is not always easily diagnosed and treatments are complicated and often arduous, sometimes beyond the family's comprehension. Serious illnesses pose unmentionable threats of loss to family systems and their complexity results in imbalances in relationships that change roles, intimacy, boundaries, and life scripts.

A biopsychosocial approach to helping families who have as their newest member a chronic illness requires that therapists and medical practitioners create a new system of functioning with each other and the family. As Rolland (1993) so aptly put it,

> Therapists and couples need to understand the beliefs and multigenerational legacies that guide their constructions of meanings about health problems and their relationship to caregiving systems. Beliefs about normality, mind-body relationship and control, what caused an illness or can affect its course, meanings or narratives developed around a health problem, and cultural/ethnic or gender-related beliefs are particularly significant. (p. 15)

They need also to begin to understand the medical progression and implications of the illness itself. Medical practitioners need to embrace families in their treatment of illness and expand their perspective from an individual model to a systemic model. In this arena, families can begin to address the changes that must inevitably take place within the context of an illness. Changes that support the interpersonal relationships within the family sustain intimacy and nurture communication create hope and foster coping.

REFERENCES

Badger, T. A. (1990). Men with cardiovascular disease and their spouses: Coping, health and marital adjustment. *Archives of Psychiatric Nursing, IV*(5), 319–324.

Baltes, M. M., Hans-Werner, W., & Schmid-Furtoss, V. (1990. The daily life of elderly Germans: Activity patterns, personal control, and functional health. *Journal of Gerontology, 45*(4), 173–179.

Bandura, A. (1977). Self-efficacy: Toward a unifying theory of behavior change. *Psychological Review, 84,* 191–215.

Brok, A. J. (1992). Crises and transitions: Gender and life stage issues in individual, group, and couples treatment. *Psychoanalysis and Psychotherapy, 10*(1), 3–16.

Chekryn, J. (1984). Cancer recurrence: Personal meaning, communication and marital adjustment. *Cancer Nursing, 7,* 491–498.

Coyne, J. D., & DeLongis, A. (1986). Beyond social support: The role of social relationships in adaptation. *Journal of Consulting and Clinical Psychology, 45,* 456–460.

Creasy, G. L., Meyers, B. J., Epperson, M. J., & Taylor, J. (1990). Couples with an elderly parent with Alzheimer's Disease: Perceptions of familial relationships. *Psychiatry, 53,* 44–50.

DiMatteo, M. R., & DiNicola, D. D. (1982). *Achieving patient compliance: The psychology of the medical practitioner's role.* New York: Pergamon.

Engel, G. L. (1977). The need for a new medical model: A challenge for biomedicine. *Science, 196,* 129–136.

Engel, G. L. (1980a). The clinical applications of the biopsychosocial model. *American Journal of Psychiatry, 137,* 535–544

Epstein, L. H. (1984). The direct effect of compliance on health outcome. *Health Psychology, 4,* 385–393.

Gwyther, L. P. (1990). Letting go: Separation-individuation in a wife of an Alzheimer's patient. *The Gerontologist, 30,* 698–702.

Haynes, S. G., Eaker, E. D., & Feinlieb, M. (1983). Spouse behavior & coronary heart disease in men: Prospective results form the Framingham Heart Study. *American Journal of Epemiology, 118,* 1-22.

Lachman, M. E. (1986). Personal control in later life: Stability, change and cognitive corelates. In P. Bender, B. Milton, & M. Baltes (Eds.), *The psychology of control and aging.* Hillsdale, NJ: Erlbaum.

Litz, B. T.;. Zeiss., A. M. & Davies, H. D. (1990). Sexual concerns of male spouses of female Alzheimer's disease patients. *Gerontologist, 30,* 113–116.

Marteau, T. M., & Johnston, M. (1986). Determinants of beliefs and illness: A study of parents of children with diabetes, asthma, epilepsy, or chronic illness. *Journal of Psychosomatic Research, 30,* 673–683.

McDaniel, S. H., Hepworth, J., & Doherty, W. J. (1992). *Medical family therapy: A bio-psychosocial approach to families with health problems.* New York: Basic Books, Inc.

Meyerowitz, B. E. (1983). Postmastectomy coping strategies and the quality of life. *Health Psychology, 2,* 117–132.

Minuchin, S., Rosman, B. L., & Baker, L. (1978). *Psychosomatic families.* Cambridge: Harvard University Press.

Mullan, F. (1983). *Vital signs: A young doctor's struggle with cancer.* New York: Farrar, Straus, Giroux.

Phares, E. J. (1987). Locus of control. In R. J. Corsini (Eds.), *Concise encyclopedia of psychology.* New York: Wiley.

Rolland, J. S. (1993, December). Helping couples live with illness. *Family Therapy News,* pp. 15, 26.

Rotter, J. B. (1966). Generalized expectancies for the internal versus external control of reinforcement. *Psychological Monographs, 90*(1), 1–28.

Sarafino, E. P. (1990). *Health psychology: Biopsychosocial interactions.* New York: John Wiley.

Schienle, D. R., & Eiler, J. M. (1984). Clinical intervention with older adults. In L. C. Eisenberg & M. A. Jansen (Eds.), *Chronic illness and disability through the life span: Effects on self and family* (pp. 245–268). New York: Springer.

Shlain, L. (1979). Cancer is not a four-letter word. In C. A. Garfield (Eds.), *Stress and survival: The emotional realities of life-threatening illness.* St. Louis: Mosby.

Shontz, F. (1975). *The psychological aspects of physical illness and disability.* New York: Macmillan.

Shapiro, J. (1986). Assessment of family coping with stress. *Psychomatics, 27,* 262–271.

Stone, R., C., G. L., & Sangl, J. (1987). Caregiving of the frail elderly: A national profile. *Gerontologist, 27,* 616–629.

Swan, G., Carmelli, D., & Rosenman, R. (1986). Spouse-pair similarity on the California Psychological Inventory with reference to husband's coronary heart disease. *Psychosomatic Medicine, 48,* 185.

Turk, D. C., & Meichenbaum, D. (Eds.). (1991). *Adherence to self-care regimens: The patient's perspective.* New York: Plenum.

Vinokur, A. D., & Kaplan, D. V. (1990). In sickness and in health: Patterns of social support undermining in older married couples. *Journal of Aging and Health, 2,* 215–241.

Wallston, K. A., Wallston, B. S., & Devillis, R. (1978). Development of the multidimensional health locus of control scales. *Health Education Monographs, 6,* 161–170.

Wilson-Pessano, & McNabb, W. L. (1985). The role of patient education in the management of childhood asthma. *Preventive Medicine, 14,* 670–687.

Index

Domestic Partner Abuse

L. Kevin Hamberger, PhD and
Claire Renzetti, PhD, Editors

This volume breaks new ground in the understanding and treatment of couples abuse. The editors and contributors expand the models of abusive relationships to include the special concerns of gay couples, mutually violent partners, and abusive women, among others.

Based on a special issue of the journal *Violence and Victims*, this book shatters myths surrounding domestic violence and sheds new light on a complex social problem. For all counselors, therapists, and social workers concerned with domestic violence, as well as for students and educators in this field.

Partial Contents:

• Domestic Partner Abuse: Expanding Paradigms for Understanding and Intervention, *L. Kevin Hamberger*

• Gay and Bisexual Male Domestic Violence Victimization: Challenges to Feminist Theory and Responses to Violence, *Patrick Letellier*

• Are Bi-Directionally Violent Couples Mutually Victimized? A Gender-Sensitive Comparison, *Dina Vivian and Jennifer Langhinrichsen-Rohling*

• Counseling Heterosexual Women Arrested for Domestic Violence: Implications for Theory and Practice, *L. Kevin Hamberger and Theresa Potente*

• Lesbian Battering: The Relationship Between Personality and the Perpetration of Violence, *Vallerie E. Coleman*

1996   240pp   0-8261-9090-1   hard cover

536 Broadway, New York, NY 10012-3955 • (212) 431-4370 • Fax (212) 941-7842

Springer Publishing Company

Multicultural Perspectives in Working with Families

Elaine P. Congress, DSW

Professionals must develop new skills in working with culturally diverse clients and their families due to an increasing number of families from backgrounds other than Western Europe. To address this issue for social work students, the Council on Social Work Education has updated their curriculum policy to mandate content on cultural diversity. Dr. Congress has developed a major textbook that focuses on multiculturalism and populations at risk, in order to expand the knowledge of practitioners as well as students.

The purpose of this book, which contains the latest information, research, and practice examples about culturally diverse families, is to decrease stereotypes and promote non-biased thinking. The author addresses many timely topics within the family including HIV/AIDS, homelessness, substance abuse, domestic violence, and child sexual abuse. This volume is written for social work practitioners, as well as social work educators and students.

Partial Contents:

Assessment—Micro and Macro Approaches. Use of the Culturagram to Assess and Empower Culturally Diverse Families • Managing Agencies for Multicultural Services

Culturally Diverse Families Across the Life Cycle. The Child, the Family, and the School: A Multicultural Triangle • Working with Poor Ethnic Minority Adolescents and Their Families: An Ecosystemic Approach • Multicultural Dimensions of the Third Shift: Employees, Mothers and Students • The Aging Family: Ethnic and Cultural Considerations

Selected Culturally Diverse Populations. Motherless Children: Family Interventions with AIDS Orphans • Working with Immigrant Families in Transition • Working with Soviet Jewish Immigrants • Redefining the Family: The Concept of Family for Lesbians and Gay Men • Machismo, Manhood and Men in Latino Families

Springer Series on Social Work
1997   376pp   0-8261-9560-1   *hardcover*

536 Broadway, New York, NY 10012-3955 • (212) 431-4370 • Fax (212) 941-7842

SP *Springer Publishing Company*

BEYOND THE TRADITIONAL FAMILY
Voices of Diversity

Betty Polisar Reigot and **Rita K. Spina,** PhD

In this innovative text, the authors present original qualitative research based on personal interviews with selected modern families. These interviews reveal the new variety of domestic relationships that are emerging today, including single mothers by choice, adolescent mothers, fathers as caretakers, homosexual parents, grandparents as parents, and parents by technology. The stories carry important implications for social policy and provide an insightful qualitative resource for professionals including sociologists, family therapists and academics in social work and psychology.

Contents:

Preface • Introduction • The Interviews

I. Single Mothers by Choice. Marjorie • Vera • Tracy • Sally and Roberta
II. Adolescent Mothers. Nola and Jackie • Manichan
III. Fathers as Caretakers. Chet • Aaron • Geoffrey
IV. Homosexual Parents. Franklin • Meg and Pat • Ben and Sean
V. Grandparents as Parents. The Flanagans • The Caplers
VI. Parents by Technology. The Martins
VII. Parents and AIDS. Denise

The Conclusion • Reference List

1995   267pp   0-8261-9030-8   hardcover

536 Broadway, New York, NY 10012-3955 • (212) 431-4370 • Fax (212) 941-7842